M000286418

Introductory Concepts in

INFORMATION SCIENCE

Second Edition

Introductory Concepts in
INFORMATION SCIENCE

Second Edition

Melanie J. Norton

ASIST Monograph Series

Published on behalf of the
American Society for Information Science and Technology by

Information Today, Inc.
Medford, New Jersey

First printing, 2010

Introductory Concepts in Information Science, Second Edition

Library of Congress Cataloging-in-Publication Data

Introductory concepts in information science / edited by Melanie J. Norton. --2nd ed.
    p. cm.
Includes bibliographical references and index.
ISBN 978-1-57387-394-9
1. Information science. I. Norton, Melanie J., 1954-
Z665.I67 2010
020--dc22

2010015715

President and CEO: Thomas H. Hogan, Sr.
Editor-in-Chief and Publisher: John B. Bryans
Managing Editor: Amy M. Reeve
ASIS&T Monograph Series Editor: Samantha Hastings
VP Graphics and Production: M. Heide Dengler
Cover Designer: Shelley Szajner

Contents

Acknowledgments

Many thanks to the new contributors to this edition, Drs. EunKyung Chung, Teresa S. Welsh, and JungWon Yoon, and Mr. Peter Zuber for their labors and patience in increasing the scope of this introductory work. I also wish to thank Samantha Hastings, ASIS&T Monograph Series editor, for her support and guidance in producing this edition. I wish to recognize the efforts and patience of John B. Bryans and Amy M. Reeve from Information Today, Inc., for their help in managing the publication of this book. I am especially grateful to Cathy J. Pruitt for her assistance and support throughout the writing and editing of both editions of this work.

Last, I wish to honor the memories of those who contributed through their lives and love to allow me to reach my goals: my parents, Mary M. Norton (1991) and Warren A. Norton (1995), who never got to see the publication of this work, and to my younger sister, Patricia G. Norton (2008).

Introduction

Melanie J. Norton

A second edition is an opportunity to add what the first edition may have missed and to address new developments in discipline thinking and research. In keeping with the scope of the original work as an "introduction" to some concepts in information, not all the new research has been addressed and not all of the potential omissions have been resolved. When Tefko Saracevic presented *Introduction to Information Science* in 1970, it contained 751 pages and presented many of the key papers of the field to that date. Succeeding attempts to present a comprehensive introduction to information science have yielded equally sizable volumes, and they are doubtless critical resource materials. However, *Introductory Concepts in Information Science* was never intended to be a comprehensive volume; it is an introductory text, a beginner's book if you must, intended to shed some light into the field of information science, which is a complex, practical, theoretical, and controversial collection of fields rather than just one.

Introductory Concepts is not all-inclusive—to cover the entire history of information and information science theory would require a sizable library; the text does not touch on every possible concept in the field, nor does it introduce the multitude of pioneers, stars, soldiers, or laborers of the field. This volume is intended to be a portal for novices, a passage through which to find and consider information using a different perspective. The volume will be criticized for not covering certain topics that another author would have included had he or she written the book. The topics included were selected because they were key and relevant in the view of the author to create an introductory book. The topics were selected for a perspective many students never consider with any particular energy.

It is not the intention here to attempt a definitive declaration of what information or information science is, but rather to stimulate a constructive and creative discourse upon both topics. An open mind and an open hand will serve as better aids in examining these complex topics than any endeavor at straitjacket definitions. This introduction to concepts in information science offers ideas, issues, examples, and projections to begin the long process of investigating the topics. It is not possible to present all the ideas, concerns, and aspects of information and information science; hence, this work is not represented as being more than an introduction.

Choices had to be made about inclusion and exclusion, depth, scope, and so on. An introduction to information as a concept and information science as a field comprise Chapter 1. Within Chapter 2 are included two reprinted articles: one from Harold Borko and one from Klaus Otten and Anthony Debons, which give perspectives on information science from an earlier time but continue to be relevant. Chapter 3 examines communication as a process closely related to information in a number of ways. Claude Shannon's *Mathematical Theory of Communication* is offered in a brief overview as a foundation concept, and the notion of redundancy is introduced. Chapter 4 opens the discussion of information retrieval as a concept and activity. Aspects of organization, classification, and the relationship among information, communication, and retrieval are identified. Information retrieval is an extremely complex set of concepts, which underlie all the practical and intellectual tasks of the field, but they are only covered here in limited form.

Chapter 5, authored by Dr. JungWon Yoon of the University of South Florida, presents an essential aspect of information science that underlies the retrieval activities of modern information-seekers, whether they recognize it or not, and it is an introduction to subject indexing, indexing language, and depth of indexing. Both manual and automatic indexing in general are discussed. This chapter also provides an introduction to additional current indexing issues: web indexing, multimedia indexing, and folksonomies. Chapter 6 initiates a three-chapter presentation dealing with information repositories, the first two of which were contributed by Dr. Teresa S. Welsh of the University of Southern Mississippi.

Chapter 6 lays a foundation that provides a basic account of the language roots and the documented history of what are now known as libraries, repositories, and information collections. To bring perspective to the notions of information and information science and its various manifestations as real elements in culture, history, and currency, the examples are developed over time in the three chapters. Chapter 7 provides introductory information about the various collection formats evident in repositories and includes a discussion of some relevant open source issues. Continuing the repository discussion, Chapter 8, written by Dr. EunKyung Chung of Ewha Womans University in Seoul, Korea, focuses on digital libraries, the most recent manifestation of information collection behaviors. In providing a brief recent history of digital library projects, this chapter emphasizes the technological elements, information service aspects, and social components involved in digital collections.

Chapter 9 introduces and describes bibliometrics with some expansion of the explanations to clarify for students and to introduce a few of the recent developments. Topics given additional consideration include Bradford's law, citation analysis, content analysis, and user studies. Chapter 10 introduces information economics, the underlying rationale for the emerging criticality of information. Broaching the topic of economics in the context of information opens the door for student consideration of information from a different and powerful perspective that they have typically overlooked. A discussion of the concepts of information value is presented in Chapter 11, expanding somewhat on how information may be viewed.

Identifying context and culture as part of that economy, Chapter 12, written by myself and co-authored with Dr. June Lester in 1998, explores the impact of information technology on the information hierarchy. Although I have revised the chapter for this edition, it remains as a source of discussion to make comparisons to the current state of information telecommunications technology's continuing impact on the information hierarchy. The specifics of the situations presented in Chapter 12 have changed over time, but they are relevant for historical, current, and future consideration. How information access impacts our business structures and behaviors continues to be a serious consideration.

This text is an attempt to provide a place to begin. The direction one travels afterward will depend on the reader's path of interest and interpretation, but there is the hope that this beginning study of information and information science provides a modest light by which to investigate these areas further.

Chapter 1

Information and Information Science

Melanie J. Norton

Information science has deep historical roots accented with significant controversy and conflicting views, from the definition of "information" to the scope of the topic to identifying the appropriate practitioners to the development and implementation of methodologies.

Traditional disputes about the appropriate discipline position for information science study include computer science, management, economics, librarianship, and others that all lay some claim to the study and correctly so. The concepts of this science may be at the heart of many disciplines, but the emergence of a specific discipline of information science has been limited to the 20th century. Protracted discussion about the definition of information, knowledge, communication, and uncertainty has created insights into the complexities of human information behaviors and the information scientist may be the best demonstrator of the science. Who the information scientists are may not even be relevant. While gaining recognition that this thing, "information," may play critical roles in our social and intellectual activities, we have overlooked the resulting depth of its integration into our existence and neglected to realize the impact it has on us as we study it. As we have gained information and knowledge about the topic, we have ignored how such progress alters our knowledgebase. While studying information, the thing that changes us most, we have become resistant to the notion of change in our view of it. Traditional disciplinary boundaries cannot absolutely control information and its sciences.

This chapter presents a grandiose view of information that encourages the discussion of information in all its possible roles; this chapter also offers a brief historical foundation of information science to provide a time frame for this discussion. The foundation is not comprehensive—that would require volumes—but the discussion highlights some situations and people who contributed to the development of information science today. Because there are many disciplines that contribute to this field, it is not possible to identify all the key figures.

The Grandest View of Information and Information Science

Information science is a study that reflects the accumulation of events and thought springing from humankind's hunger for information. As we strive to better understand the world that surrounds us and to control it, we have a voracious appetite for information. We also crave to understand this component of ourselves and our world in terms of information and information hunger. As such, many fields have improved and will continue to contribute to improving our understanding of this aspect of our character and the implications of its transformations upon us.

If information science is concerned with all aspects, properties, and behaviors of information as suggested by Borko's synthesis of Robert S. Taylor's three definitions of information science (Borko, 1968), then it certainly involves all disciplines at some level. Information could actually be construed as "existing" back to the first exchange or recombination of chemicals in the primordial ooze. Though the image may seem exaggerated, it suggests the depth and scope of information as an element in our existence, from birth to death and across the generations. The study of information and its aspects, behaviors, and properties could theoretically have started long before clay tablets and papyrus. The case could be made that early philosophers were seeking to understand information as they attempted to derive meaning from the world (Debons, 1990). It does not appear far-fetched to consider the observations of daily life as a form of information gathering, exchange, and implementation, though it seems almost too fundamental to consider. Do observations qualify as science? This is also open to debate. In discussing prescientific times, Heilprin referred to Plato's conclusions that our senses could not be relied upon: "It took centuries of mostly celestial observations by great thinkers such as Copernicus and Galileo to render sense perception acceptable" (1995, p. 575). It took centuries of observers—scientists of all kinds—gathering, reporting, and debating information before we would accept what we saw for what it seemed to be and not what some governing body, generally a religious body of some form, told us it must be; determining that the stars moved about in the sky not necessarily around the Earth as the center of all things undermined various religious theories. Forms of observation have been the basis of most early science. Consider Newton, Darwin, or Mendel, as well as Copernicus and Galileo. It was what they observed as well as what they interpreted the observations to be that formed the basis for further exploration and developing knowledge. Where would science be without the observations and mental work of these early scientists? The observations, the transactions, and the implementation of behaviors may be the subjects of study and reveal information at some level in the social or physical organism; this "forms the very basis of life" (Debons et al., 1988, p. 9). Information has been compared to energy and matter as a fundamental element (Otten and Debons, 1970).

The science, the efforts to understand and study information, came long after the observations of information began. If information science studies and investigates all the properties, aspects, and behavior of information, then it is concerned with virtually everything known, thought, considered, espoused, and imagined at some point. If, as Bates suggested in 1999, the definition of information is limited to what is "recorded" (Bates, 1999, p. 1048), the topic becomes more manageable but much less reflective of the formation of information and the characteristics that influence much of its interpretation and handling. Information is not bound to one medium of transport, and it is not limited to one form of expression or even interpretation. "What is information?" is the question that bedevils. Information is an essential aspect of our existence that we have yet to be completely comfortable explaining. Our understanding of our total environment—physical, emotional, intellectual, current, and historical—is perpetually changing. As information seems to be the thread linking us to everything else, it would make sense as our perception of knowledge changes so should our sense of information. Information is more than recorded words and languages; it comprises images, music, light, and any entity that interacts as largely as in concert with the universe or as minutely as subatomic particles. Information completely surrounds us, yet we continue to create, accumulate, evaluate, manipulate, and integrate even more information. Information is something we ignore, we are not conscious of at all times, and we do not always accept or integrate.

As you read these words, there are an enormous number of information sources available to you, consciously and unconsciously. Your body is receiving information about the room you are in: the level of light, room temperature, humidity, and airflow. Your body may also be receiving information from the previous occupants of the room via odors, dander, and such. Your body is working with this information, generally without your awareness until the information has some impact upon your system, such as overheating, allergic reaction, and chills—all responses to the information your body is receiving. At the point you become conscious of the information, you may decide to ignore it or consciously react to it. Due to physical limitations, you may not be able to exert any control over how your body interprets the information and its reactions, such as perspiring, sneezing, raising a rash, getting goose bumps, or worse, all from information you were possibly not conscious of receiving or sending.

It seems obvious that information is an essential element in the formation of all things, whether societies, human beings, or sciences. All that we are now was built on the previous use of information to create our societies, cultures, religions, machines, and knowledge. So information science is the study of all of these, at least in some respect. There are characteristics about this progression that require some mention. It has taken thousands of years of evolution of humanity and cultures to reach today. Puzzling out the meaning of life has sometimes been no more than trying to survive. Making sense of the dark and the day, as well as the changing seasons, developing group identity, and defining the boundaries for hunting and gathering, all these took time, much longer than any of us will ever live or imagine accurately. Each small piece of information, which had some value or supposed value, was kept and passed on, sometimes building upon previous information. Much information was also missed, not gathered, not retained, and not believed. As one group warred with and destroyed another, all too often the information and knowledge of the defeated group was lost. The truth is that the complexity of understanding how early humankind came to interpret the universe around them is beyond our comprehension. Today, we are born into a world filled with more information, more conflict, and more structure than any of our predecessors. We cannot imagine not having a past, just as we cannot readily grasp the future. Somehow humanity examined the world in which it lived and began to develop mechanisms to cope with the unexplainable, which involved almost everything for many centuries. Curiosity and observation led to possible explanations, impossible stories, and entrenched beliefs.

New tools have expanded our vision and our horizons. Telescopes, satellites, and space vehicles help us to look not just beyond the edge of the map, but light years away. What we see of the sky now is light from history; the distance is so great that by the time we have perceived it, the stars and the planets have already lived millions of years and are actually no longer in the sky where we see them. The boundaries of our senses have been expanded, and our access to information is limited only by time and imagination. The larger the volume of information has grown, the more complex it becomes to gain meaningful access; questions of organization become ever more critical while becoming increasingly more difficult. More tools and more time are necessary to explore and efficiently employ the information available.

Information is an all-pervasive creature available at many levels, in previously unimaginable forms, and in overwhelming quantity. Short of death, there is no escape from the need for information and no respite from the profusion of information. As populations grew and as our societies became more complex, the production and perceived needs for information expanded. As new mediums became available for transporting information, new forms of information became transportable and more information was demanded, which required more ways of transporting it. Such has been the behavior of information production and information need.

New technology has enhanced the effect exponentially. Discovering new methods of storing and retrieving information led to new methods of acquiring information. These new abilities to handle information contributed to the increase of information. With the perception, if not the reality, that more information could be handled, there grew the notion that more is needed. Attendant upon this information combustion, there have been changes wrought by its influx. Where once we glanced out the window to check the weather, we now turn on a radio, television, or computer to obtain weather forecasts, and we hope for longer sight into the day. Once we sought only familial sources of advice; now we delve deeply into self-help information, available from every bookstand, radio station, newspaper, and television channel, in web chat rooms and from anonymous electronic friends we never meet except in cyberspace. We write and read blogs, journaling our daily thoughts and political sympathies, soliciting discussion or providing only tirades. Our living rooms are not just gathering places for friends and family but for the combined powers of an entire industry of entertainment, news, marketing, and gospel. Our home computers allow another whole world of people and ideas into our lives, which we might never have experienced otherwise. We make ourselves vulnerable to wisdom and ignorance portrayed as fact, often ignoring that truth is somewhere in between, but we rarely stop to check the validity of the information. We have access to information in quantities and forms previously unknown to us. Information technology makes it possible to interact with anyone else who has technology access. The barriers of time and available bandwidth become our personal constraints.

Information employed and embedded into a context, integrated as it were, may become what we call knowledge. To know something is to possess information, but having information affects in some way what we know, or believe, may be construed as knowledge. Developing knowledge may be a cumulative affair, involving the acquisition of information over time to have a meaningful effect (Buckland, 1991). Using information as building blocks may result in knowledge, sometimes held as truth, regardless of the validity of the assumption, and sometimes denied as heresy. Galileo observed "new" stars with his telescope, which no naked eye could detect. The information was available out there, but it was not detected, not part of a belief system, not an "accepted" part of current knowledge, and not part of Galileo's belief either (Boorstin, 1983, pp. 318–327). Buckland reasons that belief is an important aspect of knowledge, not whether something is true or false, but whether it is believed. The telescope itself, which Galileo improved upon, was a building block, since it was the result of an idea of another fellow. By examining the sky, the stars, and the planets, Galileo reasoned that Copernicus' theory of some 50 years beforehand (that the Earth could not be the center of the universe) might be valid. This was contrary to Galileo's belief and the accepted knowledge of his time (Boorstin, 1983).

The particulars of how each society managed information over time would be a fascinating discussion, but it is not appropriate here. It is also not appropriate to explore at length the presence of information at all levels of existence, not just as an aspect of the human condition. The focus here shall be primarily on information in the human domain of control. To begin, we should recognize that information existed and was used, compiled, and applied long before the word was framed and long before anyone studied it. There is a relationship among information, knowledge, and belief (Buckland, 1991). So then, what does it involve, this study of information? It is the study of all the aspects of information's behavior and all that may impact information, its uses, its representations, and its applications (Borko, 1968). As we have gained information about information, we have recognized that the scope of the study, or the science, is much wider than earlier imagined. To study information, we might study social systems, human interactions, cognition, language, literature, art forms, technology, and history; essentially, we refer to any of the representations of information or knowledge, whether verbal, visual, imprinted, or electronically preserved, and how humans interact with these aspects. This is not to suggest information and knowledge are equivalent; there is a relationship between them. Sometimes information provides fuel for knowledge, and vice versa, but do not think they are one and the same. It is not sound reasoning to assume that just because ideas or stories are in print or on the web that they are "true," nor should we assume all information, or knowledge, is necessarily "true." Information assumes various characters and roles; it is an economic entity, a precursor to or cause of knowledge, a process, a thing in and of itself (Buckland, 1991), a component in virtually all transactions and surely other states or beings as yet unknown. As Buckland points out, and as we too shall subscribe, "We are unable to say confidently of anything that it could not be information" (1991, p. 50).

Generally, we can examine information science in the context of at least the following five areas: collection and storage, classification and control, access for retrieval, communication, and evaluation. How should decisions about what information to collect be made, and once made, how should it be stored? Related to storage is classification and control. Our predecessors recognized some system of classification or organization of information could make it possible to discover more about the world and retrieve what was known, implying that classification is closely related to retrieval. Being able to select an item of information from a body of information involves the tasks labeled as retrieval. Communication includes all the processes involved in the conveyance of information via many possible channels and with some very interesting complications. Evaluation is immediately noticed as being multilayered, in that an evaluation is performed to collect information, an evaluation may be performed on information to extract other information, an evaluation may somehow classify or organize information, and an evaluation is performed to retrieve information once stored. With time and experience it has become clear there are cognitive sciences involved with all five of the above contexts; components of user behavior and involvement dramatically impact information. The evolution of information technology—telegraph, telephone, radio, television, computers, and the internet—also has come into consideration in the five contexts of information science. A maturing in academic valuation of the diversity of cultures requires that social actions, reactions, and impacts be considered in the field. Information may cause change, and change should affect information science.

Information science is the study of this multifaceted and hydra-headed enigma. At this time, the primary considerations in the study focus on developing theories, empirical laws, or practical understandings and applications that may be germane to information and its roles, behaviors, or influences (Borko, 1968). The study of information engages members of many disciplines, ranging from library, computer, and cognitive sciences to sociology, economics, and statistics. In essence, there is no discipline that should not be investigating information in its implications to itself. Members of a diverse group of disciplines are studying information as information scientists, and they are producing generalizable results (Rayward, 1983). However, there will always be a need for discipline perspectives and applications of information, which may not be revealed through generic research.

Historical Foundations

Evolving Views

Information science has roots in a variety of disciplines and fields. Inquiry into the history of information science reveals conflicting views as to its origins and its relationships to librarianship, scholarship, various disciplines, and the documentationalist movement. There have been those who would argue the study of information is not a "science." Such debate has been long-winded and not particularly rewarding (Machlup, 1983; Machlup and Mansfield, 1983). For example, Machlup makes the case that the meaning of "science" has changed over time, usually in an exclusionary manner, as advocates of specific interpretations attempted to diminish the status of those who held different views. He postulated this habit was a method of equalizing and then enhancing each group's sense of superiority over the now-excluded group. Equally unsatisfying is the debate as to whether information science is a discipline, a subset of librarianship, an offspring of documentationalism, or a metadiscipline. This is not to imply that such discussion is not warranted; in fact, it is a necessary component of the development of the field and the declaration of its history, all of which are important. However, it is often presented as a negative debate attempting much the same exclusiveness that Machlup discussed as relevant to the discourse about science. It seems an awkward approach to an exciting and incredibly involved area of human endeavor to focus on all the disagreements and posturing. Kochen (1983) viewed the dispute over what discipline information studies falls into as a fruitless semantic argument. Plainly, more value would come from allowing those identified with the information disciplines to pursue the inquiry, seeking to improve our understanding. We will accept, at least for ease of this discourse, that information science is a science, and it has potential contributors from virtually every field of study, every discipline, and every practicing profession (Borko, 1968; Machlup and Mansfield, 1983; Meadows, 1987). But this does not relieve information scientists of the necessity to lay a foundation and invoke some of the mentioned conflicting views.

Perhaps some of the conflict results from the evolving nature of this "science," coupled with our own intellectual evolution. Before the printed book, the high science of memory, which allowed the retelling of history, laws, and even of early manuscript contents, required the teller to be present. The oral tradition was more than storytelling for entertainment; it was a way of transmitting information, education, moral plays, and cultural identity, but it was dependent upon the skills and availability of the human host (Boorstin, 1983, pp. 480–489). The preliterate traditions were linked to human carriers; faithfulness to completeness and accuracy in the rendition of the information was critical, as well as considered a sacred duty and much-admired skill (Riesman, 1960). The development of new tools influenced the ability to share information, and this also decreased the reliance on the human memory (Boorstin, 1983). The development of writing, even in a pictorial form, was a method for preserving what was seen or occurred, and allowed it to be shared with others without requiring both parties to be in the same place at the same time. Examples would be cave paintings in France, clay tablets from the Middle East, pottery of the Native Americans, and hand-scripted manuscripts from the Middle Ages. All of these permit the sharing of information, and indeed are themselves information as well as carriers, without requiring a human host, and often surviving the originating community (Riesman, 1960). Could not the ability to share information and to potentially influence others contribute to an expanding view and understanding, altering what was viewed as information, even what was considered knowledge and truth? As information was more widely exchanged, it challenged beliefs and the accepted knowledge systems. If what we study is something that may cause significant change, then will our study of it not change, too? As we investigate information, should our knowledge systems be challenged and changed? Is the study of medicine in this decade the identical study of medicine three decades ago? Why should the study of information remain as narrow as its original interpretation? Is it immune to the effects of its mission? Do we learn over time, recognizing new aspects of old images, ideas, and patterns?

Perhaps the issue is most simply about change and our resistance to it. As elders bemoan the unworthiness of their offspring, especially as the young dispense with that which the elder once prized, perhaps this is the root of the problem in conflicts surrounding information science. It is by necessity responsive to changes in the environment; the knowledgebase grows and technology evolves, the new information science is applied to the old, and change occurs.

Previous Considerations

Early scholars were plagued by the political turmoil of their times, sometimes forced into silence about their discoveries, frequently secretive about their work and sharing it with only a limited number of colleagues to ensure their primacy and safety (Boorstin, 1983). Restricting the flow of information has always been the prerogative of the controlling powers. Preventing new ideas from spreading among the populace safeguarded those in control. For example, Galileo's observations of the heavens through the telescope supported Copernican theory that the Earth is not the center of the universe, a concept that threatened then-current theological interpretations of the world, and Galileo was tried for heresy (pp. 327–332). Letter writing as a method of communication among interested scientists was the early distributor of discovery. Letters were more difficult to censor than books because it was easier to hide them, and if the document was not hidden, the phrasing could well be structured to conceal ideas as mere discussion. In later times, when politically acceptable and appropriately rewritten, letters discussing observations or discoveries would be published (p. 390).

The printing press expanded the availability of information by making it possible to create more than one copy of a document in an economy of time. It was no longer necessary to hand copy each document, making information available to a far wider audience than any previous tool. The growth in volume of "knowledge" created a crisis of access and communication. The need to share ideas more effectively, to better expand the universe of knowledge, and frankly, to protect an individual's claim to a new idea led to publications of scholarly letters, then papers. The awarding of prizes for discovery and the attainment of a certain celebrity caused significant competition to be identified with a discovery (Boorstin, 1983, pp. 314–318). Eventually collections of papers became journals, which produced new concerns—how to access the information in an economical and useful manner. Growth in the production of scientific works and the printed record created problems of access and discovery, which often caused important information to be overlooked. Bernal (1939) suggested that if a solution to the organization of scientific communications was not found soon, more knowledge would be lost than was gained (Meadows, 1987).

One of the promulgators of modern information science was the "explosion" of recorded material in the 19th century coupled with a lack of adequate systems to access the material. A pioneer in bibliographic construction and a wide variety of related endeavors, Paul Otlet, a Belgian lawyer in the 1890s, would significantly contribute to addressing those difficulties and be credited as the originator of the documentalist movement in Europe (Rayward, 1997). In the early 1890s in Brussels, Belgium, Otlet, working with Henri La Fontaine, began to contemplate new ways of making printed text accessible via the creation of a bibliography of all printed material. He envisioned a method of representing subject contents of printed material on cards, which could then be grouped to simulate the relationships involved. Otlet sought a method to classify knowledge to implement the proper ordering of the cards. After encountering a copy of the Dewey Decimal Classification (DDC) system, Otlet and La Fontaine became convinced and convinced others that it should be possible to create a "universal catalog of all knowledge" (p. 291). Ultimately, an association of interested parties would lead to the formation of the International Institute of

Bibliography (IIB), which would become the International Office of Bibliography in Brussels (OIB). The IIB/OIB would be the repository for the catalog to be built. Over time, the IIB/OIB became the current International Federation for Information and Documentation (Rayward, 1997).

Using a much expanded version of the DDC system, the Classification Decimale Universelle, or UDC (Universal Decimal Classification), was initiated in 1895. This was the scheme to organize all knowledge and the basis for organization of the subject cards. The UDC expanded and increased the flexibility of its antecedent DDC. The UDC structure was based on a bibliography, a subject index that permits classification of portions of materials (Foskett, 1966; McIlwaine, 1997). Rayward (1997) likens the UDC to a database management system. The UDC employed what became a complex, numerically based series of codes that were intended to represent the structures and substructures of classification relevant to a particular entry. The complexity of the numeric system and the attempt to provide associations among related items made the system too intricate for the technology of the time to fully utilize. Otlet significantly addressed some of the shortcomings of the card and cabinet database; he developed the notion of standardizing card sizes and entries, and employed colors as well as minor card size variations to contribute to the organization of the catalog and to improve the speed of searching by providing a visual structure to the database. Despite the problems of the time, the catalog, the Repertoire Bibliographique Universel (RBU), which was started in 1895, grew to almost 16 million entries by 1930. Other databases were created based on the same premise as the RBU and to supplement it. This included an image database and a "multimedia" collection of pamphlets, brochures, and hand-copied passages.

The actual manual tasks of handling the catalogs proved difficult. Early attempts at providing database search services entailed locating the appropriate cards, copying entries by hand, and refiling, which was time-intensive and tended to introduce errors in the copied material and during refiling. However, searches were performed; users were instructed in the proper phrasing applying the UDC numbers so the staff could locate the appropriate entries in the database and copy the card (Rayward, 1997). Rayward believes Otlet and La Fontaine were engaged in activities and intellectual endeavors, such as database construction (the UDC and card collection), information retrieval, and developing search strategies, which today would be encompassed under information science.

In 1903, Otlet devised the word "documentation" (Williams, 1997) to describe the intellectual and actual processes of bringing together for application "all the written or graphic sources of our knowledge ..." (Rayward, 1997, p. 299). His interest included the processes in the creation of the content of works, their collection, the analysis to describe them in detail, and the dissection of the physical material into its subject components so the parts could be placed together in relationship to similar materials to create a documentary file. Lastly, all the novel aspects of each work would essentially be classified to become part of a larger overall delineation of science (Rayward, 1997). In the context of his time, Otlet was interested in the organization, storage, and retrieval of information in all the forms in which it is preserved as well as in the intellectual and practical concerns of the tasks involved. His vision included the technology of the time and anticipated its improvement and continued application. The UDC system he devised continues to be used today in French-speaking parts of Europe, Africa, and Latin America as well as in some special libraries in English-speaking countries (McIlwaine, 1997, p. 331).

Rayward (1997) credits Otlet for proposing the device that H. G. Wells would later describe as a "World Brain" and that Vannevar Bush would designate as Memex. Indeed, what was viewed as rather wild mental gymnastics in 1903, 1938, and 1945, respectively, took form in the latter part of the 20th century. In 1945, *Atlantic Monthly* published "As We May Think" by Vannevar Bush. As director of the Office of Scientific Research and Development for the United States, Bush had coordinated the efforts of American scientists during World War II to apply science to warfare. Looking toward the end of the war, Bush urged that scientific efforts be focused on making knowledge accessible (reprinted in Meadows, 1987). Among other things, Bush proposed a device to act as a supplement to the human brain, which would permit the acquisition of knowledge from a storage unit without the cumbersome indexes of the time but rather by a manner of association, quickly and efficiently (Meadows, 1987). It could be construed that he was proposing a modern computer, perhaps a computer connected to a network that permitted the selection of information via association and via relationships. While speed or efficiency of networks or web searches are relative and could be debated, there can be no question that compared to the systems in use in 1945, today's devices are phenomenal. Over time, we learn and apply what we learn, building on previous information and knowledge. (The serious student of information science would be well-served to read both Bush's "As We May Think," and his later related work, "Memex Revisited," written in 1967.) Bush's work motivated a renewed interest in information storage, transmission, and access by a variety of disciplines (Debons, 1990). It is significant that Bush's work is still cited in reference to having a role in information science and computer science.

Warfare was another important contributor to interest in what is now known as information science and why it is by necessity a study involving many disciplines. World War II created a demand for scientific information to combat the military technology and advantage of Germany and Japan. The depth of the Great Depression of 1929 devastated the scientific efforts in all but government-sponsored situations prior to the 1941 Japanese attack on our naval base at Pearl Harbor, Hawaii. World War II gave real motivation and impetus to invigorating the research apparatus of the U.S. Technological research involved communications, cryptography, detection systems such as sonar and radar, weaponry, delivery systems, manufacturing, computers, and more. Materials, even food, were rationed, not just due to supply transport problems but to divert goods and raw materials to the war effort. Urgent and significant research efforts were undertaken, one of the most famous being the Manhattan Project, the atomic weapon research that ultimately ended the war in the Pacific with the bombings of Hiroshima (August 6, 1945) and Nagasaki (August 9, 1945), Japan. From the Manhattan Project spun out a new set of technology and information concerns.

The Cold War era also contributed to renewed interest in technology and science to prevent the U.S. from falling behind the Soviet bloc in developing technology. The launching of *Sputnik* by the Soviets shocked the U.S. and spurred a renewed interest in science and scientific communication and information, as well as in the generation of knowledge. The Cuban Missile Crisis of the early 1960s fueled the United States' concerns about Soviet military prowess. The presence of a serious nuclear missile threat, a mere 90 miles off the coast of the U.S., emphasized the importance of advancing technologic knowledge, which required investigation into the creation, transfer, and behavior of information and knowledge. Military considerations continued to fuel interest in developing more advanced methods of handling and managing information, with an emphasis on the perspective of computer information and data processing, as these devices are critical to the management of weapon systems. Space exploration significantly influenced the increased concern with information management systems, computer communications, human behavior in relation to technology, artificial intelligence, expert systems, and much more (Debons, 1990).

The need for information cannot be denied or diminished in attempts to keep peace or to fight wars. The war in Iraq (2003–) has been fought using "pilotless" spy drone planes to detect insurgent strongholds and to provide coordinates for computer guided missiles. The weapons of the 21st century are information intensive and technologically complex, but they are still imperfect. Information gathering with the intention of measuring Iraq's real potential for weapons of mass destruction will be faulted by history, as will the lack of honest representation.

Association Trails

Professional or scholarly organizations usually attract people with related interests and typically common problems, challenges, or aspirations. These organizations are often the providers and consumers of their own research because the organization addresses issues in their realm of curiosity (Norton, 1998; Pearce, 1993). Theoretically, these associations can also be indicative of movement and development of specialties or disciplines (Crane, 1972). Williams (1997) argues that the Special Libraries Association (SLA) held interests more closely affiliated with the documentalist Otlet than with the American Library Association (ALA), which is the professional organization of librarians and the group from which SLA emerged in 1909. The focus of members of the SLA was to provide for the specific information needs of their organizations' users, regardless of format. SLA members were in situations that could not be generalized under the traditional library model of the time. Their concerns included the entire information process for their particular users, and this usually involved formats or materials that would not be handled in other types of libraries.

In 1937, the American Documentation Institute (ADI) was formed, heavily influenced by the 1935 Congress of the International Institute of Documentation (Williams, 1997). SLA became one of ADI's sponsors, but ADI interests, while related to SLA's, were more general. ADI had a more national perspective; it associated with the larger research and governmental projects, and therefore, it had less specifically focused concerns than SLA. Prior to World War II, the ADI was more oriented to the dissemination of information rather than acquisition or user services, which were both issues of importance to SLA. However, their interests were more aligned than SLA felt (Williams, 1997). Shera (1966) suggested that traditional librarianship in this country, as represented by ALA, became involved in the "cult of universal education and self-improvement" (p. 36), to the detriment of some professional growth. Documentalists and SLA were open to undertaking the development of new technologies and the extension of traditional library tools to new materials. Interpretations of these alliances would be best left to the historical participants. Suffice it to say that some significant ideological differences prevented the three organizations from becoming one. The division of thought placed SLA and ADI closer and more cooperative with one another than with ALA, despite the underlying foundational interests of all three being essentially the same: "1) *acquisition* of appropriate materials, and 2) their organization and interpretation for effective use" (Shera, 1966, p. 48). While the application of the material, the special circumstances of handling various formats, and the separate missions of the institutes that members of these three associations serve may differ, they are all associations interested in information as a practical and theoretical concern. The speed at which they adapted emerging technology to address their concerns, or the willingness to experiment with different methodologies, is no more significant to their profession than it is in general society and business. Different people, organizations, businesses, and institutions approached information technology at different speeds with widely varying success.

In 1968, the ADI changed its name to the American Society for Information Science (ASIS). Its membership included SLA and ALA members, but it also included a variety of science and technology disciplines and even some that might be positioned in the humanities. Taking a multi- and interdisciplinary approach to information concerns has yielded a richer, more diverse research front. The diversity of contributors has applied novel methods to the investigation while providing improved or new approaches to the practical problems of information organization, manipulation, and access in a wider arena (Rayward, 1983).

During the writing of the first edition of this volume in 2000, there was an enlarging debate in the library and information science community about librarianship, documentation, and information science in all of its possible configurations. In April 1999, the ALA sponsored a series of online discussion topics and a national meeting called the Congress on Professional Education to examine the roles and educational criteria for the library professional. (There have been two other Congresses—2nd Congress on Professional Education: Continuing Education November 2000, and 3rd Congress on Professional Education: Focus on Library Support Staff [COPE III] May 2003). Among many issues of concern for the first congress were the implications of name changes, and potentially related curricular changes at the professional education institutions, where the word "library" was removed from the title of the school or program. A number of schools of "information" were spawned from what were/are schools of library science; removing "library" from the banner has been considered a way to be more marketable and/or to indicate a divergence from "traditional" library science. Concerns regarding the instruction of core competencies, such as cataloging, collection development, and youth services, were raised related to these banner changes. The appearance of conflict among the accrediting body and the educational institutions stirred a movement to discuss and clarify the role of the library and information professionals and educators via a series of interactions and contacts.

The various debates in and about information science continue: questions about the appropriate education to be information practitioners, contention about definition of domains, scope of interests, and so on. Librarians do not necessarily see themselves as information scientists, and many information scientists are not librarians, though many information science professionals emerge from programs previously rooted in library science. In response to the concerns raised about name changes and potential curricular impacts, the ALA adopted Core Competencies of Librarianship in August 2008, after lengthy deliberations. The American Society for Information Science and Technology (ASIS&T; formerly ASIS) approved Educational Guidelines in November 2001.

It is perhaps better to identify information science practitioners by the intellectual tasks and conceptual investigations they work with, such as organization of information, retrieval of information, access issues related to information, and any manipulation or evaluation of information objects or behaviors. As Borko (1968) and Otten and Debons (1970) point out, there must be bridges between theory and practice, application and research. The field is a growing, changing entity that requires the attention and participation of all who are willing to expand their horizons. Information science involves many disciplines and practitioners with slightly, or even extremely, differing foci and concerns. Continued advances in technology and the study of information from all its various aspects will ensure unprecedented transformations in information science and all the related professions (Debons, 1990; Debons, Horne, and Cronenweth, 1988). As our understanding of information and its effects on all elements of our lives develops, we will be forced into accepting new professional roles and responsibilities in order to remain competitive.

Summary

Information is the fundamental link among all that we are, know, and do not know. Attempting to understand all the ramifications of information is an increasingly involved and complex collection of practical and research activities. As more is discovered about information and information behaviors, the more there is yet to discover.

Information science has a much debated and tangled history. It can be demonstrated that theories and concerns currently identified as information science topics were at issue for the earliest scholars (Weinberg, 1997). Even when most information was transmitted by human carrier via memory, the issue of storage and information transfer was real (Riesman, 1960). The concerns for access to information were not decreased by the development of the printing press. If anything, the printing press created even more demand for the investigation of collection and storage, classification, retrieval, communication, and evaluation. More complex techniques had to be devised to provide for more complex document systems as well as an explosion of information. Otlet's documentalist notions are closely related to current concepts of information science and information provision, classification flexibility, and resources to access the interior subject content of documents of all formats. Otlet expanded the notion of information content to objects and graphics as well as attempting to include them in searchable systems. By applying the DDC with modification, Otlet initiated a continuing experiment in classification. He also proposed, among many other things, what later would provide the basis for Bush's Memex, which, in turn, spurred tremendous growth in the research efforts down the path toward modern automation (Rayward, 1997).

Information science is a widening study that will continue to mature and fracture into specialties, if it is not yet doing so, and that is debatable too. Information is part of the world in which we live and work. Our ability to examine it and to develop an understanding of the roles and characters it plays will contribute to future knowledge. As more information is examined, more will be found. It is unlikely the complexity of the issue will diminish. As the impact of information influences all aspects of our existence, it is clear that the study is still in its infancy, as is our comprehension of the magnitude of information as a phenomenon.

References

Bates, M. J. 1999. The Invisible Substrate of Information Science. *Journal of the American Society for Information Science*, 50(12):1042–1050.

Bernal, J. D. 1939. Scientific Communication. In A. J. Meadows (Ed.), 1987. *The Origins of Information Science* pp. 167–183. B. Cronin (Series Ed.), Foundations of Information Science. vol. 1. London: Taylor Graham.

Boorstin, D. J. 1983. *The Discoverers*. New York: Random House.

Borko, H. January 1968. Information Science: What Is It? *American Documentation* 19(1):3–5.

Buckland, M. 1991. *Information and Information Systems*. New York: Praeger.

Bush, V. July 1945. As We May Think. *Atlantic Magazine*. Retrieved May 8, 2010, from www.theatlantic.com/magazine/archive/1969/12/as-we-may-think/3881

Bush, V. 1967. Memex Revisted. In V. Bush (Ed.), *Science Is Not Enough* pp. 75–101. New York: William Morrow.

Crane, D. 1972. *Invisible Colleges: Diffusion of Knowledge in Scientific Communities*. Chicago: The University of Chicago Press.

Debons, A. 1990. Foundations of Information Science. In M. C. Yovits (Ed.), *Advances in Computers* 31:325–371. Boston: Academic Press.

Debons, A., Horne, E., and Cronenweth, S. 1988. *Information Science: An Integrated View*. Boston: G. K. Hall.

Foskett, D. J. (Ed.). 1966. *Documentation and the Organization of Knowledge*. By Shera, J. H. Hamden, CT: Archon Books.

Heilprin, L. B. 1995. Science and Technology: From Prescientific Times to the Present. *Journal of the American Society for Information Science* 46(8):574–578.

Holley, R. P. 2003. New Realities, New Relationship. The Ivory Tower as Preparation for the Trenches: The Relationship Between Library Education and Library Practice. *C&RL News* 64(3):172.

Kochen, M. 1983. Library Science and Information Science. In F. Machlup and U. Mansfield (Eds.), *The Study of Information: Interdisciplinary Messages* pp. 371–377. New York: John Wiley & Sons.

Machlup, F. 1983. Semantic Quirks in Studies of Information. In F. Machlup and U. Mansfield (Eds.), *The Study of Information: Interdisciplinary Messages* pp. 641–671. New York: John Wiley & Sons.

Machlup, F., and Mansfield, U. (Eds.). 1983. *The Study of Information: Interdisciplinary Messages*. New York: John Wiley & Sons.

McIlwaine, I. C. 1997. The Universal Decimal Classification: Some Factors Concerning Its Origins, Development, and Influence. *Journal of the American Society for Information Science* 48(4):331–339.

Meadows, A. J. (Ed.). 1987. *The Origins of Information Science*. B. Cronin (Series Ed.), Foundations of Information Science. vol. 1. London: Taylor Graham.

Norton, M. J. 1998. Volunteer and Business Organizations: Similar Issues for Collaboration. In *Proceedings of the 1998 American Society for Information Science Midyear Meeting*, Orlando, FL, May 16–20, 1998, pp.78–83.

Otten, K., and Debons, A. 1970. Opinion Paper. Towards a Metascience of Information: Informatology. *Journal of the American Society for Information Science* pp. 89–94.

Pearce, J. L. 1993. *Volunteers: The Organizational Behavior of Unpaid Workers*. New York: Routledge.

Rayward, B. W. 1983. Library and Information Sciences: Disciplinary Differentiation, Competition, and Convergence. In F. Machlup and U. Mansfield (Eds.), *The Study of*

Information: Interdisciplinary Messages pp. 343–364. New York: John Wiley & Sons.

Rayward, B. W. 1997. The Origins of Information Science and the International Institute of Bibliography/International Federation for Information and Documentation (FID). *Journal of the American Society for Information Science* 48(4): 289–300.

Riesman, D. 1960. The Oral and Written Traditions. In E. Carpenter and M. McLuhan (Eds.), *Explorations in Communication* pp. 109–116. Boston: Beacon.

Shera, J. H. 1966. A Review of the Present State of Librarianship and Documentation. In D. J. Foskett (Ed.), *Documentation and the Organization of Knowledge* pp. 21–53. Hamden, CT: Archon Books.

Saracevic, T. (Ed.). 1970. *Introduction to Information Science*. New York: R. R. Bowker.

Taylor, R. S. 1966. Professional Aspects of Information Science and Technology. In C. A. Cuadra (Ed.), *Annual Review of Information Science and Technology.* vol.1. New York: John Wiley & Sons.

Weinberg, B. H. 1997. The Earliest Hebrew Citation Indexes. *Journal of the American Society for Information Science* 48(4):318–330.

Williams, R. V. 1997. The Documentation and Special Libraries Movements in the United States, 1910–1960. *Journal of the American Society for Information Science* 48(9):775–781.

Chapter 2

Two Perspectives on Information Science Reprinted

The discussion of what information science is and what role it will have in our world has been an ongoing debate for several decades. Two historical papers frequently cited in this discussion are reprinted here. The authors, Harold Borko, and Anthony Debons and Klaus Otten respectively, among the 20th century pioneers in the field, proposed key concepts for the discussion that are still considered relevant today.

In 1968, Harold Borko, wishing to prepare an answer to inquiries about the meaning of the name change of the American Documentation Institute to the American Society for Information Science, wrote "Information Science: What Is it?" With his permission the entire paper is included here for review and discussion. Not so oddly, the question of what information science is persists. Borko's remarks remain very pertinent if not slightly prophetic. He identified several reasons existing institutions were "inadequate to meet the communication needs of society." These included factors we recognize today, 40 years later, as still critical; almost all of the reasons relate to the speed of change in technology, the development of related knowledge, and the dissemination of both, as well as the larger implications to further growth. A key factor was and still is the need for continuous renewal of skills to cope with the speed of change, which also involves the continuing growth of membership from different constituencies in the information science fields.

Eugene Garfield proposed and effected the name change for the professional organization most closely linked to information science: the American Documentation Institute. The name was changed to the American Society for Information Science (ASIS) in 1968. Garfield advocated another name change for the Society to the American Society for Information Science and Technology (ASIS&T), which was approved by the society body and took effect in 2000 (History of ASIS&T, www.asis.org/history.html). In Garfield's Inaugural Address as incoming president of ASIS&T in 1999, he reiterated fundamentally the same observations about the future of information science in 1999 as in his 1962 essay, "Who are the information scientists?" (Garfield, 1962). Though discussing the need to make the professional society more available and more appealing to a broader group of disciplines in 1999, he observed that his 1962 essay "forecast that one day every laboratory scientist and scholar would become an information scientist. Today, almost all scholars are totally dependent upon information technology … We have to find a way to get outside the confines of the LIS world to reach this bigger audience" (Garfield, 2000, n.p.). His underlying contention was that the name change would better signal to the larger scholarly community the recognition of technology as an intrinsic component of information science (www.asis.org/Bulletin/Jan-00/garfield.html). The emergence of significantly more complex technologic tools to implement information processing, the application of technology to larger and larger arenas of endeavor, the integration of information technology into educational, cultural, and political landscapes should make it clear that there will be no escaping either the mechanisms of information as expressed by the technology or the much larger and inclusive effect of information itself upon our societies. Information and related technology (which might be argued is basically all technology) to analyze, move, and access information continues to evolve at an increasing speed; one discovery or technological innovation spawns multiple other advances. While the digital divide may continue to grow as an expression of economic disparity, the integration of technology tools and toys into our society and economy continues unabated, demanding more of the information scientist and the field.

Borko identified nine categories, based on those defined by (at that time) *Current Research and Development in Scientific Documentation*. These categories seem to still be representative of the areas of study in the field: information needs and uses; documentation creation and copying; language analysis; translation; abstracting, classification, coding, and indexing; system design; analysis and evaluation; pattern recognition; and adaptive systems. Though much expanded in the area of coverage in 1999 than in 1968, these categories still provide extensive coverage of information science.

In 1970, Klaus Otten and Anthony Debons published an opinion paper, included here with permission, for review and discussion; it attempts to formulate information science as a metascience, a superscience from which a common framework could be devised for all the scientists and participants in the information science fields to work within. This paper depicts information as a commodity and a basic phenomenon, much the same as energy or matter, an entity in and of its own with many adjunct characteristics. It expands on the disciplinary inclusiveness of information science, drawing into it mathematics, computer science, engineering science, library science, psychology, and linguistics. What should also be added are all the cognitive and social sciences, economics, and physical sciences; basically, there is no discipline that is not impacted by information and its science. Otten and Debons disagree with such a broad definition of information science: "Definitions of information science have been suggested that are all inclusive: as sciences concerned with all aspects of information. Our definition of metascience of information should clearly not be misunderstood as one of an all inclusive science. We view the metascience of information as a very specific science, concerned only with the foundations of information-related science and technologies and not concerned with the content of these specialized disciplines" (1970, p. 117). But since information is a component of everything and every science, it is obvious that information science is all-inclusive. It is in specific practice and specific context, however, that a refinement in information science has to be considered. Information in a nuclear reaction is not measured in the same context as information in a baseball game. Implementation of information available to analyze a DNA sample is not the same as analyzing a chess game; therefore, it may be reasonable to report information science as all-inclusive at a meta level; it is critical to recognize that as with other metafields, there are contextually sensitive and essential differentiations to be made.

The following two papers present a sound historical basis to begin the investigation of information and information science and obviously have colored the tone of this volume. While these papers were offered within an academic and scientific context, it is important to recognize that information has those aspects, but it is pervasive, invasive, persistent, and resistant in all areas of endeavor. Information is the link. While it is possible to discuss the identification of laws and try to characterize information in comparison to what is known, care should be taken. Information is the underlying aspect of everything, known and unknown. It is not merely the electronic energy associated with bits and computers. It is what is at the root of how everything, every cell, every object, every atom exists, and continues to exist. It does influence everything in ways not even recognized. Information units are DNA, the messages to create and replicate cells; information units are electrochemical exchanges within brain cells across synapses; information can replace confusion, reduce uncertainty, and create new uncertainty, and information about information is not a contradiction but a fact. In its complexity and its simplicity, information is the link to all that we are, as beings, as creatures in societies, as members of organizations, as units in a larger universe, and as single individual generators of information. Studying information is to determine more about it and how it affects not just our organizations and systems and technologies but how those things in reaction are affected by us.

Information Science: What Is It?[1]

Harold Borko

*Information Systems Technology Staff System Development Corp.,
Santa Monica, California*

Reprinted with permission: *American Documentation*—January 1968, pp. 3–5.

In seeking a new sense of identity, we ask, in this article, the questions: What is information science? What does the information scientist do? Tentative answers to these questions are given in the hope of stimulating discussion that will help clarify the nature of our field and our work.

Introduction

Now that the American Documentation Institute has voted to change its name to the American Society for Information Science, many of us have been forced to try to explain to friends and colleagues what information science is, what an information scientist does, and how all of this relates to librarianship and documentation. Those of us who have tried to make such explanations know that this is a difficult task. As an exercise I decided to prepare an answer to these questions at leisure rather than under the pressure of a direct inquiry. Let me state at the outset that I don't think I have *the* answer. It is hoped that this paper may provide a focus for discussion so that we can clarify our thinking and perhaps be more articulate about who we are and what we do.

Definition

The term "information science" has been with us for some time. In his chapter on the "Professional Aspects of Information Science and Technology" (1) in the *Annual Review*, Robert S. Taylor provides three definitions of information science. These have many points in common as well as some differences in emphasis. The definition that follows has been derived from a synthesis of these ideas.

Information science is that discipline that investigates the properties and behavior of information, the forces governing the flow of information, and the means of processing information for optimum accessibility and usability. It is concerned with that body of knowledge relating to the origination, collection, organization, storage, retrieval, interpretation, transmission, transformation, and utilization of information. This includes the investigation of information representations in both natural and artificial systems, the use of codes for efficient message transmission, and the study of information processing devices and techniques such as computers and their programming systems. It is an interdisciplinary science derived from and related to such fields as mathematics, logic, linguistics, psychology, computer technology, operations research, the graphic arts, communications, library science, management, and other similar fields. It has both a pure science component, which inquires into the subject without regard to its application, and an applied science component, which develops services and products.

If this definition seems complicated, it is because the subject matter is complex and multidimensional, and the definition is intended to be all-encompassing.

Obviously information science is not the exclusive domain of any one organization. Traditionally, the American Documentation Institute has been concerned with the study of recorded, that is, documentary, information. This is still our main emphasis; however, the work is now embedded in a larger context. Librarianship and documentation are applied aspects of information science. The techniques and procedures used by librarians and documentalists are, or should be, based upon the theoretical findings of information science, and conversely the theoretician should study the time-tested techniques of the practitioner.

The Need for Information Science

Information science as a discipline has as its goal to provide a body of information that will lead to improvements in the various institutions and procedures dedicated to the accumulation and transmission of knowledge. There are in existence a number of such institutions and related media: These include *books* for packaging knowledge; *schools* for teaching the accumulated knowledge of many generations; *libraries* for storing and disseminating knowledge; *movies* and *television* for the visual display of knowledge; *journals* for the written communication of the latest technical advances in specialized fields; and *conferences* for the oral communication of information.

These institutions have served, and continue to serve, very useful functions, but they are inadequate to meet the communication needs of today's society. Some of the factors that contribute to their inadequacies are:

1.   The tremendous growth in science and technology and the accelerated pace at which new knowledge becomes available and old knowledge becomes obsolete;

2.   The fast rate of obsolescence of technical knowledge, so that the old graduate must go back to school and update his skills;

3.   The large number of working scientists and the large number of scientific and technical journals which exist today;

4. The increased specialization which makes communication and the exchange of information between disciplines very difficult;

5. The short time lag between research and application that makes the need for information more pressing, and more immediate.

As a result of these pressures, the existing methods for exchanging information have been found wanting. Information science has not kept pace with other scientific developments, and now there is a need to concentrate efforts in this field and to catch up. If communication and information exchange procedures are not improved, all other scientific work will be impeded; the lack of communication will result in a duplication of effort and a slowing of progress.

The importance of information science and the reasons for the current emphasis upon this discipline are thus clear: The need to organize our efforts and meet the new challenges finds a concrete expression in the American Society for Information Science.

Information Science Research and Applications

As was pointed out in the definition, information science has both a pure and an applied aspect. Members of this discipline, depending upon their training and interests, will emphasize one or the other aspect. Within information science there is room for both the theoretician and the practitioner, and clearly both are needed. Theory and practice are inexorably related; each feeds on the work of the other.

The researcher in information science has a broad field in which to pursue his investigations. A glance through the 566 pages (excluding the Glossary and Index) of the last issue (No. 14) of *Current Research and Development in Scientific Documentation* (2) shows a staggering range of projects being studied. The 655 project statements are organized into nine categories as follows:

1. *Information Needs and Uses*
   Behavioral studies of users; citation studies; communication patterns; literature use studies.

2. *Document Creation and Copying*
   Computer-assisted composition; microforms; recording and storing; writing and editing.

3. *Language Analysis*
   Computational linguistics; lexicography; natural language (text) processing; psycholinguistics; semantic analysis.

4. *Translation*
   Machine translation; translation aids.

5. *Abstracting, Classification, Coding and Indexing*
   Classification and indexing systems; content analysis; machine-aided classification, extracting and indexing; vocabulary studies.

6. *System Design*
   Information centers; information retrieval; mechanization of library operations; selective dissemination of information.

7. *Analysis and Evaluation*
   Comparative studies; indexing quality; modeling; test methods and performance measures; translation quality.

8. *Pattern Recognition*
   Image processing; speech analysis.

9. *Adaptive Systems*
   Artificial intelligence; automata; problem solving; self-organizing systems.

In essence, information science research investigates the properties and behavior of information, the use and transmission of information, and the processing of information for optimal storage and retrieval.

Theoretic studies should not, and in fact do not, take place in a vacuum. There is a constant interplay between research and application, between theory and practice. As in most every scientifically based discipline, the researchers form a small but vocal minority. The bulk of the membership is applications oriented. These members deal, on a daily basis, with the problems and practices of information transfer. They are responsible for making the system work in spite of all inadequacies, and they develop improvements within an operational context. They need to be informed about the new techniques being developed and when these are proven, they need to apply them and evaluate them under operating conditions. Yet, it is important to recognize that, particularly in information science, there is no sharp distinction between research and technology. It is a matter of emphasis, and all members share a concern over a common set of problems.

Every scientific discipline needs an academic component, and so it is important to note that information science is now a recognized discipline in an increasing number of major universities. The subjects taught vary from school to school, probably more as a function of available professorial skills rather than any real difference of opinion about what should be taught. Such diversity is desirable. The field is too young, and it is too soon to standardize on a single curriculum, for a variety of programs encourages exploration and growth. As students graduate, they will exert a unifying and maturing influence on the educational program.

Summary

By way of a summary, I will restate the questions and answers that led to this essay on information science. Again, I would like to add the caveat that these are not meant to be final answers but rather to serve as foci for further discussion and clarification.

What is information science? It is an interdisciplinary science that investigates the properties and behavior of information, the forces that govern the flow and use of information, and the techniques, both manual and mechanical, of processing information for optimal storage, retrieval, and dissemination.

What then is documentation? Documentation is one of many applied components of information science. Documentation is concerned with acquiring, storing, retrieving, and disseminating recorded documentary information, primarily in the form of report and journal literature. Because of the nature of the collection and the user's requirements, documentation has tended to emphasize the use of data processing equipment, reprography and microforms as techniques of information handling.

What does an information scientist do? Information scientists may work as researchers, educators, or applications specialists in the field of information science; that is to say, they may do research aimed at developing new techniques of information handling; they may teach information science; and they may apply the theories and techniques of information science to create, modify and improve information handling systems.

Information science is an important emergent discipline, and the information scientist has an important function in our society.

Postscript

This article was written and submitted to the Editor of American Documentation in September 1967. Clearly the members of ASIS are not the only people worried about the vocabulary of information science and technology, for in October 1967, Mr. Samuel A. Miles, a member of the Society of Technical Writers and Editors and also a member of ASIS, published a paper entitled "An Introduction to the Vocabulary of Information Technology" in Technical Communications, the journal for STWP. The general purpose of this paper was to familiarize the technical writer with the activities and the vocabulary of the information processor. To do this, Mr. Miles selected ten basic terms and their definitions from the proposed ASA standards and from the DoD glossary. These terms are similar to and supplement the terms in the Information Science article.

In this ecumenical atmosphere, it is good to know that other societies are equally concerned with the workings of information science, and it is a pleasant duty to reference the work of Mr. Samuel A. Miles.[2]

References

1. Taylor, R. S., Professional Aspects of Information Science and Technology, in C. A. Cuadra (Ed.), *Annual Review of Information Science and Technology*, Vol. 1, John Wiley & Sons, New York, 1966.

2. National Science Foundation, *Current Research and Development in Scientific Documentation*, No. 14, Office of Scientific Information, NSF-66-17, Washington, D.C., 1966.

Endnotes

1. This paper was prompted by the suggestion, made by ADI Headquarters to the members of ADI, that the diversity of members and interests of the organization would be better represented if the name of the society were changed to American Society for Information Science.

2. Samuel A. Miles, *An Introduction to the Vocabulary of Information Technology*, *Technical Communications*, Fall Quarter 1967, pp. 20–24.

Opinion Paper

Towards a Metascience of Information: Informatology

Klaus Otten and Anthony Debons[1]

Reprinted with permission of John Wiley & Sons, Inc.: Published in the *Journal of the American Society for Information Science*, January–February 1970, pp. 89–94.

Arguments are advanced to suggest that information and operations on information are phenomena, the principles of which provide the basis for a metascience of information (informatology). The fundamental character of the phenomena is evidenced in the operations executed during the processing and communication functions. The role of the metascience is dictated by several factors, namely, the need for a common basis upon which all information-oriented specialized sciences and technologies can be understood and studied, a common framework and language for all scientists and technologists concerned in some form or other with information, and the need to integrate various theories that concern themselves with the phenomena of information on one side and man's relationship to the phenomena on the other side. The content of the postulated metascience of information is circumscribed by a list of specific questions and problems for which the science has to provide answers and solutions. It is suggested that an educational concept responsive to the needs of metascience of information be developed and implemented.

Introduction

The emergence of a new discipline concerned with theories on information has been proposed by Gorn (1) and others. The importance of the new discipline for all sectors of human activities and development, especially in education, has been discussed. In this paper, an attempt is made to outline the nature and content of this new discipline in the hope that it might provide the basis for further examination and discussion.

Information, both as a commodity and as a basic phenomenon is gaining importance in all activities of man. We seek information, we exchange information, we "use" information, in many contexts. We have developed entire technologies centered around information and its dissemination, e.g., the arts of recording (writing and printing), of broadcasting (advertising, publishing, radio and TV broadcasting), of transmitting (postal systems, telephone and telegraph, satellite communications), and of processing information (computers), to name just the more important ones. As a phenomenon in its own right, we have been made aware of the pervasion of information and operations on information through nature and human society, in the communication between cells of any organism, in the information exchange between living creatures and within social systems.

To explore the nature of information and operations thereupon as phenomena, two questions have to be raised: (1) Does information represent a fundamental and universal phenomenon similar to matter and energy? (2) Are the various operations performed on information based on fundamental phenomena and are they hence only different forms of some fundamental relations?

If the answers to the above two questions are essentially affirmative, then we believe that the body of knowledge describing these phenomena and relations will evolve as the subject of a new science. This proposed new science, by its nature of unifying concepts now included as part of established sciences and by the postulated need to derive formalistic descriptions, may be referred to as a metascience (2). More specifically, it may be referred to as a metascience of information.

To expand on this concept we have established several objectives for this paper. The first objective is to show that the answers to the two questions raised appear to be affirmative and that a metascience of information is emerging. The second objective is to outline the basis for the development of a metascience of information. The third objective is to state the specific goals of such a metascience and distinguish these objectives from those of existing related sciences.

Information and Operations on Information as Fundamental Phenomena

Basic Constituents of Information

First, we want to distinguish between information and operations on information. Information, like energy, can be viewed as a fundamental phenomenon. Energy is manifested in a variety of attributes (heat, electrical energy, chemical energy, etc.). Similarly, the attributes of information are experienced in various forms (knowledge, news, etc.). Energy can be described abstractly and analytically independent of its form. Likewise one might postulate that information can be approached on the same terms.

Operations on information, on the other side can be compared to the various forms by which energy can be manipulated, e.g., the conversion of heat into electricity, chemical energy into heat, etc. These manipulations on energy obey certain fundamental laws. In the same way one can postulate that operations on information will obey its own set of fundamental laws.

The various phenomena to which we refer to as "information" (i.e., human communications, computations, automated control) contain invariant components irrespective of the particular form (news, knowledge, etc.). Likewise the multitude of operations that can be performed on these phenomena appear to be composed of invariant components. It is therefore logical to pursue the development of formalistic and abstract descriptions of these invariant components as we will describe later.

All information processing operations can be performed by digital computers. To achieve this general information processing by computers, the processes have to be decomposed into a number of elementary operations. It is this set of elementary operations that constitutes the building blocks for all complex information processing in nature or machinery.

This recognition of the fundamental nature of information processing has evolved slowly. Information processing in the past has been the privilege of man. "White collar" professions, that is, professions centered around information processing activities, developed. Information processing in these professions ranges from routine clerical chores to the demanding intellectual activities of a diagnostician, researcher, or manager. The variety of information processing activities, and hence of white collar professions, increases rapidly.

Along with the diversification of information processing tasks goes a gradual takeover of information processing by machines. First, machines were invented to perform elementary calculations; that is, fundamental information processes on numbers only. It was later found that the same types of machines could handle many nonnumerical repetitive chores usually handled by clerks. Gradually computers have entered all areas of information processing. They execute a wide variety of complex operations on information that conventionally had been performed by man in the fields of business, industry, research, education, and in other areas. These complex operations are not performed by specialized machines but by computers, which can perform only a limited number of elementary logic operations.

How is it possible that many of our operations on information, such as comparing, calculating, extrapolating, analyzing, and even reading, writing, composing, and designing can be performed by one and the same machine, executing only elementary operations? We must assume that the apparently different information processing tasks all have some common basis. *This common basis must be expressable in terms of the elementary operations executed by the computer. The ability to translate complex information processing tasks into sequences of elementary operations may be accepted as evidence for the fundamental nature of information and of information processing.*

The fundamental nature of information per se can also be demonstrated by the processes of information transmission or communications in general. Any transmission link can, in principle, be used to transmit every kind of information. A communication channel provides the means for the transmission of information. This involves the transmission of a physical signal. However, this signal can be used to convey any form of information. For example, it can convey information expressed in the language of computers, information in the form of speech, of graphics, or even of motion pictures (TV). The operations performed in transmitting the various physical representations of information are one and the same; that is, the engineer can design his communication system without knowing the nature of information being transmitted as long as he knows the quality of information being transmitted. In brief: the fundamental character of information and of information processing is suggested by the nature of several operations on information. It is primarily indicated by the facts that:

1. All different forms of information processing can be performed by serial execution of a few elementary operations (computers used for simulation), and

2. Information in all of its different forms is transmittable by one and the same process (communications).

Theories Underlining the Fundamental Nature of Information and of Operations on Information

Indications of the commonality of information phenomena have, of course, been well studied from various points of view. As a result, we have a number of theories attempting either to describe selected information phenomena in a quantitative form or to establish a common basis for the study of information phenomena in two or more related fields.

Information theory is the outgrowth of an attempt to measure whatever can be transmitted over a communication channel of given measurable physical properties. Information in information theory is a probabilistic quantity, a measure of an expectation value: The probability of occurrence of an event prior to its observation. Information is viewed as the result of stochastic selection process (from a defined set of alternatives); hence, the measurable quantity is named "selective" information. Consequently, information-theory deals with one specific aspect and type of information. It does not deal with many other (particularly semantic) forms that we generally refer to as information. Most important, it does not provide a theory for "information" as used and valued by man in his daily actions.

The common concept of information is qualitative and can be distinguished from the selective information concept as that of semantic information. Ultimately, semantic information would have to be measured in terms of the conceptual system of the user; man. Linguists and semanticists are in search of a measure for semantic information but have not as yet succeeded in finding one.

Various other mathematical theories have received impetus from the rapidly developing information technologies and have resulted in the branching off of specialized information-oriented disciplines of mathematics. Examples are coding theory (evolving from set and function theories in response to needs in the field of communication), and the theory of finite automata (evolving from the theories of computability in response to needs of designers of algorithmic programs, in particular, of programs simulating human recognition functions).

Other examples can be derived from the various system theories. Theories describing the behavior of dynamic systems have evolved in response to the need for full control over the design of electric signal processing systems. These theories serve as the link between physical characteristics of system components and system responses to signals. Since signals are carriers of information, any form of signal processing is an operation on information. Theories of dynamic systems initially were derived to account for relations between electrical signals and structures of electrical components, often referred to as systems. Consequently, theories of dynamic systems have been recognized as theories describing the behavior of any signal in any systems that are analogous to electrical systems.

All of these theories given as examples attempt to describe the invariance of information and hence can be considered as building blocks of the metascience of information.

The Development of a Science of Information

The Concept of Metascience and the Functions of a Metascience

Human desires and needs lead to the development of technologies: The advancement of these technologies requires explanations to technological questions that arise. Hence, the advancing technologies stimulate research and lead to the development of sciences. As the technologies progress, research and, correspondingly, the resulting sciences become more and more specialized. More and more sciences evolve, sciences that become narrower and narrower in specialization. As a result, the chances for fertile and productive communication between related specialized sciences decrease.

In response to trends of higher and higher specialization, usually, a counteraction takes place; the need for communication between sciences leads to a re-evaluation of the foundations of related specialized sciences.

These re-evaluations stimulate the formulation of new simplifying and unifying theories that subsume the main concepts of the original theories of contributing sciences. These unified theories may be considered as the body of a new science, which may be named the metascience for those sciences for which the metascience provides the unifying foundation.[2]

Metasciences provide the common language and the means for translating concepts among divergent fields and as such, assist in unification of knowledge in general. Metasciences serve three important functions:

1. They permit the description of the common basis of related disciplines at a higher level of abstraction than possible within the framework of the individual contributing disciplines.

2. They provide a common language for scientists and technologists in divergent fields of specialization.

3. They establish the means for translating knowledge gained in one field to other related fields.

Metasciences require precise and abstract formalizations and definitions of the foundations of all related sciences, thereby strengthening the foundations of the sciences under unification through the metascience. Evolving metasciences stimulate the advancement of the specialized sciences and contribute to the knowledge transfer between otherwise isolated disciplines.

The specialization of sciences in our century has led to the evolution of several metasciences in the sense of unifying base sciences, even though they are usually not identified as such. We have already referred to the metascience of mathematics: "formal mathematics." As another example, we may cite the parallel developments of theories used for the analysis and synthesis in the fields of mechanical systems, acoustical systems, and electrical. For each of these systems, specialized theories evolved. However, the analogies between phenomena observed in these three disciplines lead to the development of the general theories of linear and nonlinear dynamic systems. These theories are equally applicable to any one of the three types of systems as well as to other physical systems. These general system theories can be considered as the "Metatheories" for the various fields of dynamic system technologies.

Other illustrations of metasciences can be obtained from linguistics, which can be regarded as the metascience for the body of knowledge on languages and their use for communication.

As metamathematics evolved in response to the divergence and growths of specialized mathematical disciplines, similarly, we anticipate the evolution of a metascience of information in response to the need for a critical reevaluation of the foundation upon which many information disciplines and technologies are based. This anticipated metascience can be viewed as the science of information (or informatology). Informatology can be defined as the study of the fundamental principles underlying the structure and use of information.

The Metascience of Information

Sciences and technologies centered around the phenomena of information are mushrooming. Diverging disciplines of ever increasing specialization grow in response to the "information explosion." For that reason, the need for a unifying science appears apparent.

Need for the existence of the metascience of information can be demonstrated by the following factors:

1. There is a need to provide a common basis upon which all information-oriented specialized sciences and technologies can be understood and studied.

2. A common framework and language must be established to serve technologists concerned with information in some form or other.

3. There is the need to build bridges between the abstract theories attempting theoretical explanations of the phenomena of information on the one side and between the (at present predominately empirical) theories describing man's relationship to information phenomena on the other side.

Information is generated, processed, and used by men. If machines are involved in handling information, these machines generate, process and use information under the control by man and for man. Thus, the metascience of information has two focal points: the phenomena of information and man's relation to the phenomena.

Man sets the limit to what can be done with information. As ultimate user and, in many cases, as generator of information, his information processing capabilities determine the usefulness of information systems to him individually or collectively. This statement concerning man as the point of reference applies even to the functions of hypothesized supermachines exhibiting artificial intelligence exceeding that of exceptional human performance.

It must be recognized however, that the complexity of man's relation to information and of his information processing, prevent man, at this time, from being the test bed for information sciences. The theories forming the body for the metascience of information may have to evolve slowly. They have to be based on elementary information relations that can be examined and verified under controlled conditions in man-made form and environment. The application of these fundamental laws and relations in more and more complex systems ultimately have to be applicable to man and always have to serve man.

The ultimate orientation of a metascience of information toward man as the user of information does not exclude the development of information processes for which neither nature nor man provide examples. The evolution of artificial intelligence in the sense of intellectual or information generating power exceeding that of man is conceivable. Yet, it always has to be under the control and submission to man as its originator and user.

Questions to Be Answered by Metascience of Information

The objectives and the content of the postulated metascience of information may become more evident if we look at the major questions for which it has to provide answers.

1. Can the concept of selective information be extended to permit the measurement of semantic or qualitative information? If so, how; if not, what concept of semantic or qualitative information allows quantitative analysis? (Information Theory, Semantics)[3]

2. Can the various forms of information processing be analyzed in the form of common elementary processes and can these processes be described by fundamental laws? (Mathematical Logic, Automata Theory, Computer Sciences)

3. How can different methods of information processings, which achieve the same results, be compared, and what are suitable quantitative measures that will enable the differentiation of the complexity and efficiency of operations on information? (Computer Sciences, Computational Linguistics)

4. How does man associate meaning with information, and what is the relationship between meaning and his established value system? (Psychology, Philosophy, Semantics)

5. What are the laws that make natural languages[4] the universal means of formulating (creating) and communicating new concepts and ideas? (Linguistics, Semantics)

    Natural languages in the widest sense (including music and forms of artistic expression) permit the creation of new concepts. Even if there exists no equivalent (in nature or in man's history) for these new concepts, they become immediately understandable to persons other than the creator by virtue of the context of the language and the situation. Are there fundamental laws that govern the conditions under which "creation" can take place and how can new creations (concepts) be understood if the description can only indirectly suggest a thought process?

6. What are the interrelations between the forms of energy, matter, and order (or structure), and the use of these forms to represent (selective) information?

    Selective information, when communicated, is always associated with some form of physical representation: as matter, or energy, or both (molecules in genetic code; energy quanta in communications via light). The degree of order of the physical form is correlated with information. What are the laws that govern the ordered use of matter or energy to represent information?

7. What are the physical limitations of communication, information processing, and information storage? (Communication Theory, Brain Research, Research in Memory Technology)

    Neither energy nor matter are continua. The smallest units of energy (quanta) and matter (atoms, nuclear particles) set absolute lower bounds to the information that can be represented by given physical systems or processes.

8. What are the laws governing the organization of information as it applies to mass information storage and retrieval?

(Experimental Psychology, Library Sciences, Computer Science, Brain Research)

9. What are the laws of information dissemination which explain the processes of cognitive perception? (Educational Psychology, Theories of Self-Adaptive Systems, Cybernetics)

10. Are there properties of information which stimulate creativity and is creativity an information processing function for which laws can be developed? (Cybernetics, Artificial Intelligence, Semantics)

11. What are the laws of information accumulation, updating, and assimilation? (Educational Psychology, Library Sciences, Computer Sciences)

The foregoing problem areas do not exhaust all the possible questions that are the domain of a metascience of information. They are suggestive of the nature of the questions and, as such, should serve to circumscribe the anticipated content of the science.

Metascience of Information and Its Relation to Other Sciences

Metascience of information, as indirectly defined by the major questions for which it has to provide answers, is a science by itself. However, it has concerns common with other sciences and disciplines. This is schematically shown in Figure 2.1. As a metascience, it shares with the related sciences the formalistic descriptions of the respective science foundations. If this were the full content of the science, it would not require separate identity. However, the metascience's main contribution is the function it plays in synthesizing the various formalistic descriptions into one unified set of theories which is equally applicable to all contributor sciences and disciplines. There are numerous new disciplines concerned directly with some selected phenomena of information. We have to investigate the differences between some of those sciences and our postulated metascience to show that none of the following sciences by itself is aimed at answering all of the questions listed above.

Computer sciences are concerned with the processing of information, particularly by digital computers. Emphasis is on the analysis and synthesis of information processing operations and on the implementation of those by computers. Questions concerning the communication of information and the use of information by man are of secondary importance. The focal points are algorithmic processing and computer technology. Computer sciences are concerned principally with information and information processes as is the

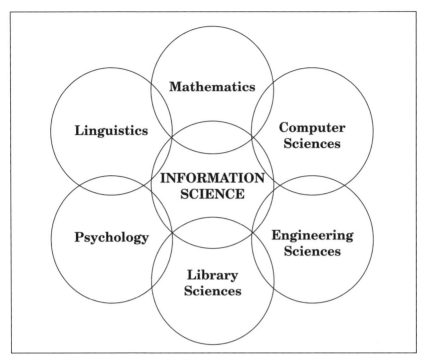

Figure 2.1 Information Science and Related Sciences. (Schematic two dimensional representation of an n-dimensional relationship—only the most important related sciences are shown.)

metascience of information. However, the information-oriented problems in computer sciences are centered around computers as processor and are hence specialized. The metascience of information, in contrast, is studying and describing the fundamental concepts of information and operation on information regardless of its main function—its theories must be equally applicable to computers, biological systems, man, social systems and man-made information systems.

A comparison of the metascience of information with cybernetics is difficult, since cybernetics has different meanings to different people. Let us refer to cybernetics by Wiener (3) ("Cybernetics as science of control and communication in the animal and machine.") Cybernetics, according to this definition, is centered around control and communication: control of systems to achieve desired objectives, and communication of information to support the control functions. The focal point for cybernetics is control. Information in its various forms is essential to the cybernetician, but always as the means to exercise or achieve control. In contrast, the postulated metascience has information, per se, not its use, as its focal point. The particular use of information and information processing is of secondary interest. Cybernetics can perhaps be viewed as the metascience of purposeful dynamic systems in general.

Finally, we have to comment on the various forms of "information science" ranging from the narrowly defined library and documentation science concepts to the all-inclusive claims for an information science. Information science, in the sense of documentation and library science, is oriented toward one sector of the postulated metascience: the laws of classification and of mass information storage and retrieval. To date, this library-oriented information science has been preoccupied with developing improvements of documented message handling and has not been able to devote much effort toward the study of the laws underlying these operations. Therefore, information science in the library science sense represents primarily a technology, with some science-oriented aspects that can be considered as sub-fields of the postulated metascience.

Definitions of information science have been suggested that are all inclusive: as sciences concerned with all aspects of information. Our definition of metascience of information should clearly not be misunderstood as one of an all inclusive science. We view the metascience of information as a very specific science, concerned only with the foundations of information-related sciences and technologies and not concerned with the content of these specialized disciplines. Any claim for all-inclusiveness would lead to superficiality and therefore would not serve any purpose.

Training Requirements for a Metascience of Information

Based on the foregoing, we will argue that the training for future information scientists should be started now by the development of an integrated information science curriculum in which information science is understood as the evolving metascience of information.

The metascience of information requires a special training for its successful development. Information scientists, in contrast to information technologists, need to be oriented toward the objectives of integrating present and future knowledge of the laws inherent in information phenomena. They require carefully developed inter-disciplinary skills. Tools and concepts from engineering, computer science, library science, and psychology should be coupled with an understanding of fundamental sciences such as mathematics. In this way, students can apply their understanding to the formulation of meaningful research, which may help in establishing the laws and theories for the metascience discussed in this paper.

Acknowledgments

Appreciation is expressed to Dr. Carlos Crocetti, Rome Air Development Center, Rome, N.Y., and to Dr. Vladimir Slamecka, of the Georgia Institute of Technology, for their helpful comments and suggestions.

References

1. Saul Gorn, The Computer and Information Sciences and the Community of Disciplines, *Behavioral Sciences*, 12:433–452 (1967).

2. Stephen C. Kleene, *Introduction to Metamathematics*, D. Van Nostrand Co., Inc., Princeton, NJ, 1950.

3. Norbert Wiener, *Cybernetics*, The M.I.T. Press, Cambridge, Mass., 1948, 1961.

Endnotes

1. Respectively, The National Cash Register Company, Dayton, Ohio, and Dept. of Information Science, University of Dayton, Dayton, Ohio.

2. The evolution of formal mathematics (which is referred to as metamathematics) is an example of this type of science evolution. Metamathematics provides the unified foundation of all specialized disciplines of mathematics.

3. Specific disciplines are quoted in parentheses, which are concerned with the specific area.

4. Natural languages are codes of communication resulting from an evolutionary process of culture. In the narrow sense these are spoken languages, e.g., English, French, etc., in the wide sense they include, e.g., music and art.

Chapter References

ASIS&T. [n.d.]. History of ASIS&T. Retrieved February 15, 2010, from www.asis.org/history.html

Garfield, E. August 1962. Who Are the Information Scientists? *Essays of an Information Scientist* 1:2. Current Contents, August 7, 1962. Retrieved February 15, 2010, from www.garfield.library.upenn.edu/essays/V1p002y1962-73.pdf

Garfield, E. 2000. Dr. Eugene Garfield's Inaugural Address. From 1950s Documentalists to 20th Century Information Scientists and Beyond. Retrieved February 15, 2010, from www.asis.org/Bulletin/Jan-00/garfield.html

Chapter 3

Communication

Melanie J. Norton

One of the most frequent causes of confusion about information's identity is that information is communication. While information and communication are intricately connected and have some aspects that seem similar, they are not the same. Communication involves process, or the movement of information, or potential information. Information and communication are impacted by context. Context may provide dimensions to information or to communication; these dimensions influence the outcome of the communication or the interpretation of the information. Technical aspects of communication compared to human communication, such as the signal quality versus the content and interpretation of the signal, are context dependent. One of the more influential theories of communication originated with a question about an electronic signal transmission. Modifying that theory to be more applicable to the human communication and information models provides insight into the special issues of information and human communication.

Communication and Information

In the context of an electronic signal, communication is the process whereby a signal is transmitted from a source via some channel to a recipient. The signal is sent from a beginning point through a channel, such as a wire or cable, to a receiver. For example, an electrical signal, generated by dialing a phone number, is carried over phone wires to the appropriate telephone set where the signal is received (Schramm, 1973). This perspective on communication is credited to Norbert Wiener's book *Cybernetics*, and Claude Shannon's paper "The Mathematical Theory of Communication" (Young, 1987). It was in the context of an electronics and engineering problem for which Shannon proposed the mathematical theory of

41

communication, a theory to measure the amount of "information" in a signal. His theory revolved around a statistical formula to determine the amount of deviation from a code the signal could tolerate and be received in a state that could be correctly decoded. Shannon's interest was in the quality of the transmission, not in the meaning of the signal (Ritchie, 1991; Schramm, 1973; Young, 1987). Noise in the channel, such as static, would interfere with the clarity of a signal so the receiver would have difficulty distinguishing the intended signal from other signals. Such difficulty would complicate decoding the signal correctly. In the context of an electronic transmission, a disruption in the signal causes a communication failure. Shannon resolved this problem essentially by determining how much redundancy was necessary to ensure the electronic signal could be correctly interpreted. Consider attempting to have a phone conversation with someone while the phone was malfunctioning so you actually understood only every third word. You would be attempting to reconstruct what the caller was saying, despite the omissions; the degree of success would be dependent on a variety of factors, including your existing knowledge of the caller, the potential message, and your skill at interpreting cryptic messages. Perhaps you were able to have the caller repeat the information enough times to fill in the missing parts; redundancy in transmission whether electronic or human communication can improve the likelihood of information being transmitted successfully.

Shannon opposed the application of his theory to other than its specific problem (Bar-Hillel, 1964; Ritchie, 1991), though it was the coauthor of Shannon's book *The Mathematical Theory of Communication*, Warren Weaver (1949) who suggested the theory could be applied to other areas of communication (Ritchie, 1991; Severin and Tankard, 1992). There continues to be controversy about the appropriateness of the extension of Shannon's theory outside of the specific domain of its original development. Nonetheless, this theory has been the basis of many new interpretations of activities in a variety of disciplines (Shera, 1983; Tribus, 1983; Young, 1987).

In a generalized context, the concepts underlying Shannon's theory may be extended to a broader vision of communication. Communication involves the sending of a signal of some type through some medium to a receiver (Schramm, 1973). When a cat cries, the sound itself is a signal; the sound is carried through the air (the channel) and received by your eardrums, which the sound causes to vibrate. When you speak, your voice is a signal carried by the air to the ears of whoever is present; they are the receivers. However, if you stand perfectly still and say nothing, you are still communicating, or sending a signal, via a different medium, perhaps visual rather than audible or perhaps chemical. The signal may be construed as information. Information is a concept that is difficult to define, and we subscribe to the notion that there is nothing that is not information. In this framework, communication then is a process involving the transmission of information, in whatever form via whatever vehicle, to a receiver, or decoder. Information is a component in the process of communication. Information may be the core of the activity, as in trying to distribute research information; it may be incidental to the process, as in "small talk." Communication may be the result of processing information, or the cause of processing it, such as when someone tells you a riddle, and you attempt to process the information into a solution.

Schramm states that "information is the stuff of communication. It is what distinguishes communication from, say swimming or bouncing a ball ..." (1973, p. 38). Schramm views communication as an activity essential to the organization of human society, culture, relationships, and survival. The movement, exchange, and processing of information are the underlying, and possibly unconscious, impetus to engage in acts of communication. Such acts are part of building a community, defining a standard of conduct, establishing an identity within a group, or even being in touch with one's self.

How is it that the movement of information is so involved with humanity and seems so important? Information may describe, characterize, or model the world. The color of the sky informs us of aspects of the weather—a clear blue sky tells us of a different sort of weather than a gray-black cloudy sky. Experience helps us to identify which of these colors indicates good weather or bad weather. How is the information shared without the experience? It is done by the communication of others who relay this measure of weather to us, as we compare their information to our experience at a later time. The shape of a mountain may convey information about its formation just as the color of a gem or mineral indicates its origins in the earth. The information may reside in the object, it may be inferred, or it may be communicated by human exchange or merely by human observation and interpretation. Schramm (1973) makes the point that information and communication are not limited to languages, or words. There are verbal and nonverbal communications that transmit information, and they may be culturally specific. Information may be communicated not necessarily by what is said but by the fact that someone finds it important enough to say. Information may also be gleaned from how it is communicated, such as choice of words, level of excitement, tone of voice, speed of speech, the pitch of music, or even movements and moments of silence. Communication involves a transmission or sending something, not necessarily words, or electronic tones; it may be images, physical signals such as hand or flag waving; it may be sound, or not, but it has a source and a recipient.

Information, Uncertainty, and Communication

Information has been defined in many ways, including the grand explanation in the first chapter, but it is necessary to clarify how the word and its adjuncts will be considered here in context with communication (Dervin and Nilan, 1986). Information in a communication application is input from any source that has the potential to affect, reduce, or supplement a state of uncertainty, which is a lack of information, to allow decisions to be made or new communication to occur. Yes, this is a circular statement because information can influence existing information, causing or requiring more information to be moved. Uncertainty has many circumstantial definitions, but in the context with which we are concerned, it can be construed as the probable amount of useful information available. The availability and usefulness of information can be influenced by all the factors that characterize it, including presentation, recipients' ability to capture what they need, and all the noise that will contribute to the interpretation. The greater the uncertainty, the less recognizable information is available to make a decision. In the 21st century, there is an overabundance of information, but that does not make it recognizable to deal with decision making or solving problems. It is possible to have so much information that it is not possible to recognize the useful information needed to solve the problem. Consider how many news resources are available via television, internet service providers, webpages, social networking sites, radio, and so on; can one sort through all of those sources and extract only the pertinent information, or even the accurate information?

An example of an abundance of information that concealed useful information is the January 28, 1986, space shuttle *Challenger* explosion 73 seconds after rocket ignition. The information collected about the impact of weather on the space shuttle was extensive; there were more than 20 successful launches at the time with data available about various factors suspected of impacting system performance under a variety of test conditions. Retrospectively, analysis of the prelaunch charts (13 of them) indicates that information was not displayed in a fashion to clearly indicate the likelihood of a dangerous failure after a night of sub-freezing temperatures, though the information was available, distributed, and discussed. Persuasive evidence against launching based solely upon those displays was not apparent; the information was there, but the presentation did not clearly relate the temperature to potential failure. Tufte (1997) reported "In 13 charts prepared for making the decisions to launch, there is a scandalous discrepancy between the intellectual tasks at hand and the images created to serve those tasks. As analytical graphics, the displays failed to reveal a risk that was in fact present" (p. 45). The information should have reduced uncertainty; it did not.

Decreasing uncertainty requires gaining more recognizable/useful information, but increasing information is not always sufficient. Uncertainty may be the measure of how many alternatives are available and the possibility of their outcome. When deciding which road to follow at a complex intersection, the user considers the amount of uncertainty related to the number of roads at the intersection and how much other information is available about the roads. The uncertainty could be reduced if there were a sign on any one of the roads indicating whether it was a north–south or east–west road, or if a sign displaying miles to a specific town were available. However, a sign about the local movie theater would probably not contribute much, unless it was what you were looking for and you knew the neighborhood; more information was available but not what was necessary.

Adding information to the situation may decrease the uncertainty and improve the decision process. If you see a bird and think it is a bluebird but you are not certain, the method to solve the question is to consult a birding book. What if upon checking the book you find that the bird is indeed not a bluebird, but you have no idea what type of bird it is? The information that solved whether it was a bluebird did not provide the answer to the real question of what type of bird it is. You have decreased uncertainty by ruling out one type of bird, but over-all, you have not resolved the problem. In the case of the bird, if you continue to look at pictures and ask bird experts, you are likely to resolve the problem and reduce uncertainty to zero. At some point, you may be able to determine without a doubt the identity of the bird by selecting alternatives and accepting or ruling them out. The amount of information you can bring to the investigation about size, color, geographic location, time of day, time of year, and weather conditions can be compared to known characteristics of potential candidates.

There are many situations, especially in science, management, and finance, where it is not possible to reduce uncertainty completely or to acquire perfect information. For example, when selecting a stock, you may perform extensive research to evaluate a given company's historical stock performance, the behav-ior of the management team, and the current and predicted status of the market in which it operates. You could even statistically analyze the last 30 years of stock prices, but you will not be able to eliminate all uncertainty. Possession of all this information will not ensure that the stock goes up, as you cannot be in possession of all the information that influences the stock market. You will not be able to eliminate all the possible alternatives or their outcomes. Some of the reasons for uncertainty have to do with communication. The movement and availability of information to resolve all the uncertainty in such a complex sys-tem are currently beyond our capacity to control. Information and communica-tion have a complex relationship, but they are not the same. Communication moves information, and information may reduce uncertainty; communication has a relationship to uncertainty via information. But communication may even contribute to uncertainty. The actors in the communication system may influ-ence how information is transmitted, by what channels, and how it is received. What if it were suggested that one of your favorite stocks is about to crash? How you received the information, who sent it, and how sensitive you are that day to such a threat will influence how you respond to the information, whether you accept it or reject it. This contextualization that provides a framework to infor-mation creates relevance to the individual for the information and influences decisions and uncertainty. Context will impact the success or failure of infor-mation transmission, but does it constitute a failure to communicate?

Passive or Active, It Is Communication

Information exposure may be passive, that is, the potential recipient or user is exposed but does not necessarily pursue or consciously apply the information.

An example would be television commercials that were seen but not consciously noted, yet did influence a shopping choice via recognition of a product name. An act of communication did occur: The television was the sender, and your unconscious mind was the receiver. Indirect application of information would be unintentional retention of information in memory and use of this unrecognized information in resolution activities. Or, information exposure may be active, where the information is pursued and/or applied consciously. In this case, the television commercial caused the recipient of the information to look for a specific product or consciously seek to purchase such a product. Again, an act of communication occurred, and it had a conscious effect.

Direct application of information is intentional storage in memory or acknowledgment of information received. When information is stored in memory, an act of communication has occurred from the external world to the mind's internal world. Another direct application would be the use of the information to cope with a specific problem, decision, or uncertainty reduction process. Information pursuit, or use, is actively attempting to obtain some value from information. Information seeking is a process involving a behavioral activity, or a set of activities, to obtain information believed to be necessary to affect a state of uncertainty or to evoke a communication. Each of these information-related notions is entwined with communication. Acts of communication may be directed actions undertaken to gain information to decrease uncertainty, or they may be passive acts where information is transmitted and received without overt effort on the part of the recipient. Information moves.

Channels

The medium by which information is transmitted is the channel. A person carrying messages may be a channel; a radio or a billboard may be a channel. There are also information roles in the communication act: The person carrying the messages is an information transmitter if all he or she does is carry the message. However, if the messenger also located and collected the information, he or she might be an information provider, an economic context of the communication act and the information dynamic. The radio, however, is a technological channel. The radio announcers may be channels, or information providers, or information producers or information seekers attempting to gather information for application, but they are actors in a communication-information exchange.

Two hundred years ago, the stagecoach was an information channel, a part of a communication system. The riders carried newspapers, letters, and information collected on the ride, the state of the passage. They also carried news of the places from which they traveled and from the people with whom they had spoken. Strangers traveling in this country years ago would be invited to stop to visit, as they were sources of information about places they had been, or people they may have encountered, or just the gossip of the time. As much of the knowledge of the West was not written, Indian scouts and wagon train masters who had traveled the West and were familiar with the special difficulties of an area were accorded a certain respect for the information they possessed. There was more faith in a person than in the words of a book that many could not read and few trusted with their lives. Access to information was limited by time and distance. Later, the wireless (telegraph) was a monumental new channel for carrying information, but word of mouth and long-delayed letters were maintained into the 20th century as potent information sources.

Modern channels of communication such as the telephone, television, radio, computer networks, telecommunications, fax machines, and daily newspapers allow us to obtain information much faster than in the days of the stagecoach. However, more than speed, these new channels opened other doors and changed our society. Industrialization changed the work roles and social structures of this country, so too have changes in the technology of communication and information affected our lives. Instead of Pony Express mail, we can fax materials to be received within minutes of transmission or send via email, text messaging, or Twitter within seconds. Instead of waiting for European newspapers to arrive in ports and travel across country, we can see the news in virtually any corner of the globe by turning on the television or accessing the web. The Indian scouts and wagon masters have been replaced with maps that are available in the supermarket next to the guidebook of interesting sights or online at your internet service provider's portal. The maps replaced one aspect of the scouts and wagon masters' knowledge but not their stories and insights missed by the map or what physical information they brought. Maps do not contain the accumulated experience that allowed the scouts and wagon masters to survive the unexpected and to make choices to preserve their charges. A person armed with a map can follow a route but does not have the added resource of the experienced guide who can make decisions when the weather goes foul or the map is out of date. The map is a communication medium, but its information content is dependent upon the user's ability to extract information from the object. Possession of information yielded power when only a select few could read a map, which imbued them with power. The increased availability of maps and their potential information create the illusion that anyone can access the information. In theory, this is true, but in fact, using the information requires prior knowledge, which is not automatically available by mere possession of the map. Assumptions about individuals' ability to use information tools create new complications for effective communication.

Much of what was carried in oral traditions is now printed material or visual media. We read stories from books to our children; we watch re-enactments of life on video, DVD, and the web. A stranger is not considered a potential message carrier and is not invited to visit without a great deal of unease. Our society has tended to believe the printed word over the spoken word; contracts are drawn to protect us so that we can debate them in court. Some communications have been formalized into special situations that tend to cause them to be perceived as more valid, such as statements in a court of law, the communication between doctor and patient, or the exchange between religious guide and supplicant. Whereas once we relied upon and trusted only the human communication system, we now substitute artifacts in print and other media. However, technology is changing this too. The new media are influencing communication and impacting our social behaviors with and about information.

Human Experience, Information, and Communication

Schramm (1973) characterizes communication as a manner of extending one's senses and improving one's ability to interact with the surrounding world. Schramm expanded upon Shannon's theory of information and communication to overcome the limitations of the basic model provided by the sender-channel-receiver pattern. Invoking human qualities, Schramm includes human experience as part of the system of both the sender and receiver in human communication. Further, Schramm, unlike Shannon, was interested in the meaning of the signal sent through the channel. Schramm suggests human experience contributes to channel "noise"; this and the added feature of feedback together impact the transmission and decoding of signals (Severin and Tankard, 1992). If someone has never seen or heard of an elephant, it might be difficult to comprehend the size or appearance of the creature. Few of us have ever walked on the moon; most of us can only imagine the way the moon-ground feels beneath our feet or how it feels to lumber about in spacesuits. Because of the limitations of inexperience, it is difficult for the nonmoon walkers to understand when moon walkers discuss it. Those who have firsthand experience of war, such as soldiers, nurses, civilians, and some journalists, may find it impossible to convey their sense of the experience to those who have not been there. This is not because the senders are inarticulate but because the recipients cannot imagine and cannot typically associate the information to something they have experienced. Information in the human model is not sterile and neither is the communication process (Schramm, 1973). When Schramm expanded the electronic communication model, adding accumulated human experience and feedback (Severin and Tankard, 1992), he was attempting to include aspects of our humanity that have potent effects upon our ability to transmit, receive, and interpret information. He was endeavoring to account for our prior experiences, our roles in social settings, and our identities as aspects of any communication system.

Kenneth Boulding (1956/1973) discusses the relevance of accumulated experience in *The Image*. By locating himself in space and time, reflecting upon who he is, what has made him who he is, and what comprises his identity, he defines his knowledgebase or his "image." Boulding contends that the image each of us has, our knowledge base, our identity, is composed of our accumulated experiences, interpretations of those experiences, and the effects of the total of our experiences. Essentially, we are the product of our past environment, education, and experiences, and we filter all information through these. If you were raised in West Texas, where there are sand dunes and desert scrub brush and the trees are rarely taller than the houses, you may find it hard to imagine the giant red-woods of northern California or the enormous pines of the northeastern Atlantic seaboard. You might not find it possible to envision twelve-foot-high drifts from lake effect snow near Buffalo, New York. The experience of a hurricane would not be yours so long as you remained in West Texas, although you would probably be very familiar with tornadoes and dust storms. Though you may have vicarious information, having seen a film or read a book, the information content and its integration into your being would not be the same as if you had experienced these activities. Those experiences contribute to the relevance assessments you will make about information, which, in turn, will determine whether you accept or reject related information. Your lack of experience or your experience will create a texture in the channel, the noise, and it may prevent you from acquiring or recognizing information.

In some ways, we all remain naive, limited by the boundaries of our experiences and by those who first contributed to our image. We see and perceive the world through what we have already known. What we have not known or cannot associate to something similar, we may ignore or create an artificial association for or allow someone else to "give" us an association for it. Our image is composed of the information that has been communicated to us from all the various sources possible, and we deal with it in relation to where this information fits into our image. Some of this image may be the genetic or biochemical product of our heritage. Our personal chemistry may impact our information receptivity, such as when someone is depressed or intoxicated. We associate with people who are like us. We do not intentionally spend time with people who hold political views completely opposite of our own. We spend time with people who enjoy the same activities, the same sports, or the same music. We tend not to interact closely with people with whom we have not established some minimal sense of community. "A fundamental principle of human communication is that the exchange of ideas occurs most frequently between individuals who are alike, or homophilous" (Rogers, 1995, p. 286). Our image/identity is our past as well as our present, and it can influence our future. Our image includes the people with whom we associate or identify, our cultural and social identities, and even social customs. This image has a significant effect upon our personal information and communications systems and actions.

An example of the role of social and cultural identity and its capacity to influence our communication and information behavior can be found in diffusion research. Everett Rogers' *Diffusion of Innovation* reviewed more than 500 studies about the movement of new ideas, or innovations, into general acceptance with the intent of finding the "common threads running through all the research traditions on the diffusion of innovation" (1995, p. 6). An innovation is information new to a particular setting or individual, regardless of the actual novelty of the information to another individual or in another setting. Diffusion of the new information (innovation) is the process or path of communication, movement of the information. The process is influenced by circumstances governing the transmitter, the person initially having the information, the person(s) receiving the information, the recipients and the channels, or social/cultural environments surrounding the individuals involved, as well as the content of the information message. Time is also a factor in this process. Individuals may adopt innovations at different rates, often related to their position in the social/cultural environment and other characteristics not yet understood.

Adoption of an innovation is the integration of the information or activity into common use or acceptance. Rogers' (1995) review of works suggested the social/cultural environment has significant influence upon the adoption of innovations. His work also identified categories of adopters based upon their speed of adoption. An aspect of his work especially relevant here is cultural norms: common patterns of behavior, conduct, or belief within a social system. These patterns may even be how one cultural group differentiates itself from another. At a global level, Christians are those who believe Jesus Christ is the Supreme Being; at a much more local cultural level, the details of that belief can be substantially different. Consider two Christian groups, such as the Baptist faith in comparison to the Lutheran faith. In fact, unless you are a student of theology or have friends in both faiths, you may not have sufficient knowledge about their beliefs to make a comparison. Such is the limitation of social/cultural environments and norms.

In the context of social/cultural norms, these patterns may not only define groups but may define information acceptability for members of the groups. You are more likely to accept information as valid from someone you know rather than someone you do not know. You are more likely to listen to the ideas of people you respect or with whom you agree than the ideas of people you do not respect or with whom you do not agree (Haslam, McGarty, and Turner, 1996; Rogers, 1995). Think of your political affiliation: Do you often find yourself agreeing with the members of other political parties? Do the relationships you have with people influence how you value or devalue their opinions and ideas? The point being, one's position in a social system and relationship to others does influence what information you accept (Rogers, 1995). If you politically identity yourself as a Republican, you are saying you basically believe and subscribe to the political agenda the party espouses. Depending on how closely your personal political views coincide with the party view or how closely your image places you in this system, you may find yourself unable, or unwilling, to believe events presented by someone who is not a member of the Republican party, especially about topics considered to differentiate Republicans from Democrats. Effectively, all political information coming to you is filtered through this image and is affected by your perception of the sender. If the sender is a Republican, he or she is likely to affirm what you already believe, or if he or she challenges it, he or she will be given the opportunity to communicate. Alternately, if the sender is a Democrat, regardless of what he or she suggests, you are likely to doubt and/or even disregard the communication. This is not to suggest that there is no reasoning or thinking involved in this, but rather, the information from a member of

member = acceptance of info

your own group is given more credibility than that of a nonmember. In fact, some studies indicate even information typically resisted by an individual may be received more openly if presented by someone from their identity group, but there seems to be a conscious evaluation involved regardless of the source (Haslam, McGarty, and Turner, 1996). Another situation where an outsider's information may be accepted, as suggested by Boulding (1956/1973), would be if somehow the information or communication creates an emotional state, which may make the recipient receptive to information that normally conflicts with his or her image. *emotional state*

Methods of communication, such as choice of channel, direct or indirect, demonstrative or passive, may also influence whether you accept information. Are you likely to believe someone means you well if they are yelling at you and using abusive language? This is not to imply we never communicate or accept information from those unlike us. Indeed, it is much the opposite; we do communicate and accept information from people not like us, but our rate of acceptance or our agreement with the information is not the same as when dealing with communicants who are culturally or socially similar. The acceptability of the information, how closely it resembles something we already believe or accept, also contributes.

Boulding (1956/1973) suggests there are three general responses the image may experience in response to information: The image may be unaffected, the image may change slightly, or the image may undergo a very significant change. One's image may remain unaffected by the morning weather report. One's image may be slightly changed by understanding how to operate a computer software program, but that does not really change how one lives or views the world. Firsthand experience of a war, however, may dramatically influence how you view yourself, your faith, and the world; therefore, your image would be significantly impacted. Taken in the context of Rogers' (1995) work, your image also has a place in a social/cultural environment, and your receptivity to new information is partly formed by the environment's affect on your image. Despite the role of the individual, extraneous information communicated via the social/cultural environment will be received consciously or subconsciously. Perceived information that seems irrelevant will be suppressed or dismissed as "noise"; however, it may remain with the recipient subconsciously until it has a useful application or emerges as part of a social/cultural experience. All of these components contribute to who you are and consequently how willingly you accept information, regardless of the method of communication. An entire new field of communication studies will have to be undertaken to investigate how blogs, wikis, Facebook, MySpace, and similar social networking situations will influence individual receptiveness to information, interpretations of relevance, and truthfulness.

Communication and Information Transfer

How do the concepts of uncertainty, information, communication, Schramm's model of communication, Boulding's image, Rogers' innovations, and social/cultural environments all tie together? These are all concerns that must be included in any information transfer model, that is, in any communication system. Schramm added accumulated experience and feedback to the model because we interpret whatever is communicated to us through the veil of our past experiences, through our image as Boulding suggests, and because we evaluate and respond more critically to information that seems contrary to our social/cultural environment or social groups belief (Boulding, 1956/1973; Haslam, McGarty, and Turner, 1996; Rogers, 1995; Schramm, 1973). The transfer of information then is going to be limited or accentuated by characteristics of the participants, their perceptions of themselves, the presenters, and the information presented. The quality of the information transferred may be modified by these perceptions.

Communication is one of the processes or methods for making information available. Information may reduce uncertainty. But our image, as explained by Boulding (1956/1973), and our position in a given social or cultural information situation impact what information we will consider accepting into our belief system. The combination of who we believe ourselves to be, who we believe our peers to be, and the degree of our rigidity of belief in certain social and cultural constraints will contribute to our ability to integrate "new" information into our image and/or belief system. Communication may be significantly impacted by all the resulting "noise." The noise may be composed of the image, stature, or social position of the sender as well as of the recipient. The noise may be an unconscious bias, as in genderism, ageism, sexism, or racism. The noise may be entrenchment, wherein the participants hold their beliefs as inviolate and cannot accept any deviation or suggestion thereof. The noise may be an inability to comprehend the information, due to physical constraints or intellectual limitations. The sender and the receiver may have social, cultural, or identity issues or physical constraints that will influence the quality of the communication act and the success of the information transfer. Just as an electronic communication system may have physically limiting characteristics that contribute to noise, so too can human communications have physical, social, and environmental limitations. When someone speaks, he or she can only determine if the information transfer has been successful if the feedback from the recipient yields some indication of comprehension. However, the original speaker may be misinterpreting the feedback. Information transfer becomes an extremely complex process, dependent upon the participants, the communication methods and protocols, and the total communication environment. Evaluating the entire information and communication environment may assist in improving information transfer. Determining all the aspects of the environment that require detailed study is still underway as we learn more about information and communication systems and behaviors.

Summary

The human communication and information transfer model is significantly more complex than the essential electronic communications model Shannon proposed. Accepting that individuals have membership in a social/cultural environment, which also places them in a delimited individual image/identity relationship with themselves and others, has important implications in human communication. The basic electronic model does not adequately portray all the characteristics and aspects that may influence human communication. Information possession and transmission involve a variety of processes, environmental factors, and systems, which need to be taken into account when evaluating information and communication structures. It is not sufficient to recognize that there is a relationship between information and communication; the relationship must be explored and evaluated.

References

Bar-Hillel, Y. 1964. *Language and Information: Selected Essays on their Theory and Application*. Reading, MA: Addison-Wesley.

Boulding, K. 1956/1973. *The Image*. Ann Arbor, MI: University of Michigan Press.

Dervin, B., and Nilan, M. 1986. Information Needs and Uses. *Annual Review of Information Science and Technology* 21:3–35.

Haslam, A. S., McGarty, C., and Turner, J. C. 1996. Salient Group Memberships and Persuasion: The Role of Social Identity in the Validation of Beliefs. In J. L. Nye and A. M. Brower (Eds.), *What's Social About Social Cognition? Research on Socially Shared Cognition in Small Groups* pp. 29–56. Thousand Oaks, CA: Sage.

Ritchie, D. L. 1991. *Communication Concepts 2: Information*. Newbury Park, CA: Sage.

Rogers, E. 1995. *The Diffusion of Innovation* (4th ed.). New York: The Free Press.

Schramm, W. L. 1973. *Men, Messages, and Media: A Look at Human Communication*. New York: Harper & Row.

Severin, W. J. and Tankard, J. W. Jr. 1992. *Communications Theories: Origins, Methods, and Uses in the Mass Media* (3rd ed.). White Plains, NY: Longman.

Shannon, C., and Weaver, W. 1949. *The Mathematical Theory of Communication*. Urbana, IL: University of Illinois Press.

Shera, J. H. 1983. Librarianship and Information Science. In F. Machlup and U. Mansfield (Eds.), *The Study of Information: Interdisciplinary Messages* pp. 379–388. New York: Wiley & Son.

Tribus, M. 1983. Thirty Years of Information Theory. In F. Machlup and U. Mansfield (Eds.), *The Study of Information: Interdisciplinary Messages* pp. 475–484. New York: Wiley & Son.

Tufte, E. R. 1997. *Visual Explanations: Images and Quantities, Evidence and Narrative*. Cheshire, CT: Graphics Press.

Young, P. 1987. *The Nature of Information*. New York: Praeger.

Chapter 4

Information Retrieval

Melanie J. Norton

This chapter presents a broad traditional overview of information retrieval. Aspects of organization, classification, and the relationship among information, communication, and retrieval are briefly discussed.

Information retrieval refers to the processes and activities involved with making it possible to obtain information from some source. Currently, it is typically associated with computer-based retrieval, but that is not the only form of information retrieval available (Goffman, 1968/1970; Salton, 1982). Even with computerized systems, certain aspects of the overall processes involved must be understood. When we ask someone a purposeful question, we are seeking information and engaging in an act of information retrieval. In the human inquiry, it is easy to understand that information retrieval involves forms of communication (Schramm, 1973). It may be less obvious with interactions between human and machine, or human and information systems (such as libraries), that elements of the communications processes are involved.

When we consult someone, we are attempting to retrieve information from that person's collected store of information. A component of retrieval is intimately related to the collection of materials, in particular, whether the collection consulted has the information desired and whether it is retrievable. A collection may hold the desired information, but if it cannot be located, it might as well not be present. The ability to locate an item after it has been stored is based on the organization and subsequent representation employed to describe it for potential retrieval (Fayyad, 1996; Lubetzky and Hayes, 1969/1970; Salton, 1982).

How do we locate information? Association seems to play a large role in cognition, and it has been a powerful influence in the design of classification systems. When information is collected and stored, the issue of locating a specific item of interest at a later time becomes a major concern (Foskett, 1977; Rowley,

1992; Taylor, 1999). How does one go about finding a book in a library or locating a particular subject or author? How can information within documents, video, or other media be handled so an interested party can access it? What enables the retrieval of information from databases or the web?

Organization and representation are key components of information retrieval. These are critical aspects of the retrieval equation, but they are impacted by human communication considerations as well as by cognitive judgments. This chapter briefly discusses some aspects of organization and classification, and the relationship among information, communication, and retrieval.

Organization as Access

Why are the fruits and vegetables usually located together in a market? Why not have the apples on the shelf next to the applesauce, apple pie filling, and apple juice? Or why not have the market arranged by alphabetic order: The first aisle could be all the "A" things, and the last aisle could hold all the "Z" things? Or why not just unload the trucks and put everything in the store in the order it comes off the truck on any given day? Why are standard phone books arranged by alphabetic order rather than by numeric order? Simply, it makes it easier to find things if they are organized in some manner. Since fruits and vegetables require refrigeration and are valued for their freshness as well as appearance, it seems reasonable to keep them together, usually on countertop displays to maximize the refrigeration and presentation. They are also usually sorted into fruit, with all the apples next to one another and all the pears next to one another, while the vegetables are also grouped together, such as red, yellow, and white onions, and different types of squashes, and so on. This is organization by association. But why not put all the apples with the applesauce and the apple juice? Are the applesauce and the apple juice next to one another on the shelf? Depending on the organization of the market perhaps, but it is just as likely that the juices are grouped together while the fruit sauces are also all together. There may be rows of apple juice next to rows of grape juice. This indicates levels of association, the relationship of juices to juices being closer than that of raw apples to grapes, at least in this particular hierarchy.

If the store were arranged alphabetically, there would have to be agreement about what each item would be called. It would mean that bandages and birdseed would be on the same aisle, as would baloney, bananas, baby powder, and buttons. It could work, but where would we put facial tissue since most people call it by a particular brand name? Should the shelves be arranged alphabetically by the brand name and then the common name? Some brands are regional, some national, some international, and not all stores carry all brands. What about unloading the truck and leaving it in the order of the truck today? What if every truck is not packed in the same order? Every day, things would be in a different order, at least compared to the things unloaded the day before; how would anyone find anything?

There are, of course, phone books arranged by the phone number. It is a reverse phone book for locating who belongs to a number; but the standard phone book works using the alphabet because the user is most likely to know the person's name rather than his or her number. These may seem to be silly and unimportant details, but consider how much time would be wasted in the market where every day there was a different arrangement. How would one look up a phone number if the only information available were the last name? Essentially, without an organizational scheme, large collections become inaccessible. The same principles apply to information collections.

Organization, or the imposition of some structure, improves a person's ability to locate things. In the context of information containers, such as books, newspapers, correspondence, films, videos, computer files, and the many mediums now available, organization is critical to locating information. By imposing a structure, preferably one with clear criteria for inclusion, with rules for placement and association, a blueprint is created to permit the location of items based on the rules that position them in the collection. Additionally, agreed-upon rules and criteria for placement make retrieval possible by other than the original organizer (Rowley, 1992). If the agreed organization of a collection of books puts all paperback books together alphabetically by author's last name, then we only need to know that the book is available in paperback and the author's last name. However, what if the author has a compound last name or no last name? This consideration should be documented, and a rule for how to locate the book in the collection should be recorded. What about hardbound books: Should they also be alphabetized by the author's last name? It could work. However, what if you do not know the author's last name? And what if you want a book about a particular subject?

A blueprint based on only a few physical characteristics of a book is not sufficient to locate items by subject. In fact, now the problem of location becomes much larger. If there are many books and many subjects, how can the subjects of the book be located without physically examining each book each time there is an interest? One method is to use a surrogate, something to provide information about the book but is not the book, such as a piece of paper, a card, or an entry in a computer file. But then, there still needs to be a way to connect the book to the surrogate for the surrogate to refer to the physical book in a specific location (Foskett, 1977; Rowley, 1992). What if the book is about more than one subject? What if the book has information that might be useful in a variety of subjects? Using a surrogate system, it is possible to have several cards or such referencing one book. But how does one determine what the book is about and where it should be positioned in the collection relative to the other parts of the collection?

Since Plato, it has been theorized there is a natural order that should provide a framework for the organization of all knowledge. This framework would provide an arrangement from the general to the specific; entities would be arranged based upon characteristics similar to each other as well as dissimilarities to other entities, and those characteristics would be essential and unchanging aspects of the entity (Shera, 1965). This hierarchical and relational-based notion of a classification framework continues today, though it is not the only system of organization or classification available.

With the impossibility of organizing all knowledge aside, it has been useful to arrange entities by characteristics that define their uniqueness and their similarity in comparison to other entities. For example, vertebrates are creatures with backbones, as opposed to nonvertebrates, which are creatures without backbones. Mammals are warm-blooded vertebrates that give birth to live young to whom they feed milk, as opposed to reptiles that are cold-blooded vertebrates that lay eggs and do not feed milk to their offspring. These characteristics or attributes describe the entities in such a way that similarities and differences make it possible to group the entities. The more detailed the characteristics known, the more precisely we can group the entities. Given the information that something is a vertebrate mammal with four legs (which is actually a great deal of information), this indicates the animal has a backbone, has all the characteristics of a mammal, and has four legs. With this information, it is clear the animal is not a human being and not an amoeba, but this information is not sufficient enough to be able to name the animal. Given enough information, such as it has claws, typically weighs less than 20 pounds, has significantly larger relatives, prefers to hunt at night, and generally prefers to be solitary, you might be able to guess the type of creature based upon what you know about animals and their characteristics. There is a scientific classification system that could be employed as well that would describe it: Kingdom: Animalia, Phylum: Chordata, Subphylum: Vertebrata, Class: Mammalia, Order: Carnivora, Family: Felidae, Genus: Felis, Species: Domesticus (Braungart and Buddeke, 1960). Kingdom being the most general of the classifications in this method, and species being the most specific, this is a domestic cat. However, each of the groupings—kingdom, phylum, subphylum, class, order, family, genus, and species—indicates certain similarities and differences for the creature to fit into each group level. This means it is possible to locate where an animal belongs in the classification system using the knowledge of the animal combined with the criteria of each group.

This type of hierarchy has inherited attributes, meaning the characteristics of the higher group appear in the lower level group. All members of the family of Felidae are carnivorous and mammals with backbones. Such a structure also means it is possible to locate related animals at different levels of relationship. For example, there are characteristic criteria for belonging to the class mammal and to the order carnivore; only animals with certain specific characteristics will be in the mammal class and carnivore order. However, unless we are familiar with this scientific naming convention, we would not recognize either the hierarchy or the implications of each group level, and this classification method might not yield any useful information. This does not change that this classification system does present significant information to those versed with it, and it does provide a way of identifying entities based upon like and unlike attributes. Botany uses the same hierarchical, kingdom-to-species approach to classify plants.

The hierarchical grouping system based on relationships, likeness, and unlikeness has some shortcomings. What characteristics form the basis for the evaluation of the relatedness, likeness, and unlikeness? Should all four-legged creatures be grouped together, or should only warm-blooded, four-legged creatures be grouped together? Should all the aspects of any discipline that has anything to do with information be grouped under information science? Are all blond-haired children related to each other? Using too few characteristics makes it difficult to arrange items usefully and limits access to the structure by dictating what information the user must have to employ the system. Further, there is an underlying question of the value of relating items on certain characteristics. One would not assume all blond-haired children are all related. Would there be any value in grouping all blond children together as a category based upon these criteria? It would depend upon what information was being sought and what other attributes or characteristics were being considered. Other methods of classification might be more meaningful or more flexibly applied.

The criteria for organizing, whether for surrogates, physical objects, or ideas, has to be based upon the intended use of the materials and the anticipated users. They have to take into account what descriptive or relationship information is available about the entities and how useful organizing the material is based on those criteria. The organizational structure has to have the capacity to expand and the flexibility to provide multiple access points, and be reflective of the intended users' cognitive levels and interests (Loucopoulos, 1992; Mylopoulos, 1992; Rolland and Cauvet, 1992; Rowley, 1992).

The application of organizational criteria is part of providing access, creating a method for pulling information out of a collection. If all books bound in blue were about law enforcement, then putting all the blue books together would place all the law enforcement volumes in one place. If you knew all the blue books were about this one subject and you needed information about the subject, you would only examine the blue books, not the red, not the black, and not the green. If the blue books were also arranged alphabetically by the last name of the author, then it might not be necessary to examine all the blue books if you knew the author's last name. However, if you only knew the title, you would still have to look at each book, unless the books were arranged by title instead of author.

Since an item can only be in one place and the arrangement of the books is not likely to change based on what we do or do not know, the use of a surrogate becomes more powerful. In theory, many surrogates can be created to refer to the one item based upon the method of description. The method of description, or the classification, has to be agreed upon. Each surrogate for each item in the collection will have sufficient information to distinguish one item from another. It would also be very helpful if each surrogate used an agreed-upon reference for locating the item in space. For example, before electronic databases, the access points to a library collection were defined by the catalog card system, a card being a record and a document surrogate. Each card had a referent number, or call number, which was a method for locating the item on the shelf. Each document had as many card records as the system determined appropriate. Typically, a title card, author card, and some subject cards were included. Each of these cards would be an access point; if one knew the title or the author or had an idea of the subject, it was possible to locate the document. The cards basically became a database of entries descriptive of the contents of the collection. Each surrogate card was a record referring to an item in the collection.

In electronic database construction, the records are composed of fields or categorized characteristics, which describe the physical entity, or subject entity, to which the record refers. For example, documentary materials are classified using characteristics such as title words, citations and references, subject keywords, and author. These are characteristics or attributes to describe the document. In a database, the record for such an entity might be retrievable by any of the fields, or attributes, depending upon the design of the retrieval system and the database. The record would refer back to the actual document, as in how to locate it via a document number, journal citation, or call number. Other types of collections are characterized by attributes that describe the basic collection entities, or subjects of the database, such as customer databases. The customer is the entity or subject, and attributes are the aspects to describe the customer, such as address, purchasing history, income, gender, age, and so on. How well the attributes describe, or represent, the entity and the relationship of that representation to the user's knowledgebase will significantly impact the user's ability to retrieve the appropriate record using the attributes as access points (Fayyad, 1996). If we are seeking information about cats and the attributes for animals are all in Latin, then the records cannot be located if we do not know Latin.

Organization, Details, and Retrieval

Implementing an organization and classification system requires agreement about the criteria and their application: the definition of the vocabulary to be employed, the methods for selecting the content of an item, and the format of presentation for the records. Details about how to determine the subjects, attributes, or descriptors of items need to be established. What will be the primary entities, what are the most useful descriptors, and what depth of detail should be employed? In a documentary system, will subjects be determined by frequency of meaningful words and/or phrases or derived from titles and abstracts? In a customer database, will the primary entry be the customer, the item purchased, the account number, the sales contact, or a combination of these? Should the record be kept in a numerically coded format or natural language or a combination of both? All of these questions, necessary to create a data dictionary or an authority file, provide standards employed to permit retrieval and require answers.

The details required to make useful organization and classification schemes are numerous and usually create a complex artificial structure. These schemes are then applied to a collection that produces an imposed structural organization that should allow information to be retrieved by applying an understanding of the structure via an inquiry system. In a library catalog card system, the user searches by looking in the card file via the access points, the author, title, or subject file, depending upon what information the user has available. The user seeking information is actively undertaking an inquiry. This user may be seeking a specific book or additional information about a specific subject. In another environment, the user might be trying to trace a purchase order or a customer billing address. The searcher's ability to manipulate the system will be dependent upon how well the information entered into the system complies with the structure and how well the user understands the structure and the scheme. The ability to retrieve information from the collection will depend on how well the organizational structure is understood and how the subject of interest is represented in that structure. Historically, the use of classification structures has resulted in using intermediaries especially trained with the systems imposed, or training users in how to use specific systems successfully. The lack of generality in systems has sometimes required significant investment in training with every advance in technology.

Classification and organization schemes may limit access points in trying to uniformly implement the scheme. The access points may have been identified by people who are not experts in the given discipline. When determining a subject for a document, experts in the field may have a different orientation than novices or librarians, and this can cause difficulties. For example, when a user is subject searching in a library catalog, the subject identification is limited to what is selected by the cataloging department. This sometimes means the user has to outguess the catalogers to locate an item or rely upon the catalogers' interpretation of a subject area. The use of thesauri, indexes, and "see also" entries help with this problem, but they do not ameliorate it. However, recent research suggests that subject experts do not achieve significantly improved retrieval over nonexperts (Wilbur, 1998), which would lead to the conclusion that the need for catalogers to have extensive subject knowledge may have been an erroneous assumption. It does not negate the need to train users in specific database retrieval systems or interfaces to achieve results. While library organizational schemes have a history and a certain amount of uniformity to the application of classification and description, no such constraints direct other types of databases.

In early electronic databases, the cost of space and memory limited the number of access points, thereby leaving the user still highly dependent upon the skills of the database designers and programmers. The controlled structure of a classification scheme, or controlled vocabulary, encouraged the application of information technology. Machines can manipulate controlled vocabulary and follow rules with less effort than is required to handle natural language.

Machine limitations and the advantages of classification schemes affected early database design from both input and retrieval perspectives. Space and memory limitations restricted the quantity and method in which information could be stored. Information was abbreviated and arranged to maximize space savings; coupled with the characteristics of the schema used, the need for intermediaries was perpetuated. In library settings, the most visible databases were the Online Public Access Catalogs (OPAC) and the vendor databases rendered via Dialog- or LexisNexis-like corporations. The vendor database access offered by the library translated into library staff accepting information inquiries from patrons, inventing strategies to query the databases, and offering the result to the patron who would determine relevance. Behind the scenes, databases supported the acquisitions, circulation, and administration requirements of the facility. These were also limited by structures imposed at the database design stage, which ideally should have incorporated an organization and descriptive system appropriate to the specific intended uses. In nonlibrary organizations, the intermediaries would be data processing personnel, programmers, and analysts who would implement information requests via programming or searchers trained to use the databases. The retrieval of personnel, customer, payment, circulation, vendor, and acquisition records is as dependent upon the adequacy of the organization and representation as documentary records, and perhaps more in some cases. A document record that misdirects the user is hardly as important as a personnel record that misdirects a check, Social Security, or tax payment information.

Designing for Retrieval

There are several factors involved in the design of any information retrieval system. The intent or purpose of the collection as to how the information will be used will affect the structure of the database, the formats for storage, input and output, the design of the user interface (the computer screens, card catalogs, or whatever method by which the user interacts with the system), and other issues such as security and currency. Those characteristics of the information that will be most useful to satisfy the intention will contribute to the structure of the database, as well as influence formats and input and output. Who will the users be and what characteristics about them may influence the system? This question seeks information specific to the application and its relationship to the users, and the users to the application, all of which may require attention in the design of the system at all levels.

The use of the collection is important in the design because it will indicate what information and what formats of information are needed to build the collection. In the context of a database, what information is to be stored in records and what attributes will be employed to best describe the primary entity the record is intended to reflect? The planned application of the database should influence these decisions. Will natural language or controlled vocabulary be used to place information into the system? Natural language, or language the way humans normally speak or write, has nuances and meanings that are affected by context and a degree of currency. This makes it more difficult for computers to use natural language and may require more manipulation or programming at the interface and storage level to make it work transparently for the user. Where is the information coming from? Will it be downloaded from another source, or will it be collected over time and input as it arrives? This influences the format for input and any interface display consideration. Who collects the information, verifies it if necessary, and evaluates the integrity of the input could also impact the format of the record as well as the interface.

Another important question is what characteristics of the information will be most useful to satisfy the purpose of the collection? These characteristics establish the parameters for the information set to be collected and may also define the structure to be employed. Concerns, such as any space limitations, may contribute to selecting the most useful characteristics and omitting others judged as less critical. The potential for overlooking an essential piece of information is much higher when there are constraints such as space, language, or input features. Within the limitations of the technology as much flexibility as possible should be built into the structure. Decisions about potentially useful information have to be made. As technology has improved, there has been a movement toward data warehousing, or storing information collected in the normal process of business or operations. These collections may be enormous. In these cases, it is difficult to anticipate what information may be extracted from the warehouse in the future, but it further underlines the importance of planning for flexibility (Fayyad, Pietetsky-Shapiro, and Smyth, 1996).

Who will the users be: technicians, students, minimum-wage transient employees, programmers, designers, salesclerks? Just as communication may be impacted by the "image" and social/cultural environment of the sender and receiver, so too will information retrieval. The reasons that users are attempting to retrieve information, their motivation, their concept of how to use the system, and their measure of what they are seeking are all critical to the retrieval process. In fact, it will be the users who ultimately determine whether the retrieval activity, regardless of its intention, is successful; does it resolve or address the information request they posed? The structures created to organize information to make it accessible may also contribute to the complex problem of locating information. The ease of use will impact whether the users view the retrieval activity as successful. The users' competence with the system may impact the sense of success, as does the determination of whether the retrieval addresses the request. If the users are not competent with a system, they may have difficulty obtaining results, even though the desired information may actually be within the system. Another issue will be relevance, or the "aboutness" of the item retrieved. Is it related, connected, and relevant to the information inquiry? The users' competence in the area of the information request will impact whether the users perceive the retrieved results as being related to the inquiry (Gluck, 1995). The individual's skills, image, and social/cultural interpretation of the transaction will affect the retrieval of desired information and the ability of the individual to recognize the information as relevant.

Concepts of Relevance

An aspect of information retrieval under extensive study involves the notions of relevance, how individuals determine whether an information item is pertinent, useful, or about the information need they are seeking to resolve. Research into what components of an information unit trigger a perception of relevance indicates a variety of factors at play. The information need is situational and contextually dependent. The importance of the desired information influences the sources consulted. Basic criteria, such as currency, language, and even authorship, may be factors in detecting potential relevance (Barry, 1998). The initial information state of the seeker will affect the determination of relevance by providing initial gross criteria, such as currency and language. Secondary markers for relevance are more variable. Barry details 20 categories of potential relevance criteria in document selection. However, as with much of the research in relevance, the findings are not entirely conclusive. The various components of documents that may convey relevance information, ranging from titles and abstracts to final paragraphs, all elicit differing degrees of usefulness in the evaluation of relevance. Barry points out that the context of the search, as well as the user's previous knowledge of both the topic and the sources, may influence the effective detection of relevant items. It would appear that the complexity of the information need, the environment, user, and information item may make it impossible to create a definitive key field for relevance evaluation. Regardless of that possibility, identifying relevance markers may contribute to enhanced retrieval systems.

Summary

The retrieval of information is dependent upon organization or classification systems. The degree of success obtained from these systems will be based upon their relevance to the users and the representativeness imbedded in the scheme used for the subject area. These systems have to be bound to the knowledge environments, which the information seekers in the subject domain can implement to recall materials relevant to their inquiries. The activities of pulling useful information out of a collection are connected to the organizational scheme and to relationships invoked via the inquiry. Whether technologically based or not, the construction and application of a classification system must take the users into account. The parameters of the users' abilities, the relationships employed to construct the classification, and the representativeness of the descriptions all impact how well a retrieval system can satisfy users' needs. Organization of materials should be viewed as a method of access. Coupled with criteria to establish relevance, or aboutness, for the user in conjunction with the collection structures resulting from classification, it should be possible to provide a working retrieval system.

In the electronic environment, selection becomes a more individualized task. If more criteria for selection are to be applied, more ways to examine, evaluate, classify, organize, and represent materials must be developed. With more sophisticated searching tools, at least in theory, users could better frame the inquiries and obtain better results with less attention from intermediaries. Since information retrieval relevance is a user-dependent activity, it seems logical to increase the users' ability to apply a system directly.

References

Barry, C. 1998. Document Representations and Clues to Document Relevance. *Journal of the American Society for Information Science* 49(14):1293–1303.

Braungart, D. C., and Buddeke, R. 1960. *An Introduction to Animal Biology* (5th ed.). St. Louis, MO: C. V. Mosby.

Fayyad, U. 1996. Data Mining and Knowledge Discovery: Making Sense Out of Data. *IEEE Expert* 11(5):220–225.

Fayyad, U., Piatetsky-Shapiro, G., and Smyth, P. 1996. From Data Mining to Knowledge Discovery in Databases. *AI Magazine* 17(3):3754.

Foskett, A. C. 1977. *The Subject Approach to Information* (3rd ed.). Hamden, CT: Linnet Books, The Shoe String Press.

Gluck, M. 1995. Understanding Performance in Information Systems: Blending Relevance and Competence. *Journal of the American Society for Information Science* 46(6):446–460.

Goffman, W. 1968/1970. An Indirect Method of Information Retrieval. In T. Saracevic (Ed.), *Introduction to Information Science* pp. 485–492. New York: R. R. Bowker.

Loucopoulos, P. 1992. Conceptual Modeling. In P. Loucopoulos and R. Zicari (Eds.), *Conceptual Modeling, Databases and CASE: An Integrated View of Information Systems Development* pp. 1–26. New York: John Wiley & Sons.

Lubetzky, S., and Hayes, R. M. 1969/1970. Bibliographic Dimensions in Information Control. In T. Saracevic (Ed.), *Introduction to Information Science* pp. 434–444. New York: R. R. Bowker.

Mylopoulos, J. 1992. Conceptual Modeling and Telos. In P. Loucopoulos and R. Zicari (Eds.), *Conceptual Modeling, Databases and CASE: An Integrated View of Information Systems Development* pp. 49–68. New York: John Wiley & Sons.

Rolland, C., and Cauvet, C. 1992. Trends and Perspectives in Conceptual Modeling. In P. Loucopoulos and R. Zicari (Eds.), *Conceptual Modeling, Databases and CASE: An Integrated View of Information Systems Development* pp. 27–48. New York: John Wiley & Sons.

Rowley, J. 1992. *Organizing Knowledge: An Introduction to Information Retrieval* (2nd ed.). Brookfield, VT: Ashgate.

Salton, G. 1982. Information Retrieval: An Introduction. In *Introduction to Modern Information Retrieval* pp. 1–23. New York: McGraw-Hill.

Schramm, W. L. 1973. *Men, Messages, and Media: A Look at Human Communication.* New York: Harper and Row.

Shera, J. H. 1965. *Libraries and the Organization of Knowledge.* Foskett, D. J. (Ed.). Hamden, CT: Archon Books.

Shera, J. H. 1966. *Documentation and the Organization of Knowledge.* Foskett, D. J. (Ed.). Hamden, CT: Archon Books.

Taylor, A. G. 1999. *The Organization of Information.* Englewood, CO: Libraries Unlimited.

Wilbur, W. J. 1998. A Comparison of Group and Individual Performance among Subject Experts and Untrained Workers at the Document Retrieval Task. *Journal of the American Society for Information Science* 49(6):517–529.

Chapter 5

Indexing

JungWon Yoon

The main purpose of indexing is to represent documents in a way that enhances search effectiveness. In other words, indexing, as a form of document representation, should assist a user who has a certain information need to find and select relevant documents. For example, readers look through a back-of-the-book index in order to find the section efficiently in the book that seems relevant to their information needs. Library users, instead of browsing a collection of books from A-to-Z, begin with searching library Online Public Access Catalog (OPAC) systems, which include bibliographic representations to find the places where relevant books are located. Similarly, web users make use of search engines operating around representations of web documents, rather than randomly browsing web documents themselves. In short, regardless of information formats or types of information retrieval systems, an index should direct searchers to a subset of a whole (either a whole book or a whole collection) that is relevant to the searchers' needs. This fundamental function of the representations of documents is carried out by reducing search time and search space (O'Connor, 1996). In other words, representations of documents or indexes improve retrieval performance by highlighting crucial attributes of documents and omitting unnecessary attributes, the latter of which can result in information loss. Therefore, it is essential to decide which attributes should be represented and which ones should be left out. This decision is not a simple process because every current and future user will have different information needs and will interpret a document from different perspectives, depending on their needs. For example, given a document reporting psychological testing results, some users might be interested in study results, whereas others might be interested in methodology, including sampling, testing procedure, and so on. Still others might be interested in the testing material itself for reusing it. Since each user group has different expectations as to which parts of the document should be emphasized, it is a challenge to develop a representation scheme that can satisfy current and potential users' needs as well as effectively reduce search time and space.

ofness

In practice, the concept of indexing has two meanings: First, descriptive indexing represents documents with respect to physical aspects, which is called "ofness," such as author and other creators, title of the document, publication information, and so on. Second, subject indexing focuses on topics, themes, and content of documents, which is called "aboutness." The main focus of this chapter is subject indexing rather than descriptive indexing. Basic concepts, main approaches to subject indexing, and modern subject indexing approaches that have emerged with the development of digital resources and technologies will be discussed.

aboutness

Background Concepts for Subject Indexing

Aboutness

The concept of subject or aboutness is one of the key components in understanding subject indexing. Researchers have examined the concept of aboutness theoretically for more than three decades. In regards to early studies, articles by Hutchins (1977) and Maron (1977) are often referred to within the literature. More recently, Bruza (Bruza and Huibers, 1994; 1996; Bruza, Song, and Wong, 2000) and Hjørland (1992; 2001) logically investigate the notion of aboutness. When considering the aboutness of a document, two approaches have been discussed: a document-oriented approach and a user-oriented approach. A document-oriented approach sustains a point of view that the subject of a document is solely dependent on the document itself and the author's intention. In contrast, the idea of a user-oriented approach is that aboutness is determined by users as well as the document itself. Albrechtsen (1993), Fidel (1994), Bates (1998), Hjørland (2001), Mai (2001), and many other researchers support the fact that subject indexing should be determined based on the understandings of a particular group of users who are served. As Lancaster (2003) pointed out, the user-oriented approach may be more important for certain formats of documents, such as image, video, and music, because in the case of these types of materials, subjective interpretation is more directly and strongly involved in understanding documents. As related concepts, a document-oriented approach pertains to literary warrant, and a user-oriented approach relates to user warrant. Since the subject of a document cannot be determined either only by the document itself or only by users of the document, subject indexing should be a balanced work between literary and user established authority.

Indexing Language

There are two types of subject indexing language: controlled vocabularies and natural languages. Controlled vocabularies include a set of selected concepts, and those terms are organized in an orderly manner through three semantic relationships: equivalent, hierarchical, and associative relationships. Equivalent relationships identify relationships among synonyms and spelling variations by indicating authorized (preferred) terms so searchers using the controlled vocabularies do not have to try every possible synonym to obtain comprehensive search results. Hierarchical relationships demonstrate broader and narrower terms for a given concept, and associative relationships indicate any related concepts, excluding equivalent and hierarchical relationships. Therefore, when searchers are not familiar with a certain domain and they need some guidelines for selecting appropriate search terms or revising search terms, controlled vocabularies can help searchers navigate the semantic space of the domain. Because of these benefits in searching effectiveness, library communities have long been developing controlled vocabulary systems for indexing documents, such as subject headings (e.g., Library Congress Subject Headings, Sears, MeSH [Medical Subject Headings]) or thesauri (e.g., ERIC, INSPECT). However, there are disadvantages with controlled vocabularies. Developing controlled vocabularies is labor-intensive. Terms become outdated requiring searchers to monitor controlled vocabularies continuously and provide current appropriate terms, while maintaining sufficient historical terminology. Users must consult vocabularies to find authorized terms and may need training to use vocabulary tools.

Indexing systems using natural language extract index terms from a document itself. Unfortunately, a lack of indexing consistency may cause difficulties for searchers. However, by adopting natural language index terms, it is possible to increase term specificity, to use the most appropriate term (such as jargon) that is accepted in a certain domain, and to reflect emerging terminologies or concepts without time lag. The pros and cons of controlled vocabularies and natural languages have been debated for decades (see Rowley's 1994 article on the issue), but it is agreed that the two types of indexing languages are complementary, and both should be considered for increasing searching effectiveness.

Depth of Indexing

Another important concept related to subject indexing is depth of indexing. There are two kinds of depth to be considered: exhaustivity and specificity. Exhaustivity refers to the number of index terms assigned to each document. In general, an institution that generates a form of document representation has an indexing policy establishing the range of the number of index terms. Specificity refers to the conceptual detail of index terms that are available from the indexing language. Therefore, level of specificity depends on the indexing language. For example, for an article that reviews several classification schemes, one indexer can assign an index term "classification," which shows low exhaustivity and low specificity, whereas another indexer can assign "DDC, LCC, UDC, Colon Classification," indicating the various types of classification covered, which shows high exhaustivity and high specificity.

Depth of indexing is closely related to the measures of information retrieval effectiveness. Two main measures for the evaluation of information retrieval effectiveness are precision and recall. Precision evaluates how many returned documents are actually relevant to users' needs from all the potentially relevant number of retrieved citations. For example, the precision is 60 percent in a case where only six documents are relevant to a user's need among 10 documents retrieved. Recall evaluates how many of the relevant documents in the collection are actually retrieved after a search. Consider that a collection has 10 documents that are relevant to a user's certain information need, but the information retrieval system retrieves only four documents of the 10. In this case, the recall is 40 percent. Information retrieval (IR) system performance, measured by precision and recall, is affected by depth of indexing. As the number of index terms increases (i.e., with greater exhaustivity), high recall will result at the cost of precision; however, as index terms are more specific (i.e., with greater specificity), high precision will be obtained at the cost of recall.

Expectations on the level of exhaustivity and specificity may vary depending on users and their information needs. Although it is difficult to develop one absolute guideline, Lancaster (2003) offers general considerations concerning the level of indexing depth. His suggestion regarding specificity is that several specific index terms would be better than one general term. Making a decision on the level of exhaustivity is not as straightforward as specificity. According to Lancaster, the level of exhaustivity should be a cost-effectiveness consideration because high exhaustivity requires the time and efforts of indexers. In other words, when comprehensive searches are requested in most cases, a high level of exhaustivity is needed, but if comprehensive searches are rarely required, a low level of exhaustivity should be sufficient.

Two Major Approaches to Subject Indexing

There are two major approaches to subject indexing: manual indexing and automatic indexing. Both approaches are broadly adopted in representing documents, and each has its own advantages and disadvantages; therefore, many information retrieval systems adopt both approaches for maximizing retrieval effectiveness (Anderson and Pérez-Carballo, 2001).

Manual Indexing

In the process of manual indexing, which is also termed human indexing, human indexers analyze and determine the subject(s) of a document and choose subject index terms that can represent the aboutness of the document as well as help users find and select the document. Lancaster (2003) explains that the subject indexing process consists of two major steps: concept analysis and translation. These two steps can blur and can occur simultaneously or iteratively.

At the stage of concept analysis, indexers decide the aboutness of documents. Although concept analysis should be a core process in subject indexing, there is no clear and structured guidance indicating how indexers should decide the subject of documents (Langridge, 1989). The Dewey Decimal Classification (Dewey, 2003) and the ISO standard (1985) are manuals on classification and indexing that provide guidelines for indexers. These guidelines suggest that indexers should investigate various parts of documents, including title, table of contents, introduction, preface, references, and so on; however, they do not explain *how* to examine these sources or how to reflect current and potential users' needs for determining subjects (Mai, 2000). An important concept analysis method was proposed by Wilson (1968). He suggested the following four methods for determining subject and then concluded that any one of the methods by itself is insufficient to determine subject and that the usage of one method can result in different subject index terms. Four approaches for subject analysis are as follows:

- To identify the author's intention in the document

- To determine relatively emphasized aspects of documents

- To use a statistical approach, such as word frequency

- To determine what makes the document a whole

Although Wilson's approach is considered to be one of the most important subject analysis methods (Hjørland, 2001) and is frequently cited in literatures on subject analysis, it has been indicated that he omits the user-oriented approach, which has received a great deal of attention recently (Mai, 2000).

At the translation stage, indexers translate identified subject concepts to appropriate index terms for a certain system. In the case where an organization system uses natural language, an indexer extracts subject terms from a document. When using a controlled vocabulary system, an indexer extracts subject terms from a document and then selects authorized terms by consulting the controlled vocabulary system. If a system uses precoordinate indexing (e.g., Library of Congress Subject Heading), an indexer combines related concepts for representing specific and complex concepts. However, a post-coordinate indexing system (e.g., most thesauri) allows searchers to combine index terms using Boolean operators.

Automatic Indexing[1]

With the development of computer technologies, automatic indexing, which makes use of computer algorithms, becomes an interesting research area. Permuted, KWIC (Key Word In Context), KWAC (Key Word Alongside Context), and KWOC (Key Word Out of Context) indexes, which manipulate document titles and generate human browsable indexes, are known as primitive formats of automatic indexing. However, as digitized full-text documents become available, automatic indexing focuses attention on the utilization of document features, such as word co-occurrence in a single document as well as in a collection, word proximity, word location, and so on. Automatic indexing has been studied in many research fields through collaborations, including library and information science, computer science, linguistics, and artificial intelligence, and different approaches have been developed and tested. Among these approaches, natural language indexing, text categorization, and clustering have established main lines of automatic indexing research.

One manual indexing approach is to extract index terms from a given document. Natural language processing is an automatic indexing method that extracts index terms using statistical processes (Kowalski and Maybury, 2000). A number of complex and advanced algorithms have been developed for automatic extracting indexing. Since they are beyond the scope of this chapter, those detailed algorithms are not introduced here. However, there are several processes that provide foundations for natural language indexing. First, tokenization is a starting point of natural language processing. Tokenization is the process of deciding which linguistic units become basic units of retrieval. The basic unit of retrieval is usually defined as "word" separated by white spaces. In most cases, white spaces seem to identify words straightforwardly, but there are critical exceptions. For example, it is difficult to determine whether a hyphenated word should be one word or not. Other punctuations, such as slashes, underscores, apostrophes, and commas, among others, are tricky. Numbers, single words, abbreviations with punctuations, uppercase/lowercase letters, URLs, and email addresses have some complex structures. Another process designed for improving indexing effectiveness is the process of removing "stop" words. Although automatic indexing is based on word frequency, there are words that are used frequently in almost every document but are insignificant, such as prepositions, articles, and conjunctions. Since these words usually do not have an effect on retrieving relevant documents, it is common to define a stop word list so these words are ignored in any further processing. Stemming is another process for managing a set of words having a common root but in different forms. Since those terms deal with a set of closely related concepts, a stemming algorithm can increase recall of relevant documents with little cost of precision by removing prefixes and suffixes (Anderson and Pérez-Carballo, 2001).

Although natural language indexing assumes that frequently occurring terms are good surrogates for a document, a sole consideration of term frequency within the document may not suffice to distinguish a set of relevant documents from nonrelevant. Index terms are not entirely dependent on properties of any single document, but they reflect a relationship between an individual document and the collection from which it might be selected. Consider an electronic database on medical information. Terms such as disease, medicine, symptom, and others may occur in most of the resources of the medical information database. Therefore, these terms may not be useful in distinguishing individual resources in this special collection, whereas the same terms can be good index terms in public libraries or school libraries. Since unusually frequent words in a certain collection cannot be used to discriminate among documents, both individual term frequencies for a single document as well as for a given collection are combined to define good index terms. Term frequencies within a document and in a collection provide a basis for calculating a weight of index terms assigned to the document.

After performing all of these processes, most automatic extracting indexing systems create an inverted index. An inverted index consists of an alphabetical list of index terms appearing in the collection; it points to documents containing each of the index terms and usually has weights of the index terms. An inverted index greatly increases search effectiveness by allowing the information retrieval system to match queries and index terms without scanning the full text of the document or of all documents in the collection. For example, Figure 5.1 presents a simple inverted file structure. When a user sends the query "Indexing AND Theory," a retrieval system locates "Indexing" and "Theory" from the sorted inverted list and performs Boolean operations. Without scanning every document in the collection, the system returns D3, which includes both search terms [(D1, D2, D3) AND (D3)].

Text categorization, also called text classification, automatically assigns index terms from controlled vocabulary. A unique feature of text categorization

Documents	Directory	

D1 Software Indexing

D2 Introduction Indexing Abstracting Exploration

D3 Indexing Abstracting Theory Practice

Term	Document Number
Abstracting	D2, D3
Exploration	D2
Indexing	D1, D2, D3
Practice	D3
Software	D1
Theory	D3

Figure 5.1 An inverted file.

is that it uses human assigned subject index terms for automated indexing (Lewis, 2000). Text categorization is based on a training set of documents having manually assigned controlled vocabulary index terms. A computer algorithm, which is called a machine-learning algorithm, is designed to determine how those subject index terms are assigned to documents by analyzing patterns and features of documents, the "learning" aspect, and then creates an automatic classifier. Once the established automatic classifier is applied to a new document, it predicts and assigns index terms based on its learned knowledge. For better performance, various machine-learning algorithms, such as Naïve Bayes, Neural Networks, Support Vector Machine, and others, have been developed for text categorization applications.

The idea of clustering has been designed and explored by Gerard Salton and his colleagues since the 1960s. This technique involves clustering groups of similar terms (term clustering) or similar documents (document clustering) based on the co-occurrence of terms in documents. The term clustering technique has been used in developing automatic thesaurus constructions, based on the assumption that the more frequently two terms co-occur in the same documents, the more the two concepts are related to each other (Anderson and Pérez-Carballo, 2001). Document clustering is also based on the concept that documents having more terms in common are more related to each other. Depending on its operation, clustering may be divided into two types: global and local. Global clustering strategy groups documents with the consideration of the whole collection and local clustering strategy brings together retrieved documents by reflecting a current user's query and the set of retrieved documents (Baeza-Yates and Ribeiro-Neto, 1999).

Modern Indexing Approaches

Although there has been continuous research on automatic indexing and several automated indexing systems have been implemented, manual indexing by professionals (librarians, indexers, and catalogers) has been a dominant indexing method for traditional bibliographic resources. However, with the exponential growth of digital materials, it is nearly impossible for information professionals to assign value-added index terms to every digital resource. In addition, digital resources have their own unique features that are different from traditional library collections. In these contexts, some researchers have made an effort to develop automatic indexing methods appropriate for digital resources, such as web, digital image, sound, multimedia, and more. These approaches extract features embedded in media, such as color, shape, melody, and so on, and use them in representing documents. Other researchers have attempted to develop specialized metadata schemes for a particular community's information resources. From a perspective of library and information science, metadata is not a new concept. Metadata is a descriptive indexing that has been practiced for a long time in the library community. However, metadata is now a widely used term that refers to descriptive indexing schemes for diverse digital resources. In addition to these automatic and manual indexing approaches, social tagging is recently being considered as a way to supplement traditional indexing approaches. In the next section, these recent attempts to represent digital objects are briefly discussed.

Web Indexing

The World Wide Web (www or web) has brought profound changes in the way users access information. Since the web environment is different from the conventional bibliographic universe, the indexing principles and practices, which have been developed for several decades (or centuries), have been modified and extended to a new networked digital environment (Rasmussen, 2003). For instance, being dynamic is a feature of the web. The size of the web is large, the number of websites keeps growing, and the contents of websites can be easily updated, added, and deleted. It is difficult to estimate the size of the entire web; however, according to the Google Blog (July 28, 2008), Google has processed one trillion web pages, and ComScore (December 2008) counted more than one billion web surfers world wide. The web is heterogeneous in several aspects including size, content structure, formats, and language. Another significant difference between websites and library collections or electronic databases is that many websites are developed for commercial purposes, and as a result, the intention to attract people to their sites may cause a phenomenon called "indexing spamming." For example, to obtain high rankings in search results, web developers intentionally manipulate their contents. They use metatags (metatags are elements between the head tags in webpages where descriptions, format, instructions, or information pertinent to the pages are contained, but they are not visible on the public page display) or add thousands of words that are not seen by users but are still detected by indexing crawlers. High frequency of words could influence where a page is positioned in the list of search-retrieved documents. To prevent indexing spamming, search engine companies developed indexing algorithms that incorporate more complex statistical analysis, word extraction, and use of contextual information, among other tools. Hyperlink is also a defining feature of the web, and it provides useful information in web indexing. For example, documents that are linked together may have topical commonality so the term associations found in the linked documents can be used in improving retrieval results (Savoy, 1995). Also, frequently linked webpages may be used in identifying authoritative pages.

As Rasmussen (2003) addressed, it is not surprising that a search engine adopting automatic indexing is a dominant method for web indexing with consideration of the size and variety of the web. A search engine is composed of three functional parts: a crawler, an indexer, and a query processor. A crawler (or spider) is a program that traverses the web to identify new or changed websites and gather information about those pages for indexing. An indexer then creates an inverted file by following the automatic indexing procedures previously discussed. A query processor receives queries submitted by users, tokenizes the queries, searches the inverted file, and retrieves the websites matching the query. In addition to this fundamental procedure, some ranking techniques are also commonly used for increasing search effectiveness. Spink and Jansen (2004) introduced six ranking methods: 1) Click-Through-Analysis, which utilizes the frequency of users choosing, by clicking, a webpage; 2) Link Popularity, which uses the frequency of incoming links; 3) Term Frequency, which is the most common ranking method; 4) Term Location, which usually gives high weights on the terms appearing in the title, in the first paragraph, or special formatting words (e.g., bold or italicized); 5) Term Proximity, which generally assumes that documents in which query terms appear near each other are more likely relevant; and 6) Text Formatting, which analyzes internal links in the documents.

Although automated indexing is a common method for indexing the web, the value of human intellectual indexing also has been recognized. Metadata is a frequently adopted method using human intellectual judgment for web indexing. Compared to conventional manual indexing, web manual indexing is usually done by individuals or organizations creating the website by embedding metatags into the HTML source code. The Dublin Core, which has been developed for describing networked resources, is a popular metadata scheme in the web environment. Dublin Core enables people to describe information objects in an easier and simpler way by applying 15 elements to resources: contributor, coverage, creator, date, description, format, identifier, language, publisher, relation, rights, source, subject, title, and type. In addition to the Dublin Core, web creators can indicate contents of their websites by inserting Keyword or Description metatags in HTML source pages. Although the idea of metatags began in order to improve web search effectiveness, many commercial sites manipulate metatags to cause their websites to be higher ranked. Therefore, most search engines now exclude metatags in the web indexing process because of their unreliable quality.

In addition to automatic indexing and metatags, several search engines provide information access through predefined hierarchical categorization. In some cases, professional editors review and categorize websites. Yahoo! Directory is one example of categorization of the web by professionals. On the other hand, Google lets volunteer editors participate in maintaining hierarchical categorization of the web. Google Open Directory Project explains that because a limited number of editorial staff cannot maintain the fast-growing websites, they instead provide an opportunity where everybody can contribute to value-added directories. However, even with the recognition of the limitations of automatic indexing and the value of human intellectual indexing, the features of a web environment make human indexing of web documents relatively rare, at least in the public web environment (Rasmussen, 2003).

Image, Music, and Multimedia Indexing

As digital images, music, and video become valuable information resources with the advances of information technology, providing effective access to non-text digital information gains increasing importance. A conventional way to organize image, music, and video materials is to generate bibliographic records that represent materials using words. Although verbal representation using a metadata scheme is still a popular approach for digital media, it has been recognized that nontext documents have their own distinct features that cannot be expressed with words. Therefore, modern indexing approaches attempt to use inherent features of those materials, such as the color feature of image, the melodic attributes of music, and so on. This section briefly overviews modern indexing approaches to images, music, and multimedia materials.

Image indexing and retrieval methods are generally divided into content-based image retrieval (CBIR) using low-level features of an image and text-based image indexing. As expressed in the sentence "a picture is worth a thousand words," an image contains multiple levels of meanings. Therefore, for developing an image-indexing method (whether CBIR or text-based indexing), it is important to understand the features of the multiple levels of meanings involved in an image. In a sense, researchers conceptually examined attributes (or types of messages) of an image or experimentally analyzed query terms employed by image searchers. Although each researcher adopted different terminologies and categorizations, the following three categories are commonly found in this line of study: 1) low-level features, including color, shape, texture, and so on; 2) object-level, including person, thing, place, location, action, events, and so on; and 3) abstract level, such as symbolic value, atmosphere, emotional cues, and so on (Eakins and Graham, 1999; Greisdorf and O'Connor, 2002). Since each of these image attributes has different characteristics, it is suggested that various approaches should be adopted for representing each attribute (Jörgensen, 2003). For example, low-level features are directly and easily processed by CBIR automatic indexing method. Object-level is not as straightforward as low-level features, but current CBIR techniques demonstrate a great potential in representing object-level messages of an image. Most manual subject indexing tools, such as thesauri, and metadata schemes, also focus on representing object-level messages of an image. Among the three levels, the abstract level is the most problematic from an indexing perspective because abstract level is seriously affected by the individual's experiences and the socio-cultural context. It is difficult to extract abstract meanings automatically from low-level features, and it is almost impossible for human indexers with diverse personal backgrounds to assign emotional and abstract messages consistently. However, even with these difficulties, image indexing and retrieval for abstract messages is currently receiving attention from researchers.

Although verbal expressions may not fully convey meanings of an image, text-based image retrieval that makes use of keyword indexing and verbal queries is still broadly used. While Dublin Core is a general metadata scheme that can be applied for describing image objects, there are other metadata schemes that are mostly specialized for image objects. The Categories for the Description of Works of Art (CDWA), designed by the Art Information Task Force (AITF) for describing art object information, is a metadata scheme composed of 27 broad elements and 150 subelements. The Core Categories for Visual Resources (VRA Core), which is composed of 18 elements, is adapted from the CDWA for covering architecture. As can be recognized from the name, it is not intended to provide a complete set of elements but to expand the scheme in accordance with individual institutional demands (Jörgensen, 2003). In addition to descriptive metadata schemes, visual material communities also have developed thesauri for controlling subject index terms. The Art & Architecture Thesaurus developed by the Getty Vocabulary Program contains approximately 125,000 terms with a facet structure for covering art, architecture, and material culture areas. Another well-known system, the Library of Congress Thesaurus for Graphic Material (LCTGM), provides controlled vocabularies for subject and genre/format indexing. It contains more than 7,000 subject (topical) terms and 650 genre/format terms for indexing types of photographs, prints, design drawings, ephemera, and so on. Compared to text-based image retrieval, which follows a conventional text-retrieval approach, CBIR is a relatively new concept that extracts low-level features automatically from an image itself and then represents that image by analyzing the extracted low-level features. Users employing a CBIR system represent their queries either through selecting a preexisting image in the collection or drawing a rough sketch expressing color and shape. An image-retrieval system then calculates similarity between image representation and user queries. Different algorithms have been developed for effective representation and retrieval performance, and QBIC, xcavator, and Retrievr are regarded as pioneering CBIR systems. Although the development of CBIR shows a promising potential in image retrieval, CBIR communities have recently been faced with the conclusion that low-level features cannot sufficiently represent semantic meanings of an image. Therefore, approaches combining CBIR with text-based image retrieval or using available associated texts of an image are being actively proposed and tested.

Modern Music Information Retrieval (MIR) focuses on searching music through musical input. In other words, music information is represented via features of the music itself, and users send a musically expressed query, such as by humming or singing (Lippincott, 2002). Music information is composed of multiple facets, which Downie (2003) described as: 1) pitch facet, which is the perceived fundamental frequency of sound; 2) temporal facet, which is the duration between musical events; 3) harmonic facet, which occurs when two or more pitches sound simultaneously; 4) timbral facet, which concerns tone color that distinguishes musical instruments; 5) editorial facet, which is performance instruction; 6) textual facet, which is lyrics; and 7) bibliographic facet, which concerns title, composer, performer, date, and so on. According to Downie, since these facets interact with each other, it causes one of the main challenges of music retrieval, which is termed "multifaceted challenge." In addition, he identified several other challenges of music retrieval. Music can be represented in many different ways (i.e., multirepresentational challenge). Music is rarely limited by time, geography, or culture, but historical, geographical, and cultural contexts have critical impacts on expressing and comprehending music (i.e., multicultural challenge). Besides cultural aspects, each individual reacts to music differently based on personal experience and background (i.e., multiexperiential challenge).

Although music is composed of several facets, current MIR systems usually represent music through melody information, a combination of pitch and temporal facets. Music representation can be generated with different formats, and Lippincott (2002) introduced three formats used in music representation. Digitized symbolic notation encodes beginning or thematic fragments of music, and it has been a format of music representation since the beginning of the MIR system. Musical Instrument Digital Interface (MIDI) is a popular format used in recent MIR systems. MIDI is a standardized digital communication protocol, encoding music with a number of notes and control commands. However, since a MIDI file is not an audio file, it does not fully capture everything embedded in music. Full-text audio may be a format that can include the richness of musical performance and is being considered as an ultimate goal of MIR systems; however, as Lippincott (2002) mentioned, its complexity makes it difficult to be practically implemented in current MIR systems. A form of query can be either hummed audio input or keyboard input, and in both cases, the query transposes to the forms that can match with music representation. Meldex, RISM, and Tuneserver are good examples of MIR systems. In their survey paper, Byrd and Crawford (2002) remark, "although a substantial number of research projects have addressed music information retrieval over the past three decades, the field is still very immature. ... Almost all text-IR methods rely on identifying approximate units of meaning, that is words. A fundamental problem in music IR is that locating such units is extremely difficult, perhaps impossible" (p. 249). However, in spite of the inherent problem of music information, Downie (2003) concludes that some of the current MIR systems will "fundamentally alter the way we experience and interact with music" (p. 329).

Multimedia can be any form of integrated media document; however, the term generally indicates video documents that combine moving images and sound. Today, video is a popular communications medium, from movies to television broadcasts to surveillance video. Video materials include not only video and audio components but also some descriptive information such as title, date, producer, and so on. The simplest and most conventional way to index video documents may be to use structured metadata with annotations. In general, annotations are given to manually segmented shots[2] by librarians or professionals (Smeaton, 2004). Significant contents that should be included in annotations may vary depending on types of video materials. For example, a

BBC TV documentary and news program: "Pres. Bush, White House Lawn, walking toward camera, camera fixed, 90 frames" (Smeaton, 2004, p. 381). In this example, people, location, action, and camera-related information are annotated for describing the shot.

Although metadata and annotation have provided access mechanisms in video retrieval, researchers agree that, as in the case of image and music indexing, automatic indexing using visual and sound components should be improved for effective digital video retrieval. Several elements should be considered for automatic video indexing. Shot and scene[3] boundary detection is a part of the video indexing process. By adopting various techniques, a video is automatically segmented into shots, and the shots are grouped into scenes having semantic commonalities. Once a video is segmented, it is necessary to find a key frame representing individual shots. Many algorithms for finding key frames are still developed and tested (Smeaton, 2004). Then, the key frames are indexed by applying CBIR techniques as in image indexing. In addition to visual components, audio components can provide access points; in practice, there is much more progress in audio processing compared to visual processing. Audio integrated into video can be divided into spoken language audio and nonspoken language audio. Two major research areas for spoken language audio process are voice recognition and speech-generated text. Nonspoken language audio includes natural sounds, sounds associated with human activities, music, and so on. For processing natural sounds and sounds associated with human activities, libraries of sound samples are developed so that input sound can match with a sample of libraries. Since the number of sounds is large, deciding how to narrow down a set of candidate sounds during the matching process is a key issue. Although video indexing is an active research area, it is still in its infancy and many challenges remain (Korfhage, 1997).

Folksonomies

The emergence of digital formats of information objects is not the only area affected by the development of technologies and network environments. The term Web 2.0, coined by O'Reilly Media and CMP Media in 2004, presents a paradigm shift on the web that changes internet users' role to content creator. The advent of Web 2.0 also results in new library service models referred to as Library 2.0. Although it is an emerging area, Library 2.0 seems to have a potential for enhancing user-oriented library service, which has been a key issue in the library and information science field for several decades. Folksonomy is one of those 2.0 applications that make effects on information organization through user-supplied tags (or keywords).

The term folksonomy, a combination of "folk" and "taxonomy," is attributed to Thomas Vander Wal in a discussion on an information architecture mailing list (Smith, 2004). Folksonomy is referred to as social tagging, social indexing, and collaborative tagging. One of the popular systems, Delicious, explicitly illustrates characteristics of a social tagging system on its online description page. "It allows you to easily add sites you like to your personal collection of links, to categorize those sites with keywords, and to share your collection not only between your own browsers and machines, but also with others" (Schachter, 2004). That is, by assigning keywords, which are called tags, to the website, users not only organize information for their own use but also share their organized collections with others. In other words, social tagging becomes a new information organization mechanism, providing access to digital resources. In addition to Delicious, a social bookmark system, there exist many popular examples using user-generated tags. On Flickr, users store and organize their photos by means of a set of tags. Technorati and RawSugar let users assign tags to their own blogs. Connotea, CiteULike, and LibraryThing are sites where users create their own catalogs and share with others.

Key features of social tags can be found through tag analysis. For instance, the most popular tags displayed on Delicious are "design, blog, video, software, tools, music, programming, webdesign, reference, tutorial, art, web, howto, javascript, free, linux, web2.0, development, google, inspiration, photography, news, food, flash, css, blogs, education, business, technology, travel, shopping, books, mac, tips, politics, science, opensource, games, culture, research" (delicious.com as of March 1, 2010). These tags show that users generally apply keywords for representing the subject(s) of the websites. In addition, since many of these are technical terms, it suggests that users participating in social tagging are tech-savvy people. By analyzing a large set of Delicious popular sets, Golder and Huberman (2006) identified seven functions of tags: 1) what it is about (subject); 2) what kind it is (e.g., article, blog, book, and so on); 3) who owns or creates the content (author/creator); 4) qualities or characteristics (e.g., scary, funny, stupid, inspirational); 5) self-reference (e.g., mystuff, mycomments); 6) task organizing (e.g., toread, jobsearch); and 7) refining category (tags refining or qualifying existing categories).

Information loss is an essential feature of information representation, yet it is difficult to decide which information should be kept or omitted. One of the expected advantages of social tagging is that it has the potential to overcome, or at least decrease, the problem of information loss that occurs in traditional manual indexing. This is because, in folksonomies, the loss is from people having different viewpoints and is not from a single indexer's discernment (Shirky, n.d.). Also, users engaged with social tagging systems describe content with their own vocabulary without referring to any formally structured set of vocabulary. Therefore, tagging systems may reveal the conceptual structure and current terminologies of the user community (Furnas et al., 2006). In addition, by offering opportunities to find related topics and users, tagging systems can increase the possibility of discovering unexpected resources through browsing or serendipity, as well as create online communities among users having common interests (Kroski, 2005).

In spite of the benefits of social tagging systems, there have been considerable arguments concerning their drawbacks. Most of the concerns are caused by users not adopting controlled vocabularies or employing trained expert professionals, and as a result, there is no control of synonyms, homonyms, and plural and singular forms. Also, since many social tagging sites only allow single-word metadata, many compound terms are created for representing single concepts, such as "openresource" and "webdesign" as shown in the previous Delicious popular tags (Guy and Tonkin, 2006). In a sense, "tagging is a much lighter task cognitively that requires no previous consideration or training, but may result in very 'noisy' metadata as seen from a classic categorization point of view" (Furnas et al., 2006, p. 37).

Folksonomies may not be a replacement but can be a user-friendly supplement for existing information organization systems (Guy and Tonkin, 2006). Spiteri (2006) proposed the potential values that can be obtained from folksonomies: 1) users can organize personal information space; 2) user-supplied tags can supplement existing controlled vocabularies; and 3) tagging systems can create online communities of interests among users. Recent efforts have demonstrated that library services can enhance information access by using user-supplied tags (Casey and Savastinuk, 2006; Spiteri, 2007). Based on the Delicious system, the University of Pennsylvania Library has allowed users to tag records in its online catalog since 2005. Users can use tags in organizing personal information as well as sharing with others in the Penn community. Danbury Public Library connects its online catalog to LibraryThing; thus, when library users find a book, they can see tags that are created by LibraryThing users for describing the book as well as a list of related books. Although there are many unsolved research areas regarding folksonomies, especially in relation to their cognitive and behavioral aspects, it is expected that folksonomies will provide a user-friendly and interactive approach for information access.

Summary

This chapter briefly discussed fundamental concepts surrounding subject indexing and traditional and modern approaches to indexing. The advent of computer technologies affects indexing practices in many aspects: New formats of digital materials having different features with traditional materials become critical information resources, new and more complex computer algorithms are developed for extracting crucial data from documents, and even information users' roles are changing due to the development of technologies. In addition to these aspects covered in this chapter, networked information environments bring attention to information organization mechanisms that provide access across different information retrieval systems as well as across different languages. These changes seem remarkable; however, the basic principle still remains as a challenge in generating document surrogates: What is the most effective way to represent aboutness of documents that can serve current and future users?

Endnotes

1. Automatic indexing can be performed not only on text documents but also on image, sound, or multimedia documents. This section focuses on the text automatic indexing process. Automatic indexing for nontext documents will be discussed in a later section.

2. "[Shots] are defined as the contiguous set of frames taken by a single uninterrupted camera over time. ... Shots are often grouped into logical or semantic units called *scenes*" (Smeaton, 2004, p. 383).

3. Ibid.

References

Albrechtsen, H. 1993. Subject Analysis and Indexing: From Automated Indexing to Domain Analysis. *The Indexer* 18:219–224.

Alpert, J., and Hajaj, N. 2008. We Knew the Web Was Big ... The Official Google Blog. Retrieved March 1, 2010, from googleblog.blogspot.com/2008/07/we-knew-web-was-big.html

Anderson, J. D., and Pérez-Carballo, J. 2001. The Nature of Indexing: How Humans and Machines Analyze Messages and Texts for Retrieval. Part II: Machine Indexing, and The Allocation of Human Versus Machine Effort. *Information Processing & Management* 37(2):255–77.

Baeza-Yates, R., and Ribeiro-Neto, B. 1999. *Modern Information Retrieval.* New York: ACM Press.

Bates, M. J. 1998. Indexing and Access for Digital Libraries and the Internet: Human, Database, and Domain Factors. *Journal of the American Society for Information Science* 49(13):1185–1205.

Bruza, P. D., and Huibers, T. W. C. 1994. Investigating Aboutness Axioms Using Information Fields. In *Proceedings of ACM SIGIR Conference on Research and Development in Information Retrieval*, Dublin, Ireland, pp. 112–121.

Bruza, P. D., and Huibers, T. W. C. 1996. A Study of Aboutness in Information Retrieval. *Artificial Intelligence Review* 10:1–27.

Bruza, P. D., Song, D. W., and Wong, K. F. 2000. Aboutness from a Commonsense Perspective. *Journal of the American Society for Information Science* 51(12):1090–1105.

Byrd, D., and Crawford, T. 2002. Problems of Music Information Retrieval in the Real World. *Information Processing and Management* 38(2):249–272.

Casey, M., and Savastinuk, L. 2006. Library 2.0: Service for the Next-Generation Library. *Library Journal* 131(14):40–42.

Dewey, M. 2003. *Dewey Decimal Classification and Relative Index.* Joan S. Mitchell [et al.]. Ed. Dublin, OH: OCLC Online Computer Library Center, Inc.

Downie, S. 2003. Music Information Retrieval. *Annual Review of Information Science and Technology* 37:295–340.

Eakins, J. P., and Graham, M. E. 1999. *Content-Based Image Retrieval: A Report to the JISC Technology Applications Programme.* Institute for Image Data Research,

University of Northumbria at Newcastle. Retrieved February 15, 2010, from www.jisc.ac.uk/uploaded_documents/jtap-039.doc

Fidel, R. 1994. User-Centered Indexing. *Journal of the American Society for Information Science* 45(8):572–576.

Furnas, G. W., Fake, C., von Ahn, L., Schachter, J., Golder, S., Fox, K., Davis, M., Marlow, C., and Naaman, M. 2006. Why Do Tagging Systems Work? In *CHI '06 Extended Abstracts on Human Factors in Computing Systems* pp. 36–39. New York: ACM Press.

Gavin, G. 2008. Global Internet Audience Surpasses 1 Billion Visitors, According to comScore. ComScore.com. Retrieved March 1, 2010, from www.comscore.com/Press_Events/Press_Releases/2009/1/Global_Internet_Audience_1_Billion

Golder, S., and Huberman, B. 2006. Usage Patterns of Collaborative Tagging Systems. *Journal of Information Science* 32(2):198–208.

Greisdorf, H., and O'Connor, B. 2002. Modelling What Users See When They Look at Images: A Cognitive Viewpoint. *Journal of Documentation* 58(1):6–29.

Guy, M., and Tonkin, E. 2006. Folksonomies: Tidying Up Tags? [Electronic Version]. *D-Lib Magazine* 12(1). Retrieved February 15, 2010, from www.dlib.org/dlib/january06/guy/01guy.html

Hjørland, B. 1992. The Concept of "Subject" in Information Science. *Journal of Documentation* 48(2):172–200.

Hjørland, B. 2001. Towards a Theory of Aboutness, Subject, Topicality, Theme, Domain, Field, Content … and Relevance. *Journal of the American Society for Information Science and Technology* 52(9):774–778.

Hutchins, W. J. 1977. On the Problem of "Aboutness" in Document Analysis. *Journal of Informatics* 1(1):17–35.

ISO 5963:1985. 1985. *Documentation Methods for Examining Documents, Determining Their Subjects and Selecting Indexing Terms.* International Organization for Standardization.

Jörgensen, C. 2003. Image Retrieval: Theory and Research. Lanham, MD: Scarecrow Press.

Korfhage, R. 1997. *Information Storage and Retrieval.* New York: John Wiley & Sons.

Kowalski, G. J., and Maybury, M. T. 2000. *Information Storage and Retrieval Systems: Theory and Implementation.* 2nd ed. Norwell, MA: Kluwer Academic.

Kroski, E. 2005. The Hive Mind: Folksonomies and User-Based Tagging. Infotangle blog. Retrieved February 15, 2010, from infotangle.blogsome.com/2005/12/07

Lancaster, F. W. 2003. *Indexing and Abstracting in Theory and Practice.* 3rd ed. Champaign, IL: University of Illinois.

Langridge, D. W. 1989. *Subject Analysis: Principles and Procedures.* London: Bowker-Saur.

Lewis, D. D. 2000. Machine Learning for Text Categorization: Background and Characteristics. *Proceedings of the Twenty-First National Online Meeting* pp. 221–226.

Lippincott, A. 2002. Issues in Content-based Music Information Retrieval. *Journal of Information Science* 28(2):137–142.

Maron, M. E. 1977. On Indexing, Retrieval and the Meaning of About. *Journal of the American Society for Information Science* 28(1):38–43.

Mai, J.-E. 2000. Deconstructing the Indexing Process. *Advances in Librarianship* 23:269–298.

Mai, J.-E. 2001. Semiotics and Indexing: An Analysis of the Subject Indexing Process. *Journal of Documentation* 57:591–622.

O'Connor, B. 1996. *Explorations in Indexing and Abstracting: Pointing, Virtue, and Power.* Englewood, CO: Libraries Unlimited.

Rasmussen, E. 2003. Indexing and Retrieval for the Web. *Annual Review of Information Science and Technology* 37:91–124.

Rowley, J. E. 1994. The Controlled Versus Natural Indexing Language Debate Revisited: A Perspective on Information Retrieval Practice and Research. *Journal of Information Science* 20(2):108–119.

Savoy, J. 1995. A New Probablistic Scheme for Information Retrieval in Hypertext. *The New Review of Hypermedia and Multimedia* 1:107–134.

Schachter, J. 2004. Delicious About Page. Retrieved February 15, 2010, from delicious.com/about

Shirky, C. [n.d.]. Ontology is Overrated: Categories, Links, and Tags. Retrieved February 15, 2010, from www.shirky.com/writings/ontology_overrated.html

Smeaton, A. F. 2004. Indexing, Browsing, and Searching of Digital Video. *Annual Review of Information Science and Technology* 38:371–407.

Smith, G. 2004. Atomiq: Folksonomy: Social Classification. August 3, 2004. Retrieved February 15, 2010, from www.atomiq.org/archives/2004/08/folksonomy_social_classification.html

Spink, A., and Jansen, B. J. 2004. Web Search: Public Searching of the Web. Boston: Kluwer Academic.

Spiteri, L. F. 2006. The Use of Folksonomies in Public Library Catalogues. *The Serials Librarian* 51(2):75–89.

Spiteri, L. F. 2007. Structure and Form of Folksonomy Tags: The Road to the Public Library Catalogue. *Webology* 4(2).

Wilson, P. 1968. *Two Kinds of Power: An Essay on Bibliographic Control.* Berkeley, CA: University of California Press.

Chapter 6

Information Repositories: Background and Historic Overview

Teresa S. Welsh

Editor's Note: This chapter and the two that follow were selected to provide perspective in regard to the development of information collections as well as introduce the latest forms, digital repositories, and the digital library. The path of development is highlighted to establish the foundation for the following two chapters.

> Written ways of recording serve the same sorts of purposes and, like the oral tradition, it is only through the act of sharing that the written word adds to our store of knowledge or collective wisdom.
> —Lois "Lowitja" O'Donoghue (1998)

To understand a term or concept, it is useful to know the root word and original meaning. This chapter will include the origins and literal meanings of the terms "information repository" and "information," as well as an examination and discussion of tacit, preliterate repositories, and the beginnings of more traditional, physical repositories.

The role of information repositories is twofold: First, they collect and preserve information, and second, they provide access to information. No matter what the format, information is not useful unless it is stored and organized in such a manner that it can be *accessed* when needed.

What Is the Literal Meaning of Information Repository?

The word information is from the Latin *informatio*, meaning "concept or idea"; repository is from the Latin *reponere,* meaning "to put away or store." So the literal meaning of an information repository is a storehouse of information. The type of storage receptacle may vary as well as the type of information stored and the form or format of the information.

What Is Information?

Some may think of information as synonymous with data or knowledge. Data are the plural of *datum*, Latin for "something given," while the word knowledge is from an ancient Indo-European word meaning "to become aware." One way to understand the difference in these concepts is to see them as part of what is known as the DIKW Hierarchy or Pyramid (Figure 6.1).

Ackoff (1989) classified the content of the human mind into five categories by adding "understanding" between knowledge and wisdom:

- Data – symbols

- Information – data that are processed to be useful; provides answers to "who," "what," "where," and "when" questions

- Knowledge – application of data and information; answers "how" questions

- Understanding – appreciation of "why"

- Wisdom – evaluated understanding

According to Ackoff (1989), the first four categories relate to the past, while the fifth, wisdom, relates to the future because it adds vision and design.

Wisdom is understanding which knowledge to use for what purpose.

Knowledge is information which provides guidance for action.

Information comprises the basic facts with context and perspective.

Data are raw statistics and facts.

Figure 6.1   DIKW Hierarchy or Pyramid (Bellinger, Castro, and Mills, n.d.).

Preliterate, Tacit Repositories:
The Human Brain and Oral Tradition

How was information collected, stored, organized, and retrieved before writing?

Information was collected, stored, and organized in the human brain and passed down by oral tradition. Unwritten information is also known as tacit information (from the Latin *tacitus* meaning "silent"). Scholars believe that mnemonic devices such as bone notches, pictures, knots, beads, song, or rhythm were used as triggers to recall and recite large amounts of information.

Prehistoric notched bones are perhaps the earliest indication of information organization. Scientists are unsure of the type of information that was stored and whether it was related to time-keeping, such as a calendar, or to other types of record-keeping or even storytelling. Prehistoric notches may also be a notation system that could be a precursor to an alphabetic system, such as the Celtic Ogam or Ogham notched alphabet (Cowan and Marshack, 1975). For more information on the Ogham notched alphabet, see "Omniglot: Writing Systems and Languages of the World" at www.omniglot.com/writing/ogham.htm.

The oldest-known notched bone (dated about 35,000 BC) is a small piece of a baboon fibula marked with 29 notches that was found in a mountain cave between South Africa and Swaziland. Other early examples include a wolf's bone engraved with 57 notches (dated about 30,000 BC) that was discovered in Czechoslovakia and the Ishango tally bone found in the Belgian Congo (originally dated about 9000 BC and now thought to be about 20,000 BC) (Bogoshi, Naidoo, and Webb, 1987; Brooks and Smith, 1987).

Other examples of mnemonic devices used to organize information and facilitate the recall of information stored in the human brain include:

- Stone Age pictographs/pictures, such as those on the cave walls at Lascaux, France (about 40,000 BC), were of animals and humans and may be related to storytelling (Noxon, 1964).

- The ancient Incas of Peru used a system of different knots in various colored and sized cords to record, store, and transmit information. Quipus could only be interpreted by trained "rememberers" whose knowledge has been lost (Day, 1957).

- Storytelling, whether accompanied by music or rhythmic drums, was a way of preserving and passing down tribal history and memories related to cultural identity.

The Iliad and *The Odyssey* are two epic stories about the last days and aftermath of the Greek/Trojan War of about 1200 BC. The 16,000 lines of *The Iliad* and the 13,000 lines of *The Odyssey* were passed down for centuries through oral tradition and written down about 400 years later (attributed to the blind bard Homer, circa 800 BC). These poetic tales, which may have been accompanied by rhythm or music, were thought to be mythological until the late 1800s when

German archaeologist Heinrich Schliemann uncovered an ancient fortress-city near the coast of Turkey that fits Homer's literal description. Schliemann's discovery indicated that these mythic tales were likely based on a real historic battle (Wood, 1998).

In more modern times, author Alex Haley spent his boyhood summers in rural Tennessee listening to his grandmother and great-aunts recount tales about their family history that had been handed down to them since the days of slavery. In researching his family's history, which evolved into the book and miniseries *Roots: A Saga of an American Family* (1976), he traveled to the village of his ancestors in Africa. He heard the griot, or tribal historian, recite the village history back in time and recounted that Kunta Kinte (Haley's African ancestor who was captured and sold into slavery in 1767) went hunting one day and did not return *(Tennessee Encyclopedia of History and Culture, 2002)*.

The publication of the book *Roots* in 1976 and the subsequent miniseries in 1977 led to a surge in interest in genealogical research. Surveys conducted by Maritz Marketing in 2000 indicate that about 60 percent of all Americans older than 18 are interested in genealogical research, up from 45 percent in 1995 (quoted in McKay, 2002, p. 23). Examples of the continuing interest in family origins are the PBS series, *African-American Lives* (2006) and *African-American Lives 2* (2007), which traces the family history and lineage of prominent African Americans (www.pbs.org/wnet/aalives).

There has also been an increased modern-day interest in oral history projects such as the Southern Miss Center for Oral History and Cultural Heritage (www.usm.edu/oralhistory/lomp.html). With the aging and loss of World War II veterans, projects such as the Veterans History Project at the Library of Congress (www.loc.gov/vets) are an effort to collect and preserve personal experiences of historic events related to war.

Traditional Repositories: Libraries and Archives

Goethe called libraries "the memory of mankind" (Tolzmann, Hessel, and Peiss, 2001), a phrase that indicates libraries perform a function similar to the preliterate oral tradition to preserve and disseminate knowledge and culture. The word library is from the Latin *liber*, meaning "book," and a library has traditionally meant a collection of books.

The word archive is from the Greek *archeia,* or place of *archeion*, a public office. The origin of the root word indicates it was originally a storehouse of government records. The *Online Dictionary of Library and Information Science (ODLIS)* defines archive as a storage facility that preserves historical, informational, legal, or evidential records (Reitz, 2007). The earliest physical repositories discovered so far date to about 3000 BC in Mesopotamia (modern Iraq) and in Egypt, and they were associated with royal palaces and temples.

Early Repositories: Sumer Houses of Tablets

Some of the earliest writing was cuneiform (meaning "wedge-shaped"), which was done by impressing the triangular-shaped tips of cut reeds onto soft clay tablets. Many thousands of these early tablets have survived because as early city-states were conquered and burned, the tablets were hardened by the fires and covered by debris but not destroyed. Excavations in the ancient city of Nippur (formerly the religious center of Mesopotamia, located about 100 miles south of Baghdad, Iraq) have uncovered entire libraries known as "Houses of Tablets" with thousands of Sumerian and Akkadian-inscribed cuneiform tablets of administrative, legal, medical and business records, religious and astronomical texts, and the oldest-known versions (late third millennium) of literary works (Cassidy, 2002; Kramer, 1988) including the following:

- *Epic of Gilgamesh,* the account of the quest of a hero for the secret of immortality held by a survivor of a great flood. Gilgamesh (ruler of Uruk c. 2700 BC) obtains the key to immortality only to have it stolen by a serpent.

- *Enuma Elish,* or "When on high," the Sumerian account of creation, was recited annually during the New Year celebration, probably from atop a ziggurat temple.

- Hammurabi, ruler of Babylon (1792–1750 BC) amassed a large collection of clay tablets containing hymns, divination texts, mathematical texts, and myths. Hammurabi is most notable for writing the oldest-known inscribed law code, *The Code of Hammurabi,* a stone stele (an upright stone pillar used as a burial monument) that can be seen at the Louvre in Paris (Musée du Louvre, 2007).

- Ashurbanipal, King of Assyria from 668–637 BC, is considered the first librarian because his library of clay tablets is the earliest-known collection that was arranged by subject (Briscoe et al., 1986).

Early Repositories: Egyptian Houses of Life

Egypt is credited with the invention of scrolls made of papyrus, a lightweight writing material later adopted by the Greeks and Romans. The earliest fragment of papyrus (from which our word paper is derived) dates to c. 3000 BC, and the oldest papyrus with hieroglyphic text to c. 2400 BC. The earliest Egyptian glyphs in stone, recently discovered in the predynastic tomb of Scorpion I at Abydos, have been dated to c. 3400–3200 BC (Mitchell, 1999).

A "House of Life" or *per ankh* was a center of learning with a scriptorium that was connected to a temple (Baines, 1983). One of the earliest historical references to an Egyptian library (c. 2470 BC) was a tomb inscription that referred to the owner as a "Scribe in the House of Books." In the fourth and fifth dynasties

(c. 2600–2300 BC), Egypt had at least three royal "Houses of Writings," which held archives, tax records, and religious texts, and there is some evidence to support Egyptian libraries as far back as 3000 BC ("Egyptian Literature," n.d.).

King Ramses II (1300 BC) had a large library of more than 20,000 papyrus scrolls containing works of history, science, and literature. Popular literature of the time included such tales as "The Story of Sinuhe," "Story of the Eloquent Peasant," "Tale of the Shipwrecked Sailor," and "Tale of Two Brothers" (Lichtheim, 1980). On an interesting note, "The Story of Sinuhe" (similar in some respects to the Biblical story of Moses) inspired a book called *The Egyptian* by Waltari and Walford (1949) that was adapted into an epic 1954 old-Hollywood movie starring Jean Simmons, Victor Mature, Gene Tierney, and Peter Ustinov (Internet Movie Database, 2009).

Classical Repositories: Greek Libraries

The Classical Greek Period (fifth century BC) was an era associated with the development of democracy and of widespread literacy. There was an intense interest in art and architecture, science, mathematics, music, history, athletics, philosophy, theater, and literature. In *The Birds* (414 BC), Aristophanes portrayed Athenians as voracious readers who rushed out to the bookshops each morning to browse and chat with their friends. In *The Frogs*, one of Aristophanes' characters comments, "You must be very unobservant, or very uneducated; you do not even know your Aesop."

There is evidence of public libraries in Greece about sixth century BC, in addition to private collections of scholars and playwrights. Pisistratus, ruler of Athens, founded what Aulus Gellius calls "the first public library" in 560 BC. About the same time, Polycrates, tyrant of Samos, founded a public library on the island.

Bookshops and scriptoria (where clerks copied works of literature on commission) were common in Classical Athens, particularly in the agora, or public marketplace. Private literary collections became status symbols of the literati: Nicocrates of Cyprus, Euclid the Archon, Euripides, Euthydemus, and Aristotle (Tolzmann, Hessel, and Peiss, 2001).

Hellenistic Period: Great Library of Alexandria

When Alexander the Great died in 323 BC, he left a vast empire that was apportioned to his three generals. The general Ptolemy took control of Egypt, founding the last Egyptian dynasty (Cleopatra was the last of the Ptolemys and the last pharaoh of Egypt).

In 295 BC, Pharaoh Ptolemy I Sotor established the Great Library of Alexandria in Egypt. At the adjoining Museion (Greek for "shrine of the Muses" from which we get the modern term "museum"), scholars made advances in the fields of math, astronomy, geometry, medicine, and applied science, using the observatory, zoo, and botanical gardens on the grounds.

Other examples of Greek firsts related to librarianship include the following:

- Zenodotus was the first librarian at the Great Library of Alexandria and the first-known to put lists of holdings in alphabetical order.

- Callimachus compiled the first bibliography of Greek literature, *Pinakes*, or *Tables* (120 volumes).

Ptolemy II Philadelphus collected scrolls from all parts of Greece and Asia. Resident scholars translated foreign works, gathered compilations of other manuscripts, and wrote their own original works. Officials traveled throughout the region and purchased entire collections for the library.

Ptolemy III Euergetes asked world leaders to lend him their scrolls and even ordered a search of all ships for scrolls. Every known scholarly work of the ancient world was collected and translated into Greek. Considered to be the greatest library of the ancient world with a collection of 500,000 to 700,000 scrolls, the Great Library of Alexandria was destroyed by a series of fires, the first of which was in 47 BC during Caesar's invasion of Cleopatra's Egypt.

The creation of the Great Library at Alexandria was the second known attempt to establish a universal library; Ashurbanipal's Great Library at Nineveh was the first (Tolzmann, Hessel, and Peiss, 2001). Today, the Egyptian government is trying to restore the former glory of the great library with the Bibliotheca Alexandrina (www.bibalex.org/English/index.aspx); currently, its mission is primarily focused on Islamic literature.

Classical Libraries: Roman Libraries

According to the Roman poet Horace, "Greece has conquered her rude conqueror," meaning that, although the Romans conquered Greece, they admired and absorbed Greek language, literature, art, and culture. There is a record of Roman bookshops called *taberna libraria* in the Forum, or public marketplace. The first Roman libraries were private collections plundered from the Greeks as spoils of war. As with the Greeks, private libraries were usually specialized collections. Excavations at the Villa of Papyri at Herculaneum (a seaside resort near Pompeii) revealed a private library of about 1,800 scrolls, primarily the works of the philosopher Philodemus.

Rome carried on the Greek tradition of public libraries. The first public library in Rome was planned by Julius Caesar and built by Asinius Pollio c. 39 BC on the Palentine Hill. Caesar's concept of adjoining "sister" Latin and Greek libraries (a library of Greek-language documents for scholars and one of documents in Latin for commoners), *Bybliotheka Latina Apollinis* and *Bybliotheca Graeca Apollinis*, was planned by the Roman scholar Varro who had written *De Bibliothecis* (*On Libraries*).

The first Roman Emperor, Augustus, also established a public library in the Temple of Apollo on the Palatine Hill, and another, the Bibliotheca Octaviana, in the Porticus Octavia. Emperor Vespasian founded the Bibliotheca Pacis (Library of Peace) in the Temple of Peace; the library was dedicated in 75 AD and considered by Pliny to be one of the three most beautiful buildings in Rome.

The greatest imperial library was built in the Forum of Trajan by the Emperor Trajan. The two libraries of the Bibliotheca Ulpia, founded in 114 AD, faced one another across a courtyard, the Latin collection on the west and the Greek on the east (Tolzmann, Hessel, and Peiss, 2001).

Roman libraries, the model for traditional libraries in the Western world, were spacious rooms lined with wall niches that held numbered wooden bookcases called *armaria*, leaving space in the center of the room for reading tables and chairs (Tolzmann, Hessel, and Peiss, 2001). Those in charge of the libraries were called *librarii a bibliotheca*, or librarians. By c. 150 AD, Romans were replacing papyrus scrolls with codices, early books of parchment or vellum sheets (made from animal skins) laced together accordion-style with wood or leather covers. The codex had several advantages over scrolls: They were more portable and easier to reference, to store, and to read (Tolzmann, Hessel, and Peiss, 2001).

Medieval Scriptoria

Medieval is Latin for "Middle Ages," so called because it is the period between the ancient and modern worlds. It is generally dated from the fall of Rome in 476 AD until the Renaissance.

In the Islamic East, literature and libraries flourished, but in the West, the Medieval or Middle Ages are also known as the Dark Ages because of widespread illiteracy. During this time, Holy Scriptures as well as classical literature and scholarly works were preserved and copied in monastic scriptoria.

Scriptoria is the plural form of scriptorium, a room in a monastery reserved for the copying, writing, or illuminating of manuscripts and records (Reitz, 2007). In the 15th century, monks produced the *Registrum Librorum Angliae*, a catalog of 85 authors' works in 160 church libraries (Tolzmann, Hessel, and Peiss, 2001).

Important Library Milestones

Some important library milestones include the following:

- The University of Oxford Library in England, which dates back to the 14th century, claims to be the oldest English-language library.

- The first university library in the United States was the Harvard University Library, founded in 1638.

- The first public library since ancient times (small subscription fee), the Library Company of Philadelphia, was established by Benjamin Franklin in 1731.

- The British Library was established in 1753 when Sir Hans Sloane bequeathed his large collection of books and manuscripts to the nation.

- *Bibliothèque Nationale* in France was established in 1789 after the French Revolution. It was formerly the Royal Library founded by Charles V in the 14th century, but it became the National Library of the French people.

- The Library of Congress was established in 1800 as a reference library for Congress. Thomas Jefferson sold his large and valuable book collection to the Library of Congress in 1814, more than doubling the collection. Today, it is our national library, the largest library in the world, with more than 130 million items; about 1.5 million items are added each year (Library of Congress, 2007; Oswald, 2004).

One important contributor to the growth of public libraries in the United States was Scottish-American industrialist Andrew Carnegie. Born in 1835, Carnegie grew up in the coastal town of Dunfermline, Scotland. Although he only had three years of formal education, he developed a love of reading books from his father, a weaver who helped found the local Tradesmen's Subscription Library. After Carnegie's family immigrated to Pennsylvania, Carnegie worked at a textile factory and then as a telegraph messenger. During this time, he educated himself by borrowing and reading books. As he became more successful, he invested in railroads and steel. He eventually founded the Carnegie Steel Company, which he sold in 1921 for $250 million.

Since libraries had such a positive impact on Carnegie's success, he used a portion of his accumulated wealth to fund the construction of public libraries. Although Carnegie libraries were built in countries around the world, most (almost 1,700 libraries) were built in the United States. Constructed between 1886 and 1919 at a cost of more than $40 million, Carnegie public libraries can be found in every state and can be identified by their beautiful architecture and the carving of the sun's rays over the words, "Let There Be Light" (National Park Service, n.d.).

Traditional Libraries, Archives, and Special Collections

School libraries and media centers contain materials that support the school's curriculum and support literacy. Most are organized by the Dewey Decimal System. Some examples include:

- Fairbanks Alaska North Star Borough School District, www.k12northstar.org/library-media-services/library-catalogs

- Hattiesburg High School Library, www.teacherweb.com/ms/ hattiesburghighschool/library/ap4.stm

Public libraries contain materials that support general research, recreational reading, community information needs, and local history. Most are organized by the Dewey Decimal System. Some examples include:

- Library of Hattiesburg, Petal, & Forrest County, www.hpfc.lib.ms.us

- Hancock County Library System, www.hancocklibraries.info

Academic and research libraries contain materials that support both general research and the specific programs or degrees offered at the institution. Most are organized with the Library of Congress classification system. Some examples include:

- Cornell University Library, www.library.cornell.edu

- Oak Ridge National Laboratory Research Library, www.ornl.gov/info/library/library-home.shtml

Special libraries and collections contain materials that are being collected for long-term preservation or that are very specific to the needs of the institution. Some, such as corporate libraries, are not open to the public. Most are organized by the Library of Congress classification system. Some examples include:

- de Grummond Children's Literature Collection, www.lib.usm.edu/~degrum

- Folger Shakespeare Library, www.folger.edu

- Presidential Libraries, www.archives.gov/presidential-libraries/contact/libraries.html

Archives typically consist of an organization's historical records. Some examples include:

- National Archives, www.archives.gov

- Massachusetts Archives, www.sec.state.ma.us/arc

- National Bureau of Economic Research Historical Archives, www.nber.org/nberhistory

Summary

The literal meaning of information repository is a collection of concepts or ideas. These concepts or ideas may be tacit, as in the pre-literate oral tradition, or explicit as in more traditional libraries, archives, and special collections. The earliest repository was the human brain, and archaeological evidence such as regular markings on bones (dated to between 30,000 to 40,000 years ago) may be an indication of pre-literate man's organization and preservation of information.

The earliest physical repositories, Sumerian and Egyptian libraries and archives, date back to about 3000 BC. The concept of a universal library that contains all the known scholarly documents and literature originated with Ashurbanipal's Great Library at Nineveh in the seventh century BC and was revived by the Great Library of Alexandria in Egypt during the Hellenistic Period (third century BC).

These ancient repositories influenced the development of modern repositories. While the Classical Greeks were the first known to establish public libraries, the physical model of modern libraries is based on the later Roman model with tables and chairs placed in the center of reading rooms lined with bookcases. The shelves first contained scrolls and then later contained codexes (scrolls that were folded accordion-style and bound by wood or leather to form a more efficient format—a book).

Additional Reading

Ameen, K. November, 2005. Developments in the Philosophy of Collection Management: A Historical Review. *Collection Building* 24(4):112–116.

Battles, M. 2003. *Library: An Unquiet History*. New York: W.W. Norton.

Bellinger, G., Castro, D., and Mills, A. [n.d.] Data, Information, Knowledge, and Wisdom. Retrieved May 18, 2010, from www.systems-thinking.org/dikw/dikw.htm.

Casson, L. 2001. *Libraries in the Ancient World*. New Haven, CT: Yale University Press.

Dunaway, D. K., and Baum, W. K. 1996. *Oral History: An Interdisciplinary Anthology*. American Association for State and Local History book series. Walnut Creek, CA: AltaMira Press.

Harris, M. H. 1995. *History of Libraries in the Western World*. Metuchen, NJ: Scarecrow Press.

Houston, G. August, 2008. Tiberius and the Libraries: Public Book Collections and Library Buildings in the Early Roman Empire. *Libraries & the Cultural Record* 43(3):247–269.

Jones, T. 1997. *Carnegie Libraries Across America: A Public Legacy*. Hoboken, NJ: Wiley.

Kramer, S. N. 1988. *History Begins at Sumer: Thirty-Nine Firsts in Recorded History*. Philadelphia: University of Pennsylvania Press.

MacLeod, R. M. 2000. *The Library of Alexandria: Centre of Learning in the Ancient World*. London: I.B. Tauris.

Maruizi, D. 2001. Carnegie and His Legacy: The Little Libraries That Could. *Public Libraries* 40(6):346–348.

Richardson, E. C. 1963. *The Beginnings of Libraries*. Hamden, CT: Archon Books.

Staikos, K. 2000. *The Great Libraries: From Antiquity to the Renaissance (3000 B.C. to A.D. 1600)*. New Castle, DE: Oak Knoll Press.

Van Slyck, A. A. 1998. Free to All: Carnegie Libraries & American Culture, 1890–1920. Chicago: University of Chicago Press.

References

Ackoff, R. 1989. From Data to Wisdom. *Journal of Applied Systems Analysis* 16:3–9.

Ager, S. 2008. Omniglot: Writing Systems and Languages of the World. Retrieved February 15, 2010, from www.omniglot.com/writing/ogham.htm

Baines, J. 1983. Literacy and Ancient Egyptian Society. *Man* (New Series) 18(3):572–599.

Bogoshi, J., Naidoo, K., and Webb, J. 1987. The Oldest Mathematical Artifact. *The Mathematical Gazette* 71(458):294.

Briscoe, Peter, et al. 1986. Ashurbanipal's Enduring Archetype: Thoughts on the Library's Role in the Future. *College & Research Libraries* 47:121–126.

Brooks, A. S., and Smith, C. C. 1987. Ishango Revisited: New Age Determinations and Cultural Interpretations. *The African Archaeological Review* 5: 65–78.

Cassidy, K. 2002. Scholars Build Internet Dictionary to Unravel Sumerian Language. *Near Eastern Archaeology* 65(4):284–285.

Cowan, H. K. J., and Marshack, A. 1975. More on Upper Paleolithic Engraving. *Current Anthropology* 16(2):297–298.

Day, C. D. 1957. Knots and Knot Lore: Quipus and Other Mnemonic Knots. *Western Folklore* 16(1):8–26.

Egyptian Literature. [n.d.]. Retrieved December 28, 2007, from *Funk & Wagnalls New World Encyclopedia* database.

Haley, A. 1976. *Roots: A Saga of an American Family*. New York: Doubleday.

Internet Movie Database. 2009. *The Egyptian*. Retrieved February 15, 2010, from www.imdb.com/title/tt0046949

Kramer, S. N. 1988. *History Begins at Sumer: Thirty-Nine Firsts in Recorded History*. Philadelphia: University of Pennsylvania Press.

Library of Congress. 2007. *American Memory*. Retrieved February 15, 2010, from memory.loc.gov/ammem/index.html

Lichtheim, M. 1980. *Ancient Egyptian Literature*. Berkeley, CA: University of California Press.

McKay, A. C. 2002. Genealogists and Records: Preservation, Advocacy, and Politics. *Archival Issues* 27:23–33.

Mitchell, L. 1999. Earliest Egyptian Glyphs. *Archaeology* 52(2):28.

Musée du Louvre. 2007. A Closer Look at the Code of Hammurabi. Retrieved February 15, 2010, from www.louvre.fr/llv/dossiers/detail_oal.jsp?CONTENT%3C%3Ecnt_id=10134198673229909&CURRENT_LLV_OAL%3C%3Ecnt_id=10134198673229909&bmUID=1143129692514&bmLocale=en

National Park Service [n.d.]. Carnegie Libraries: The Future Made Bright. Retrieved February 15, 2010, from www.nps.gov/history/Nr/twhp/wwwlps/lessons/50carnegie/50carnegie.htm

Noxon, G. 1964. Pictorial Origins of Cinema Narrative: The Illusion of Movement and the Birth of the Scene in the Paleolithic Cave Wall Paintings of Lascaux. *The Journal of the Society of Cinematologists* 4:20–26.

O'Donoghue, L. 1998. Pathways to Knowledge. Speech to the Australian Library and Information Association (ALIA) for Australian Library Week, April 29, 1998.

Oswald, G. 2004. *Library World Records.* Jefferson, NC: McFarland & Company.

Public Broadcasting Service (PBS). 2006. *African-American Lives.* Retrieved February 15, 2010, from www.pbs.org/wnet/aalives/2006/index.html

Public Broadcasting Service (PBS). 2007. *African-American Lives 2.* Retrieved February 15, 2010, from www.pbs.org/wnet/aalives

Reitz, J. 2007. Online Dictionary of Library and Information Science (ODLIS). Retrieved February 15, 2010 from lu.com/odlis/index.cfm

Tennessee Encyclopedia of History and Culture. 2002. Retrieved February 15, 2010, from tennesseeencyclopedia.net/imagegallery.php?EntryID=H004

Tolzmann, H., Hessel, A., and Peiss, R. 2001. *The Memory of Mankind: The Story of Libraries Since the Dawn of History.* New Castle, DE: Oak Knoll Press.

Waltari, M., and Walford, N. 1949. *The Egyptian.* New York: G.P. Putnam's Sons.

Wood, M. 1998. *In Search of the Trojan War.* Berkeley, CA: University of California Press.

Chapter 7

Information Repositories: New Technologies and Trends

Teresa S. Welsh

Editor's Note: This chapter introduces the various collections formats to date with a brief discussion of open source in institutional repositories by Peter Zuber.

> Libraries today are still repositories, but now they provide *access* to information in many formats, either physically in the book and journal collections, or electronically.
> —Lois "Lowitja" O'Donoghue (1998)

While pre-electronic, traditional repositories consisted of collections of physical items generally organized and accessed by subject, author/creator, and title, the present era, known as the Information Age, or more recently, the Digital Age, is marked by an increase in the number and complexity of formats as well as descriptive categories of data (metadata).

Attributes of an information-literate individual include a familiarity with the organization and description of items in a collection or repository so relevant items can be accessed and retrieved. In addition to understanding how items in repositories are collected, organized, and described, it is vital that information specialists have a broader scope of knowledge about repository types and their definitions. It is useful, for example, to be aware of new fields such as knowledge management, which is focused on the difference between implicit and explicit information, and of how to capture or collect and integrate the two. Information specialists who have an awareness of new concepts, challenges, and future trends will be able to make more informed decisions about developing and maintaining their own collections.

One way to classify the general category of information repositories is by collection type:

- Virtual repositories (all-digital collections)

- Subject repositories (collections focused on a single topic or topics)

- Institutional repositories (collection or collections within an organization)

Virtual Repositories

What is the difference between a digital library and a virtual library?

According to the Online Dictionary of LIS (Reitz, 2007, n.p.):

- Digital library – A library in which a significant proportion of the resources are available in machine-readable format (as opposed to print or microform) accessible by means of computers. The digital content may be locally held or accessed remotely via computer networks. In libraries, the process of digitization began with the catalog, moved to periodical indexes and abstracting services, then to periodicals and large reference works, and finally to book publishing. The term is abbreviated as d-lib. (Learn more in Chapter 8, "Digital Libraries.")

- Virtual library – This is a "library without walls" in which the collections do not exist on paper, microform, or other tangible form at a physical location but are electronically accessible in digital format via computer networks. Such libraries exist only on a very limited scale, but in most traditional print-based libraries in the United States, catalogs and periodical indexes are available online, and some periodicals and reference works may be available in electronic full text. Some libraries and library systems call themselves "virtual" because they offer online services.

While some repositories consist entirely of virtual, digital information, most libraries and archives digitize selected parts of their collection, usually primary-source resources that are in the public domain.

Examples of virtual digital collections include:

- Lincoln/Net, lincoln.lib.niu.edu (a virtual collection of primary-source materials related to Abraham Lincoln)

- The WWW Virtual Library, vlib.org

- The Virtual Diego Rivera Web Museum, www.diegorivera. com/index.php

Examples of selected digitized resources from traditional collections include:

- The University of Southern Mississippi McCain Library Civil Rights in Mississippi Digital Archive, www.lib.usm.edu/%7 Espcol/crda

- The New York Public Library Digital Collections, www.nypl. org/ebooks

- Cornell University Library Windows on the Past Digital Collections, moa.cit.cornell.edu

How does one select which resources in a collection should be digitized? According to Hazen, Horrell, and Merrill-Oldham in *Selecting Research Collections for Digitization* (1998), research libraries are "eagerly embracing the digital world" by increasingly acquiring electronic materials and/or digitizing materials from their own collections. Digitization of resources can be done at a minimal level (i.e., one person digitizing a collection of historical images) or on an expansive level. A good example is the massive book-digitization project undertaken by Google with the partnership of university libraries and publishers, which involves the digitization of millions of volumes (books.google.com).

The usefulness of digital resources depends on the physical process of how well the original materials are digitized, that is, "on how well relevant information is captured from the original, and then on how the digital data are organized, indexed, delivered to users, and maintained over time" (Hazen, Horrell, and Merrill-Oldham, 1998).

One important thing to consider when digitizing materials for the web is copyright. It is vital to choose materials that are in the public domain, to obtain permission from the copyright holder, or to create and digitize one's own original material.

Another concern about digitizing multimedia for educational purposes is that it must conform to the Americans with Disabilities Act (ADA; www.ada.gov). To conform to ADA standards, digitized sound files must be accompanied by a text file for the hearing impaired, and digitized images and video must be captioned for the sight-impaired.

Subject Repositories

A subject repository is a collection that is focused on a single theme or area of study. Subject repositories may be virtual or a combination of physical and digital formats. Subject repositories are usually a part of a larger organization such as a government or academic institution. Typically, subject repositories may have some materials in the public domain available online while others may have copyrighted materials accessible only on-site or electronically via password-protection.

One example of an open access subject repository is E-LIS (eprints.rclis. org). According to E-LIS policy,

> any document related to LIS that is electronically available, in any format, can be submitted to the archive. The basic criteria for acceptance is that the document must be relevant to research in LIS fields and should be complete and ready to be entered into a process of scholarly communication. Three levels of control are in place—registered user/author; editor; site manager—to ensure inappropriate papers are not included. (eprints.rclis.org/information.html)

An example of a multiformat subject repository is the University of Southern Mississippi Katrina Research Center (KRC; www.usm.edu/katrina), which contains a physical collection of books, archival materials, multimedia, selected art objects, and artifacts, as well as an internal database of proprietary or copyrighted items that are digitized. The KRC is a contributor to and collaborative partner with the Mississippi Digital Library (www.msdiglib.net) and the Hurricane Digital Memory Bank (www.hurricanearchive.org), an open access archive of digital images, oral histories, and research data related to hurricanes.

Institutional Repositories by Peter Zuber (2006)

A shift in traditional academic publishing models has created a growing acceptance of open access systems. These include electronic peer-reviewed journals, author self-submissions, e-prints, gray literature posting, and preprint/post-print servers. Consequently, the emergence of formal Open Access Initiatives (OAI, OA) such as the Budapest Open Access Initiative (BOAI), has prompted notice from library professionals on the prospects of creating, developing, and managing a potentially significant new source of information (Yiotis, 2005). The BOAI endorsed two strategies in support of OA scholarly publication (Open Society Institute, 2002). The first was the creation of institutional repositories (IR).

An IR is typically defined as an electronic archive managed and sponsored by an academic institution's library. In this sense, an IR is intended as another resource in the academic institution's role as a supporter of leading research and creator of intellectual property. According to the Scholarly Publishing and Academic Resources Coalition (SPARC), an IR is defined as having four essential characteristics, namely:

- Is institutionally sponsored

- Contains scholarly content

- Is cumulative and perpetual

- Is interoperable with open access (SPARC, 2002)

Since their inception, institutional repositories were designed for several advantages, including allowing first publication of research, creating a forum from which comments and advice are solicited from fellow scholars, and leveraging the advantage of open access in terms of citation rate and research impact (Antelman, 2004). In addition, an IR attempts to reform current publisher copyright practices. By publishing preprints to an IR, an author effectively enables an option to negotiate to hold, rather than transfer, copyright (Harnad, 1994).

Owing to the purposes and advantages previously listed in this chapter (its relatively new introduction, its controversial nature with regard to scholarly publishing, and the growing acceptance of free, electronic access to innovative research), IRs have become a popular subject of discussion and research. Recent studies have shown increasing interest in the core subjects related to institutional repositories, namely, digital libraries and digital information. Bollen et al. conducted a trend analysis survey covering 10 years of *D-Lib Magazine* and found the highest occurrence rates among the descriptors "digital," "library," and "information" (2005).

If an academic library is considering providing support and resources for an IR, it faces several important challenges including:

- Persuading faculty to contribute important research representing large investments of time (van Westrienen and Lynch, 2005)

- Developing an article submission interface that is both intuitive and responsive

- Promotion and training

- Managing and sustaining the archive

- Understanding publication workflows and motivations for each academic discipline

The increase in traditional scholarly publication costs forces difficult decisions in the face of shrinking library budgets. This places the acquisition of information at risk. An IR is designed to provide a partial solution by attempting to re-create the older scholarly model of an "at cost" publication. Knowing the best solution to each challenge listed here is difficult, if not impossible, without additional information from case studies, practical implementations, or individuals experienced in this area (Zuber, 2006).

New Trends in Repositories

Knowledge Management

Knowledge management (KM) is interdisciplinary, primarily between information science and business management. It emphasizes the recording and sharing of human knowledge and experience within an organization.

KM, as a concept, is about the way that organizations create, capture, and re-use knowledge to achieve organizational objectives. Knowledge is created in the heads of people. It can be captured by putting it on paper, entering into a computer system, or simply being remembered. Knowledge is *shared*. When knowledge is shared and used, it leads to more knowledge creation (KIT Institute, n.d., n.p.).

In the mid-1990s, there came a realization that much institutional knowledge resides in humans and is not written but tacit. With that realization, a new field developed known as "knowledge management" or KM. According to the Knowledge Management Glossary (2007, n.p.), KM is the "systematic process of finding, selecting, organizing, distilling and presenting information in a way that improves an employee's comprehension in a specific area of interest."

KM includes both explicit information and implicit information so that information has context as shown in the following:

- Explicit information

  - Structured repositories, such as databases and expert systems with search aids such as indexes, keywords, and controlled vocabulary

  - Unstructured repositories, such as project reports searchable by free text

- Implicit or tacit information

  - Human repositories, or knowledge and experience that resides in the heads of people; the tools to access this knowledge include telephone directories, annotated company directories, and other listings (KIT Institute, n.d.)

Tacit information has been defined as "the often-undocumented wisdom possessed by expert practitioners" (Crowley, 1999, p. 282). According to Crowley (1999, 2001), recent studies in the research literatures have expanded the definition of tacit knowledge to include such factors as:

- Personal in origin and related to personal context

- Valuable to the possessor

- Able to be transmitted through interpersonal contact but difficult to articulate fully

Crowley maintains that tacit, implicit information is capable of becoming explicit knowledge and is intertwined with explicit knowledge along unstable knowledge borders. In other words, most explicit information, such as a textbook, has certain implicit assumptions embedded in the mind of the author that may not be adequately or fully expressed.

Storytelling, an ancient tool related to oral tradition and long used by librarians and teachers as an effective teaching strategy, has re-emerged as an effective knowledge management strategy (Welsh and Wright, 2007). According to Denning (2005), roles of storytelling within an organization include capturing, preserving, and sharing tacit knowledge such as organizational history; building organizational culture and instilling values; training new and existing members; and facilitating organizational change.

Learning to use storytelling in a purposeful way is an effective leadership strategy and can facilitate collaboration and stimulate creativity (Welsh, 2008). Stories are related to visualization. Mental images triggered by stories tend to stick, thus facilitating knowledge transfer that is more accurate and meaningful.

One example of KM is the Library of Congress (LC), founded in 1800 as a reference library for the U.S. Congress. The LC has changed its mission to collect not only printed works published in the U.S., but to capture and preserve cultural artifacts such as images, stories, music, and oral histories, particularly of dialects and languages that are disappearing (Library of Congress, 2010).

As another example, the National Laboratories realized in the 1990s that as the World War II era scientists died or retired, valuable corporate and historical information about the Manhattan Project and the early years of atomic energy development was lost. Although the National Labs had the scientists' project notebooks, much of the written materials were incomplete, and images from that time lacked descriptive data. The National Labs began a series of oral history projects, such as the *Human Radiation Experiments: Oral Histories*, to capture and preserve this information (U.S. Department of Energy, n.d.).

Although "knowledge has more to do with brains than with bits" (KIT Institute, n.d., n.p.), there are particular technologies that promote organizational KM and knowledge-sharing such as:

- Document management and electronic publishing systems

- Relational and object-oriented databases

- Information retrieval engines

- Push technologies, such as RSS or agents

- Data warehousing and data-mining tools (KIT Institute, n.d., n.p.)

Abell and Oxbrow (2001) list traditional information management skills of librarians that can be applied to knowledge management such as identifying, acquiring, and structuring internal sources; and sourcing, acquiring and evaluating external sources. Librarians or information specialists with an understanding of knowledge management are better able to integrate internal and external sources in order to deliver relevant information to the user or patron (Ganguly, 2007, p. 14).

Corall (1998) detailed specific knowledge management strategies of coordinating and integrating tacit and explicit knowledge by:

- Designing knowledge repositories (explicit knowledge) of physical objects

- Designing knowledge maps (tacit and explicit knowledge) – Pointers to people, document collections, and datasets that can be consulted

- Designing knowledge networks and discussion groups (tacit knowledge) – Providing opportunities for face-to-face contacts and electronic interactions, for example, establishing chat facilities/talk rooms, and so on (Ganguly, 2007, p. 15)

Multimedia Resources

According to Edgar Dale's "Cone of Learning" (1946, 1954, 1969), the more senses that one can engage in the learning process, the greater the retention rate. Repositories are responding to this by digitizing primary-source multimedia materials. Examples of locally produced multimedia projects include:

- Book of Gregorian Chant, library.umkc.edu/spec-col/chant book/main.htm – A multimedia digitization project by the University of Missouri Kansas City Miller Nichols Library and Dr. Janet K. Kraybill

- Brush Creek Follies, library.umkc.edu/spec-col/follies/main.htm – One of the digitization projects from the Miller Nichols Library Marr Sound Archive that uses audio and video clips

Commercial databases and database consortiums are increasing the availability of multimedia resources for educators and students:

- Net Library, company.netlibrary.com/aboutus.aspx – A subscription service of an ebook collection that is available online through libraries that subscribe to the service

- History Reference Center – A full-text database, available through EBSCO*host*, that contains more than 1,000 reference books, encyclopedias, and nonfiction books; 60 history magazines; 58,000 historical documents; 43,000 biographies of historical figures; more than 12,000 historical photos and maps; and more than 80 hours of historical video (University of Southern Mississippi Cook Library, 2007)

- Literary Reference Center – A full-text database, available through EBSCO*host*, that contains information on thousands of authors and their works including plot summaries, synopses, and work overviews; articles of literary criticism; book reviews; 25,000 classic and contemporary poems; 11,000 classic and contemporary short stories; full text of more than 7,500 classic novels; 3,000 author interviews; more than 1,000 images of key literary figures; and a literary timeline with interactive links and images (University of Southern Mississippi Cook Library, 2007)

User-Generated Content, Web 2.0, Library 2.0

Web 2.0, a phrase coined by O'Reilly Media in 2004, refers to a perceived second generation of web-based communities and hosted services, such as social networking sites, blogs, and wikis, that facilitate collaboration and sharing among users (O'Reilly, 2007).

Library 2.0, a term adapted from Web 2.0, describes a reorganization of library priorities toward more service-oriented values, a move away from maintenance of primarily print-centered collections and toward more patron-centered policies and new technologies that serve patron needs in multiple formats: print, periodical, digital, and online (Eden, 2007, p. 40):

- Interactive webpages not only present information in a digital format, such as an Online Public Access Catalog (OPAC) but include interactive patron services.

  - University of Tennessee Library AskUsNow!, www.lib. utk.edu/refs/askusnow – A reference service by phone, email, or instant messaging (IM)

  - USM Cook Library Services for Distance Education, www.lib.usm.edu/services/distance_education.html – Includes electronic document access, such as e-reserves and e-delivery of interlibrary loan items

- Weblogs or blogs are webpages that provide publication of web links or comments on a specific topic, often in the form of short entries arranged in reverse chronological order. Some blogs accept postings from its readers (Reitz, 2007).

  - Library of Congress Blog, blogs.loc.gov/loc

  - LISNews, www.lisnews.org

- Wikis, based on a Hawaiian term meaning "quick" or "informal," are a web application that allows users to add content to a collaborative web resource (coauthoring) and permits others to edit that content (open editing) (Reitz, 2007).

- Library Success: A Best Practices Wiki, www.libsuccess.org

- Second Life Education Wiki, www.simteach.com/wiki/index. php?title=Second_Life_Education_Wiki

- User-generated content or UGC allows users to create web content.

  - Social networking sites allow educational or any special interest group to form its own social space. Examples include Ning (www.ning.com); LibraryThing (www.librarything.com), which is a social network for book lovers; and Twitter (twitter.com), which is a free social messaging network that allows users to communicate by sending and receiving real-time updates or tweets.

  - Photo-sharing sites include Flickr (www.flickr.com) and Picture-Trail (www.picturetrail.com).

  - Video-sharing sites include YouTube (www.youtube.com) and Educational Podcast Network (EPN; www.epnweb.org).

Push Technology and Personalized Services

Push technologies are related to econtent that is personalized and sent from the internet server to the client:

- My Library is a personalized library portal.

  - MyLibrary@NCState offers My Alerts, which sends an auto-alert when a new issue of a journal of interest is available.

  - My Library at Virginia Commonwealth University, www.library. vcu.edu/mylibrary – Offers alerts when books or articles on topics of interest are available.

- RSS, which may stand for either "rich site summary" or "really simple syndication," delivers news items to a computer. It is a free subscription service and an example of push technology that delivers specialized information to users.

  - What is RSS?, www.whatisrss.com – Lists links to free RSS readers that may be downloaded

  - The Chronicle of Higher Education, chronicle.com/blog/Wired-Campus/5/rss – Offers RSS feeds on various topics

  - LibWorm: Education, www.libworm.com/rss/librarianfeeds/ subjects/Education.xml – An RSS feed related to librarianship and education

- Intelligent agent is a software agent that assists users and will act on their behalf in performing computer-related tasks.

  - Intelligent Software Agents Lab at Carnegie Mellon University, www.cs.cmu.edu/~softagents – Includes information and publications related to intelligent agents

  - Intelligent Agent 101 by the University of Maryland, Baltimore County, agents.umbc.edu – Contains basic information about intelligent agents

- Smart Systems are databases that provide guidance to help the user locate specific items by offering sets of choices.

  - Evidence Matters database, www.evidencematters.com – A collection of peer-reviewed medical research, in which the user is guided by a series of menu choices to find relevant outcomes of clinical studies related to specific diseases or treatments

- Relevance ranking is a feature of some search software that weights the documents or records retrieved in a search according to the degree to which they meet the requirements of the query (Reitz, 2007). A common feature related to relevance ranking is the option to "find more items like this one."

  - Google's search engine pioneered relevance ranking, www.google.com/technology/pigeonrank.html

Challenges and Future Trends

Digital Quality and Preservation

Sridhar maintains that the boom in content in digital format is "diminishing the demarcation between published and unpublished as well as published and gray literature. More and more digital content is pouring in public domain without [being subjected] to editorial quality control or refereeing process" (2007, p. 47).

One problem with the ever-expanding amount of digital information available online is the preservation of those online materials, disappearing links, and changing website content. One solution to this problem is the Internet Archive (IA; www.archive.org/index.php). According to Edwards (2004, p. 3), IA was founded by Brewster Kahle in 1996 as a nonprofit organization whose purpose was to archive and preserve website content. Robotic web crawlers search the internet and archive webpages' content by date. Users can enter a webpage address (URL), and, if the page is archived, a graph will appear with a listing of the dates that the webpage was archived. Users may then click on the desired date to view website content as it existed at that time.

Future Trends

Future trends in information repositories include open access, collaboration, information sharing, and information in content. According to Dr. Carol Tenopir, the future of publication (and repositories of those publications) is interactive linking, such as citation linking and link resolvers. Scholars need to share data sets, such as in institutional or subject repositories. These new models of information repositories require new forms of peer review, such as quality stamps or open peer review (Tenopir, 2006).

Tenopir cites the increasing number of scholarly articles and journal titles (more than 20,000 listed by *Ulrich's Periodicals Directory*, about half of which are both print and e-format, and more than 4,000 in e-format only). With increasing pressure for scholars to read more, there is a need for delivery of "good" information via professional blogs that summarize information, listservs, alerting services, structured text with executive summaries, and informative abstracts (Tenopir, 2006).

Web 3.0: The Semantic Web

According to the *Online Dictionary of Library & Information Science* (*ODLIS*; Reitz, 2007), semantics is the branch of linguistics "concerned with the *meaning* of the words, signs, and symbols that constitute the elements of change and evolution in a spoken or written language," and "the branch of semiotics that deals with relationships of meaning between signs, and between signs and their referents, within a system of communication" (see Table 7.1).

The Worldwide Web Consortium (W3C, 2008) defined semantic web as one that "provides a common framework that allows data to be shared and reused across application, enterprise, and community boundaries. ... It is based on the Resource Description Framework (RDF)."

The developer of the World Wide Web, Tim Berners-Lee, described the semantic web (Web 3.0) in an article in *Scientific American* (Berners-Lee et al., 2001) as a more intelligent and useful web in which software agents roaming across the web can carry out tasks, infer when information is needed, and provide that information. According to the authors:

> For the semantic Web to function, computers must have access to structured collections of information and sets of inference rules that they can use to conduct automated reasoning. Artificial-intelligence researchers have studied such systems since long before the Web was developed. Knowledge representation, as this technology is often called, is currently in a state comparable to that of hypertext before the advent of the Web: it is clearly a good idea, and some very nice demonstrations exist, but it has not yet changed the world. It contains the seeds of important applications, but to realize its full potential it must be linked into a single global system. (p. 37)

Table 7.1 Semantic Relationships

Relation	*Description*	*Example*
Active	Action, process, or operation directly performed by one on the other	Scanner/barcode
Associative	Linked conceptually but not hierarchically	Library statistics/bibliometrics
Causal	One responsible for occurrence of the other	Acquisitions/collection growth
Generic	Genus to species	Library/academic library
Hierarchic	One a logical subclass of the other	Bookbinding/binding
Locative	One located at, in, or on a place specified by the other	Mainz Psalter
Partitive	Part to whole	Chapter/book
Passive	One influenced by or subjected to the action of the other with no reciprocal influence	Library collection/selection criteria
Antonymous	Opposite in meaning	Selection/deselection
Synonymous	Having the same or nearly the same meaning	Booklet/pamphlet

ODLIS, "Semantic Relation," lu.com/odlis/odlis_s.cfm#semanticrelation

A related idea is information in context. MacPherson, in "Digitizing the Non-Digital: Creating a Global Context for Events, Artifacts, Ideas, and Information" (2006) makes the case for a new paradigm for an open source system, Context Driven Topologies (CDT), which organizes information in themes including where data originate geographically, where they belong, and how they relate to similar information over time. These themes would be similar to a museum exhibit in which information related to a particular theme would be linked or interconnected.

Cox et al. (2007) advocates similar solutions for archives but from a user perspective. He cited Samuels (2006) who maintained that new technologies, such as TEAL (Technology—Enhanced Active Learning), wikis, simulations, and ePortfolios can be used to help users assemble their own collection of related materials. "Archivists need to use wisely the machines available to them and take the riches of their repositories into the world" (Cox et al., 2007, n.p.).

Summary

Repositories are collections of materials, and those materials may be very specialized, such as a collection of digital materials on a particular topic, or more comprehensive, such as an institutional repository of various collections in a variety of formats (manuscripts, images, artifacts, audio-recordings, and video). Repositories may be open access (in the public domain) or proprietary (restricted access). Many large repositories have mixed levels of access with items in the public domain accessible online to the public, other items with limited user access, and still other items in a "dark archive" (sensitive items that are stored but not accessible by users).

The trend in repositories is toward multimedia resources and greater access to primary resources. Librarians and information specialists must be mindful of issues related to those trends such as copyright issues and ADA compliance.

Additional Reading

Bailey, C. W. (2006). *Institutional Repositories*. SPEC kit, 292. Washington, DC: Association of Research Libraries, Office of Management Services.

Jantz, R., and Wilson, M. (2008). Institutional Repositories: Faculty Deposits, Marketing, and the Reform of Scholarly Communication. *The Journal of Academic Librarianship* 34(3):186–195.

Landis, W. E., and Chandler, R. L. (2006). *Archives and the Digital Library*. Binghamton, NY: Haworth Information Press.

Peters, T. (2002). Digital Repositories: Individual, Discipline-based, Institutional, Consortial, or National? *The Journal of Academic Librarianship* 28(6):414–417.

Xia, J. (2008). A Comparison of Subject and Institutional Repositories in Self-archiving Practices. *The Journal of Academic Librarianship* 34(6):489–495.

References

Abell, A., and Oxbrow, N. 2001. *Competing with Knowledge: The Information Professional in the Knowledge Management Age*. London: Library Association Publishing.

Antelman, K. 2004. Open-access Articles Have a Greater Research Impact? *College & Research Libraries* 65:372–382.

Berners-Lee, T., Hendler, J., and Lassila, O. (2001). The Semantic Web. *Scientific American* 284(5):34–43.

Bollen, J., et al. 2005. Trend Analysis of the Digital Library Community. *D-Lib Magazine* 11 (1). Retrieved February 15, 2010, from www.dlib.org/dlib/january05/bollen/01bollen.html

Cleveland, H. 1982. Information as a Resource. *The Futurist* 16(6):34–39.

Corall, S. 1998. Are We in the Knowledge Management Business? *Ariadne* 18. Retrieved February 15, 2010, from www.ariadne.ac.uk/issue18/knowledge-mgt

Cox, R. J., et al. 2007. Machines in the Archives: Technology and the Coming Transformation of Archival Reference. *First Monday* 12:11.

Crowley, B. 1999. Building Useful Theory: Tacit Knowledge, Practitioner Reports, and the Culture of LIS inquiry. *Journal of Education for Library and Information Science* 40:282.

Crowley, B. 2001. Tacit Knowledge, Tacit Ignorance, and the Future of Academic Librarianship. *College and Research Libraries* 62:565–584.

Dale, E. 1946, 1954, 1969. *Audio-Visual Methods in Teaching.* New York: Dryden.

Denning, S. 2005. *The Leader's Guide to Storytelling: Mastering the Art and Discipline of Business Narrative.* San Francisco: Jossey-Bass, Inc.

Eden, B. 2007. Library 2.0. *Library Technology Reports* 43(6):40–46.

Edwards, E. 2004. Ephemeral to Enduring: The Internet Archive and Its Role in Preserving Digital Media. *Information Technology and Libraries* 23:3–8.

E-LIS. 2007. E-prints: The Open Archive for Library and Information Science. Retrieved February 15, 2010, from eprints.rclis.org

Ganguly, S. 2007. Changing Paradigm for Information Professionals in Knowledge Management Age. *DESIDOC Bulletin of Information Technology* 27:5–16.

Harnad, S. 1994. Scholarly Journals at the Crossroads: A Subversive Proposal for Electronic Publishing. *ARL Issues in Scholarly Communication.* Retrieved February 15, 2010, from www.arl.org/scomm/subversive/intro.html

Hazen, D., Horrell, J., and Merrill-Oldham, J. 1998. Selecting Research Collections for Digitization. Washington, D.C.: Council on Library & Information Resources. Retrieved February 15, 2010, from www.clir.org/pubs/reports/hazen/pub74.html

KIT Institute. [n.d.]. What Is Knowledge Management? Retrieved February 15, 2010, from www.kit.nl/smartsite.shtml?ch=fab&id=4612&Part=InDepth

Knowledge Management Glossary. 2007. Retrieved February 15, 2010, from www.knowledgepoint.com.au/starting_out/glossary.html

Library of Congress. 2010. History. Retrieved May 18, 2010, from www.loc.gov/about/history.html

MacPherson, D. L. 2006. Digitizing the Non-Digital: Creating a Global Context for Events, Artifacts, Ideas, and Information. *Information Technology and Libraries* 25:95–102.

O'Donoghue, L. 1998. Pathways to Knowledge. Speech to the Australian Library and Information Association (ALIA) for Australian Library Week, April 29, 1998.

Open Society Institute. 2002. Budapest Open Access Initiative. Retrieved February 15, 2010, from soros.org/openaccess/read.shtml

O'Reilly, T. 2007. What Is Web 2.0: Design Patterns and Business Models for the Next Generation of Software. Retrieved February 15, 2010, from www.oreillynet.com/pub/a/oreilly/tim/news/2005/09/30/what-is-web-20.html

Reitz, J. 2007. Online Dictionary of Library and Information Science (ODLIS). Retrieved February 15, 2010, from lu.com/odlis/index.cfm

Samuels, H. W. 2006. Educational Technology: A Documentary Tool? *Academic Archivist* 23:4–9.

SPARC. 2002. The Case for Institutional Repositories: A SPARC Position Paper. Retrieved February 15, 2010, from www.arl.org/sparc/bm~doc/ir_final_release_102. pdf

Sridhar, M. S. 2007. Information Management in Digital Environment: A Librarian's Perspectives. *DESIDOC Bulletin of Information Technology* 27:45–50.

Tenopir, C. 2006. The Future of the Journal. Presentation at the Mississippi Library Association Annual Conference, Tunica, October 24–27, 2006.

U.S. Department of Energy. [n.d.]. Human Radiation Experiments: Roadmap to the Project. Retrieved February 15, 2010, from hss.energy.gov/healthsafety/ohre/roadmap/histories/index.html

U.S. Department of Justice. 2007. Americans with Disabilities Act. Retrieved February 15, 2010, from www.ada.gov

University of Southern Mississippi Cook Library. 2007. Browse Databases by Title. Retrieved February 15, 2010, from www.lib.usm.edu/find_items/article_databases/browse_databases_by_title

van Westrienen, G., and Lynch, C. A. 2005. Academic Institutional Repositories; Deployment Status in 13 Nations as of Mid 2005. *D-Lib Magazine* 11(9). Retrieved February 15, 2010 from www.dlib.org/dlib/september05/westrienen/09westrienen.html

W3C. 2008. Semantic Web activity. Retrieved February 15, 2010, from www.w3.org/2001/sw

Welsh, T. S. 2008. Using Organizational Storytelling as a Creative Leadership Strategy. Presented at the 8th International Creativity Conference, University of Greenwich, U.K., July 4, 2008.

Welsh, T. S., and Wright, M. S. 2007. Organisational Storytelling as a Creative Strategy. In K. Rajah (Ed.), *Business Creativity: Practitioner's Handbook*. Greenwich, UK: Greenwich University Press.

Yiotis, K. 2005. The Open Access Initiative: A New Paradigm for Scholarly Communications. *Information Technology and Libraries* 24(4):157–162.

Zuber, P. 2006. Publishing Patterns on Institutional Repositories by LIS Journals. Master's Project, The University of Southern Mississippi.

Chapter 8

Digital Libraries

EunKyung Chung

In 1945, Vannevar Bush envisioned that information would be available at our fingertips; a relationship-based automated system of electronic records would respond to our queries. Approximately 40 years later, with technology approaching some of the capabilities Bush described, the possibilities of digital libraries—an electronic collection of records—were being discussed and practices considered for operating them. In the 1990s, a wide variety of digital library practices and related research topics were exploding (Borgman, 1999; Tedd and Large, 2005). Due to the increasing availability of born-digital contents (created originally in a digital format) and increased digitization projects, digital libraries have expanded rapidly in terms of both concepts and practices.

In general, the topics and issues related to digital libraries are wide ranging. As Lesk (2005) points out, building a digital library is similar to the process of organizing machines, people, and even a culture, rather than simply piling up computer files. An appropriate way to approach the current issues and problems in digital libraries is to understand their multiple facets. When discussing key features of digital libraries, the primary topics include technological elements, information service aspects, and social issues. The technological elements are composed of digital library software systems, digitization and preservation issues, interoperability (the capability of information interchange with dissimilar digital libraries) within a set of digital libraries, and information storing and access. While the technological aspects of digital libraries are relatively new, information service topics, such as user needs, evaluation, information organization, and collection building and management, have existed and are discussed in line with the perspective of traditional libraries. On the other hand, the social aspects of digital libraries can be considered in terms of funding issues of digital library projects, sustainability, and intellectual property issues. Accordingly, the discussion in this chapter focuses on the topics and issues of three key features in digital libraries: technological elements, information service aspects, and social components.

History, Definitions, and Elements

A good starting point is to explore some history of digital libraries. One of the earliest attempts in digital libraries was the Mercury Electronic Library project at Carnegie Mellon University from 1989 to 1992 (Tedd and Large, 2005). The Mercury project focused on implementing a library application in a distributed fashion to reduce the high cost of mainframe computers (Covey, 2003). Since then, digital library projects, professional interests, and research endeavors of all sizes have grown rapidly. One of the most important of these was the first phase (1994–1998) of the Digital Library Initiative (DLI-1) by three federal agencies: the National Science Foundation (NSF), the National Aeronautics and Space Administration (NASA), and the Defense Advanced Research Projects Agency (DARPA). During the first phase of DLI-1, the Digital Library Initiative funded six digital library projects primarily focusing on research, rather than on digital libraries implementation and practices (Tedd and Large, 2005). The second phase (1999–2004) of the Digital Library Initiative (DLI-2) included more agencies in order to broaden its perspectives in regards to practical implementations of digital libraries. As a result, the DLI-2 funded 36 digital library projects with a focus on practical digital library implementations (www.nsf.gov/pubs/1998/nsf9863/nsf9863.htm). One recent digital library project is a multinational consortium called the World Digital Library (www.wdl.org/en) that is taking off to provide significant information resources from different cultures to the world via the internet under an initiative of the Library of Congress.

In a sense, it is very difficult to define the concept of digital libraries from a single, uniform perspective. According to Borgman (1999), there are two distinctive areas for digital libraries: research and practice. While research fields in digital libraries are likely to focus on the contents for users' communities, practice fields tend to consider digital libraries as institutions or services, rather than only focus on the digital contents. On the other hand, in order to demonstrate the diversity in digital library definitions, Schwartz (2000) identifies 64 different definitions of digital libraries. Since digital libraries have been viewed and implemented from and within various contexts, almost every definition has its own characteristics. These various definitions generally range from simplified to more detailed ones. For instance, a simplified definition can be stated as "a collection of electronic/digital materials," while a broader definition can consider diverse aspects in digital libraries, from software systems to intellectual property issues. The following definition from the Digital Library Federation can be considered relatively complex because it contains several aspects, including collection, management, information access, and users in digital libraries:

Digital libraries are organizations that provide the resources, including the specialized staff, to select, structure, offer intellectual access to, interpret, distribute, preserve the integrity of, and ensure the persistence over time of collections of digital works so that they are readily and economically available for use by a defined community or set of communities. (Digital Library Federation, 1998)

In addition, Schwartz (2000) points out that more casual definitions can be found in announcements and calls for papers for digital library-related journals. These definitions simply view a digital library as one with an electronic collection containing diverse media types and disciplinary fields. On the other hand, a digital library definition from a practical developer's perspective can be considered as well. Many digital library project managers agree with the characteristics emphasizing management, persistence, and longevity of digital collections. In the same line with Borgman's (1999) insights, practical viewpoints in digital libraries focus on organizational and administrative features rather than the contents.

Based on these various definitions of digital libraries, at least five elements can be pulled out for discussion: collection, users, organizational structure, networked access, and digital contents (Schwartz, 2000). First, collections of digital libraries are considered to have rich contents with multiple media types and information organization (Borgman, 1999; Schwartz, 2000). Second, users for most digital libraries are supposed to be identified as a community of users or set of communities. Depending on targeted user groups or communities, relevant services and policies, such as specified collection development, user interfaces, and system features, can be provided accordingly. Third, just as traditional libraries require a unified and logical structure, digital libraries need coherent organizational supports. Fourth, digital library services are provided via networked and distributed systems (i.e., the internet) in order to maximize accessibility for users. As the last element, the contents in digital libraries are generally expected to be digital. Due to born-digital contents (text, image, graphics, audio, video, and so on) and a number of digitization projects, the digital contents are easily accessible.

Technology

Open Source Software for Digital Libraries

In order to build and manage digital contents for digital libraries, several kinds of commercial content management and open source software should be considered. Commercial content management software involves systems designed in order to collect, manage, and make digital information available in various formats and presentations. In general, a content management system consists of a master format and a corresponding metadata record in order to provide versatile formats, presentation, and access of information objects. While there are no unanimously accepted systems for digital libraries yet, CONTENTdm by OCLC has been applied within a number of academic libraries and museums. Since CONTENTdm is a commercial package, the software price and maintenance fees depend on the collection size. On the other hand, open source software systems for digital libraries are increasingly being considered as an alternative to commercial content management systems and have been applied to a wide variety of digital library collections. Open source software for digital libraries is of great benefit in terms of applicability and affordability. In general, open source software provides a number of language supports, and it supports various operating systems, including Linux, another open source operating system, to ensure worldwide applicability. The affordability of open source software is guaranteed via its free distribution, redistribution, and modification of software and open source code policy. However, using open source software does include some level of responsibility and commitment of the institution. Once the institution belongs to the specific open source software user community, the community as a whole expects to contribute to the knowledge base of source codes, documentations, and usage examples. More specifically, since open source software does not provide sufficient training, technical supports, and necessary documentations for operation, the burden to keep up with the software depends entirely on the user community.

There are similarities between open source software and the information-sharing culture in the library and information science field. More specifically, Tennant (2000) points to four specific explanations for the popularity of open source software in digital libraries. Using open source digital library software, it becomes an easy process to produce a prototype for new digital library collections or services. Along with open source software for digital libraries, associated open source software, such as the Apache Web Server and MySQL database management system, are easily used to provide digital library services to users. In addition, it is relatively easy to modify features according to specific institutions' needs since by nature the software development process is supposed to cooperate with involved developers. The last reason (though not the least) that Tennant (2000) points out is cost. Since the open source software is distributed free of charge, it would be possible to try out several kinds of open source software before committing to specific software. However, it should be noted that invisible costs such as maintenance, upgrading, and contributions to user communities are expected.

One example of popular open source software is Greenstone (www.green stone.org). From an evaluation of digital library open source software using 12 categories, Greenstone was found to be the best performer (Goh et al., 2006). According to the evaluation checkpoints provided by Goh et al. (2006), the five aspects are content management, user interface, user administration, system administration, and other requirements. Greenstone was developed by the New Zealand Digital Library Project at the University of Waikato with a focus on university libraries and other public service institutions in order to build large digital collections (Bainbridge, Thompson, and Witten, 2003). Fedora (www.fedora-commons.org) was developed by Cornell University and the University of Virginia Library with support from Andrew W. Mellon and the NSF. In 2003, Fedora released its first version with the intention of creating a production quality system using XML and web services technology to provide digital content services to users. EPrints (www.eprints.org) launched as the first Open Archives Initiative (OAI) compliant digital library software in 2001 in terms of open access software. EPrints was developed in the U.K. with the intention of providing open access to research materials such as documents, image, video, and data sets to interested users. DSpace (www.dspace.org) has been adopted in more than 200 academic institutions and museums as a digital repository for articles, books, courseware, journals, websites, and theses/dissertations. It was developed jointly by MIT Libraries and Hewlett-Packard in 2000. These open source digital library systems—Greenstone, Fedora, and DSpace— have their own characteristics in terms of preservation, metadata, access, and system features. According to Han's (2004) findings, for preservation consideration issues, Greenstone provides some features to keep the original file formats with supporting multiple corresponding common files, but DSpace and Fedora have more sophisticated preservation features that include keeping the original file names, versioning features, and scalable storage. From the perspective of metadata, Greenstone and Fedora were found to be flexible because they support any metadata sets as long as the desired metadata schema is provided. On the other hand, DSpace is relatively limited because it supports only Dublin Core. In terms of external access, Greenstone has the flexibility of supporting two standard protocols: a traditional library community protocol (Z39.50) and an internet-oriented protocol (OAI-PMH). Greenstone is easy to install and supports multiple languages, while DSpace and Fedora are relatively difficult to install in comparison.

Digitization of Text Images, Images, and Multimedia

Analog objects, which are not born-digital, are supposed to be digitized in order to serve as digital contents for specific digital collections and libraries. For images, some basic concepts and terminology are necessary to understand the fundamental aspects in digital imaging technology (Western States Digital Standards Group, 2003). Dots per inch (DPI) and pixels per inch (PPI) are frequently mentioned in digital imaging and scanning software and hardware. DPI can be used in terms of representing how many dots are produced per inch in output devices (i.e., printing devices). More dots usually translate to more detailed printing quality. On the other hand, PPI is considered in terms of scanning devices (i.e., scanners) and display devices (i.e., computer monitors). Similar to the DPI concept, more pixels produce better display quality and scanning quality. Digital images have specific file formats when converted into digital formats or born-digital images. Basically, file formats for digital images can be categorized into compressed and uncompressed. Compressed images are reduced image files in terms of file sizes in order to store and transmit them efficiently, while uncompressed images are the original image files. It is this compressed feature that enables the former to be stored and transmitted more efficiently than uncompressed files. Generally speaking, there are two approaches to compression: lossless and lossy. With lossless compression, the image does not lose any components in its original file and is more desirable for high-quality images. In contrast, lossy image compression deletes some redundant components in an image file. Popular image file types are .tiff or .tif, .jpg, and .gif. Since Tagged Image File Format (.tiff or .tif) includes uncompressed lossless file formats with supporting multiple files, it is generally recognized as high quality. When dealing with images for archiving and preservation, TIFF file format (.tif) is normally considered for preservation purposes. On the other hand, the Joint Picture Expert Group (.jpg) and the Graphics Interchange File (.gif) file formats are more likely to be used for presenting thumbnails and web versions of the original files (Cornell University Library Research Department, 2003).

In addition, audio and video multimedia contents can be considered for digital libraries. While it is relatively easy to digitize audio content, as evidenced by the popular availability of CD types, video contents are still more of a challenge depending on the size of the files. Since audio contents are generally created in the form of digital CDs, the audio in CDs is relatively easily convertible into a wide variety of digital file types, such as MP3 and RealAudio, depending on user needs and service purposes. On the other hand, video formats demand a great deal more space, especially compared to text, such as when it is produced in the digital format in the creation phase of video. Alternatively, after the creation of a video or movie, the video contents can be converted to digital formats, such as MPEG file types (MPEG stands for Motion Picture Experts Group, an audio- and video-encoding standard).

Digital Archiving and Preservation Issues

Digital archiving and preservation involve a wide variety of issues and topics to be considered when building and managing digital collections and digital libraries. From the perspective of an information life cycle, Hodge (2000) surveyed cutting-edge digital library project managers to identify best practices for digital archiving. During the information life cycle management process, standards for digital contents and metadata records, collection policy, migration plans, rights management, and version controls are considered core issues for digital archiving. As we progress through digital archiving and preservation projects, there are questions regarding selection among a variety of content standards and metadata options, the extent of collection and migration decisions, and how copyright issues are handled with copyright holders. In attempting to answer these questions, best practices should be considered. In addition,

Lopatin (2006) surveyed the current literature to identify the issues and guide-lines in digital preservation projects. In various digitization projects, their find-ings identify several key issues relevant to digital archiving and preservation. These include financial sustainability, specialized staffs, collection policy, intel-lectual property law, metadata schemes, and interoperability. In order to build and manage digital libraries successfully, financial supports should be sustained during the projects and continued even after the projects are completed. Sources for financial support can be sought, such as institutional supports, external dona-tions, charging users, and advertisements (Lesk, 2005). With financial supports, since digital preservation and archiving require several areas of expertise, these projects can be managed by specialized staff. Once specialized staff is involved, collection policy can be maintained, and copyright issues can be resolved appro-priately. But there also exist many options for metadata schemes even within the same subject area. Selecting an appropriate metadata scheme out of several can-didates is crucial in terms of interoperability with other archives as well as effi-cient information organization.

Levels of Interoperability

Interoperability is generally defined by emphasizing the interchange between involved dissimilar parts. Moen (2001) points out that when interacting between different systems, threatening factors in interoperability must be considered to improve the quality of interoperability. For instance, different operating sys-tems, protocols, and information retrieval systems affect the interoperability between multiple systems. On another level, different metadata schemes and data formats also impact interoperability. Moreover semantic levels, different vocabularies, ontologies, and disciplines can be obstacles to the interoperability of multiple systems. Okusel and Sheth (1999) distinguish these interoperability issues with four distinctive levels: semantic interoperability, structural interop-erability, syntactic interoperability, and system interoperability. While struc-tural, syntactic, and system interoperability deal with the functional levels between disparate digital libraries, semantic interoperability is concerned with the meanings of interchanged information. In this networked digital information age, users generally expect higher levels of interoperability when obtaining search results. Although the search procedure requires several information sys-tems or digital libraries, users are likely to expect to receive a single set of results according to their single query. The search results for a single query are supposed to be seamless without any critical information loss, while different systems interchange information in terms of meanings as well as functional aspects in digital libraries. A few mechanisms of interoperability in digital libraries include use of standard protocols and metadata schemes. Interoperat-ing with other digital libraries can be possible when using standard protocols, such as Open Access Initiatives-Protocol for Metadata Harvesting (OAI-PMH) and Z39.50. OAI-PMH is a relatively new protocol of exchanging data originally from EPrints servers. Currently, OAI-PMH has become an internet-oriented protocol for exchanging data between various digital libraries and repositories. By contrast, Z39.50 is a traditional protocol for exchanging data within library communities. Using a standard protocol between multiple digital libraries can guarantee some level of interoperability. In addition, application profiles and metadata schema registries can be used to improve the interoperability of diverse digital libraries and collections (Liu, 2007). An application profile can be described as a mixed-matched combination of metadata elements from a metadata scheme or multiple metadata sets for specific domains or collections. By declaring metadata elements and their usage via an application profile, an application profile can serve a package to local needs in a standardized way. Yet, metadata schema registries are also a way of managing metadata schemas and application profiles. Once metadata schemas or application profiles are declared, they can be stored and managed in metadata schema registries. Via metadata schema registries, users with specific metadata and application needs can search for the best fit for their needs.

Information Services

Digital Libraries in Various Contexts

In reality, digital collections and libraries exist in diverse settings, ranging from those having a geographical framework to multidisciplinary frameworks. The research issues and implementation topics in digital libraries are a global concern. Countries are involved in digital library development and service endeavors via the internet in many ways. The World Digital Library project is one of the more recent collaborative efforts involving several countries in one digital library project. The Library of Congress leads this initiative, but several countries worldwide participate in various aspects. The primary purpose of the World Digital Library is to collect significant materials from the cultures around the world and provide information services to the world. But digital libraries and collections have been built in a variety of fields and information communities such as museums, archives, and so on. The areas involved in building digital libraries can include diverse contents from academic fields to oral recordings of the events on September 11, 2001. The focal point should be placed on integrating various aspects of digital libraries and collections while embracing their own cultural backgrounds and contexts. For instance, a museum-oriented digital library requires some consideration in terms of collections, information organization, and user needs. The collection in a museum-oriented digital library can contain many multimedia contents including images and photographic representations of museum objects. Accordingly, the method of organizing information can have museum-specific considerations such as exhibition history and loan history as well as descriptive information organization. In addition, a museum-oriented user aspect, including user needs, can reflect on user interfaces and system features.

Collection Building and Management

Collection principles for digital libraries are discussed in terms of seven elements in the National Information Standards Organization (NISO) guidelines (NISO Framework Advisory Group, 2007). These seven principles are policy, appropriate collection information, collection sustainability, collection availability, intellectual property rights, usage report mechanisms, and consistency within the larger context. Principle one recommends that an agreed-upon collection policy should be established before the project begins. Principle two suggests that since diverse digital collections are available on the internet, it should be crucial to provide adequate collection information such as scope, formats, and copyright-related statements. Principle three points out that in order to sustain the digital collection over the funded period, the internal and external funding should be maintained. Principle four identifies that the collection should be provided to the public without any obstacles to use. Principle five focuses on the intellectual property rights in terms of respecting the rights of copyright holders. Principle six recommends mechanisms for measuring the usefulness of the collections. Principle seven emphasizes the integration into a larger context, such as the National Science Digital Library, if it is a science-related collection. In this sense, the collection policy contains these principles in statements. A policy for digital library collection development should be tightly related to its own organization's missions and policies in order not to stand in isolation from the collection as a whole. One example of a digital library collection policy is found at Library and Archives Canada (www.collections canada.ca/collection/003-200-e.html). This policy deals with selection and acquisition criteria, cooperation/collaboration, and purposes. Another example is the Digital Library of Georgia collection development policy (dlg.galileo.usg. edu/colldev.html), which focuses on primary aspects of digital collection development such as accessibility, use, copyright, mission, diversity, value, and technology.

Information Organization Via Metadata Schemes

Structured information has value especially when accessing, searching, identifying and exchanging information in a standard way. An appropriate way to structure information is to produce proper metadata records for information objects or resources. Via metadata records, users are able to search, access, identify, and exchange information. Depending upon information communities and contexts, a variety of metadata schemes have been developed and applied. In spite of this variety, there exist core components. These core components, consisting of a metadata scheme, are considered to be elements, semantics, and syntax. Elements are the labels used to provide meanings for information items; these elements can be strings, numbers, or codes, depending on the metadata schemes. Semantics refers to the assignment of the right information to the right elements. In the Dublin Core metadata standard, the Creator element is supposed to show "an entity primarily responsible for making the content of the resource" (Hillmann, 2005). Syntax can be considered as the overall record structure in which the records can be processed and exchanged. For instance, once XML is chosen as the syntax for a specific metadata scheme, the records should be expressed in the valid form of XML documents.

In general, metadata schemes can be categorized into several types: descriptive metadata, administrative metadata, technical metadata, structural metadata, preservation metadata, and rights management metadata. While it is difficult to distinguish between different types of metadata with distinctive lines, each metadata type contains its own characteristics and purposes in regards to the management of data in a structured way. Descriptive metadata is intended to represent the intellectual contents of an information item. Administrative metadata contains information metadata records, such as the date of the metadata record and the creator of the metadata record. Technical metadata is intended to describe the aspects of hardware and software related to specific information items. Structural metadata includes information about complex file organization and configuration, since various complicated structured information items have increased in terms of 3D objects, interactive software, and so on. Structural metadata schemes are necessary to describe the structure and configuration of complicated files. Preservation metadata emphasize the management of information items to describe appropriate relevant information with the purpose of preservation. Finally, rights management metadata focuses on information regarding restrictions on use, permission, copyright notice, and so on.

A few selected metadata schemes provided by NISO Framework Advisory Group (2007) are explained briefly here. Dublin Core is considered a simple and generic element set applicable to a variety of digital collections. Encoded Archival Description (EAD) is taken as a set of rules to represent archival finding aids in terms of the intellectual and physical parts. Learning Object Metadata (LOM) is used for learning objects and educational resources. MARC 21 is used for bibliographic data in a library community. With the capability of wrapping information, Metadata Encoding and Transmission Standard (METS) is used for structural, descriptive, administrative, and technical metadata in the form of XML. Metadata Object Description Schema (MODS) is the XML format that is compatible with MARC 21. For multimedia contents, the Visual Resource Association (VRA) Core Categories are used for images and MPEG-7 for multimedia as a whole. The VRA Core Categories are used for art, architecture, artifacts, and other visual resources that consider multiple representation features such as the original painting and a slide of the painting. On the other hand, MPEG-7 is a content description standard for audio and video materials. It includes nontextual information such as color, movement, shape, and sound as well as textual-based descriptions.

User Needs and Services

Because digital libraries exist within vast contexts, it is not possible to choose a single way to understand user needs and evaluation methods. In this sense, Choudhury, Hobbs, Lorie, and Flores (2002) investigate users' preferences for digital library services in terms of digital image services, full-text search features, delivery time, and cost for services. This study identified that users prefer images, full-text searches, and fast delivery time for the digital libraries, and want all of this free of charge. Manduca et al. (2005) explore user behaviors regarding the portal service of digital library collections. Based on user behaviors and needs in relation to a geosciences digital collection portal, Manduca et al.'s findings revealed that users tend to trust colleagues' recommendations for resource selections for teaching purposes. Accordingly, they proposed the communication and collaboration features in the portal site based on the findings. By nature, digital libraries do not exist physically, which brings attention to the question of virtual/digital reference services in digital libraries that are used to fulfill users' questioning and answering. These virtual/digital reference services happen synchronously (i.e., real-time chat) and asynchronously (i.e., email communication) (Tedd and Large, 2005).

Social Aspects

Funding Models in Digital Library Projects

In general, digital library projects require funding for software, hardware, specialized staff to build and manage the collections, and operation costs. The funding sources for digital library projects can be divided into two parts: first, external grants, and second, the institution's own budget. One of the major external funding sources for digital library projects is the Institute of Museum and Library Services (IMLS), a federal agency, established in 1996 to accommodate preservation and digitization needs in museums and libraries (Chepesiuk, 2001). While IMLS funding is still ongoing, other external funding sources, such the Digital Library Initiatives Phase 1 and Phase 2 by the NSF, ended in 1998 and 2004, respectively. In 1994, the four-year term of the first phase launched, and six research projects were conducted, with the second phase between 1999 and 2004 supporting 34 digital projects (Tedd and Large, 2005). According to the survey by the Metropolitan New York Library Council and OCLC (2005), the other main funding source for digital libraries is an institution's own budgets. Whether the funding sources are external or from internal budgets, one of the most critical issues in digital library projects is the sustainability of the projects beyond the funded period. In addition to an institution's own budget for digital libraries, additional funding sources may be provided by donations, user fees, and advertising campaigns that solicit financial support (Lesk, 2005).

Intellectual Property Rights

Digital library projects generally should resolve copyright issues relevant to specific collections or materials. More important to digital libraries are the legal issues in dealing with digital transmission (Besek, 2003). Intellectual property can be categorized into two parts in terms of digital library projects: first, materials under copyright protection, and second, materials in the public domain. Materials in the public domain can be used freely, such as with Project Gutenberg (www.gutenberg.org). Project Gutenberg includes ebooks and audiobooks from copyright-expired materials, such as Jane Austen's works. In addition to these copyright-expired materials, U.S. government publications are under public domain and can be legally digitized for users. One of the popular exceptions to copyright protection of materials is fair use. The main purposes for implementing this fair use exception are for educational and scholarly reasons. However, it is agreed that the fair use arguments are not always easily or successfully made (Wherry, 2002). Fair use is often decided in the courts on a case-by-case basis. Under U.S. copyright laws, determining the length of copyright protection is complex and may be influenced by the original date of copyright as well as the original ownership and subsequent amendments, such as the 1998 Sonny Bono Copyright Term Extension Act.

From a global perspective of intellectual property rights, copyright issues become far more complicated. There is no single "international copyright," though there are some international agreements such as the Berne Convention and the Universal Copyright Convention. Depending on the country and the type of material (i.e., books, photos, and so on), the periods under copyright protection vary from as few as 25 years to the life of the author, plus 50 years (Baker and McKenzie, 2002). However, not all countries participate in copyright agreements.

Summary

Vannevar Bush's (1945) futuristic visions of digital libraries have become real in terms of knowledge organization and the provision of remote access in order to improve science and engineering. Research and concepts in digital libraries have been applied and implemented and are ongoing. Research topics and practical issues in digital libraries contain various aspects of technology, collections, information organization, information services, and social and economic elements. Along with the internet infrastructure, digital library systems, such as open access software (i.e., Greenstone, Fedora, DSpace, and EPrints) and commercial packages have been introduced and applied. In addition, digital library collections are diverse, not only in disciplinary fields, but in media types too, such as text, audio, image, and motion picture. As a way of organizing information resources, various metadata schemes can be utilized depending upon the contents and types of collections. Information services are primarily dependent on targeted user groups and user needs. In addition, social and economic aspects of digital libraries, such as sustainability of digital library projects and intellectual property issues of information resources, have been discussed.

References

Bainbridge, D., Thompson, J., and Witten, I. H. 2003. Assembling and Enriching Digital Library Collections. *Proceedings of the 3rd ACM/IEEE-CS Joint Conference on Digital Libraries* 323–334.

Baker and McKenzie. 2002. *Guide to Regional Intellectual Property Laws for Librarians.* Singapore: National Library Board.

Besek, J. M. 2003. *Copyright Issues Relevant to Digital Preservation and Dissemination of Pre-1972 Commercial Sound Recordings by Libraries and Archives.* Council on Library and Information Resources and Library of Congress. Retrieved February 15, 2010, from www.loc.gov/rr/record/nrpb/pub135.pdf

Borgman, C. L. 1999. What Are Digital Libraries? Competing Visions. *Information Processing and Management* 35:227–243.

Bush, V. 1945. As We May Think. *The Atlantic Online.* Retrieved February 15, 2010, from www.theatlantic.com/doc/print/194507/bush

Chepesiuk, R. 2001. Digitizing Rare Materials: Special Collections Go Global. *American Libraries* 32(5):54–56.

Choudhury, S., Hobbs, B., Lorie, M., and Flores, N. 2002. A Framework for Evaluating Digital Library Services. *D-Lib Magazine* 8(7/8). Retrieved February 15, 2010, from www.dlib.org/dlib/july02/choudhury/07choudhury.html

Cornell University Library Research Department. 2003. Moving Theory into Practice: Digital Imaging Tutorial. Retrieved February 15, 2010, from www.library.cornell.edu/preservation/tutorial/contents.html

Covey, D. T. 2003. Mercury Electronic Library Project. *Encyclopedia of Library and Information Science.* Retrieved February 15, 2010, from www.informaworld.com/smpp/content~db=ai~content=a713532002

Digital Library Federation. 1998. A Working Definition of Digital Library. Retrieved February 15, 2010, from www.diglib.org/about/dldefinition.htm

Goh, D. H-L., Chua, A., Khoo, D. A., Khoo, E. B-H., Mak, E. B-T., and Ng, M.W.-M. 2006. A Checklist for Evaluating Open Source Digital Library Software. *Online Information Review* 30(4):360–379.

Han, Y. 2004. Digital Content Management: The Search for a Content Management System. *Library Hi Tech* 22(4):355–365.

Hillmann, D. I. 2005. Using Dublin Core. Dublin Core Metadata Initiative. Retrieved February 15, 2010, from dublincore.org/documents/usageguide

Hodge, G. M. 2000. Best Practices for Digital Archiving: An Information Life Cycle Approach. *D-Lib Magazine* 6(1). Retrieved February 15, 2010, from www.dlib.org/dlib/january00/01hodge.html

Lesk, M. 2005. *Understanding Digital Libraries.* San Francisco: Elsevier.

Liu, J. 2007. *Metadata and Its Applications in the Digital Library: Approaches and Practices*. Westport, CT: Libraries Unlimited.

Lopatin, L. 2006. Library Digitization Projects, Issues, and Guidelines: A Survey of the Literature. *Library Hi Tech* 24(2):273–289.

Manduca, C. A., Iverson, E. R., Fox, S., and McMartin, F. 2005. Influencing User Behavior Through Digital Library Design: An Example from the Geosciences. *D-Lib Magazine* 11(5). Retrieved February 15, 2010, from www.dlib.org/dlib/may05/fox/05fox.html

Metropolitan New York Library Council and OCLC. 2005. 2004 METRO Digitization Survey: Final Report. New York: Metropolitan New York Library Council and OCLC.

Moen, W. E. 2001. Mapping the Interoperability Landscape for Networked Information Retrieval. *Proceedings of 1st ACM/IEEE-CS Joint Conference on Digital Libraries* pp. 50–51.

National Information Standards Organization Framework Advisory Group. 2007. *A Framework of Guidance for Building Good Digitization Collections*. 3rd ed. Baltimore: NISO.

Okusel, A. M., and Sheth, A. 1999. Semantic Interoperability in Global Information Systems: A Brief Introduction to the Research Area and the Special Section. *SIGMOD Records* 28(1):5–12.

Schwartz, C. 2000. Digital Libraries: An Overview. *The Journal of Academic Librarianship* 26(6):385–393.

Tedd, L. A., and Large, A. 2005. *Digital Libraries: Principles and Practice in a Global Environment*. München: K.G. Saur.

Tennant, R. 2000. The Role of Open Source Software. *Library Journal* 125(1):36.

Western States Digital Standards Group. 2003. Western States Digital Imaging Best Practices. Retrieved February 15, 2010, from www.bcr.org/dps/cdp/best/wsdibp_v1.pdf

Wherry, Timothy Lee. 2002. *The Librarian's Guide to Intellectual Property in the Digital Age: Copyrights, Patents, and Trademarks*. Chicago: American Library Association.

Chapter 9

Bibliometrics

Melanie J. Norton

Bibliometrics uses quantitative methods, such as statistics and mathematical analysis, to examine documents, media, communication surrogates, and processes. Bibliometrics may also employ qualitatively descriptive methods. Bibliometrics is concerned with the relations that might be derived or inferred related to the production, manipulation, or redistribution of information (Buckland, 1991; Pao, 1989; White and McCain, 1989). The word bibliometrics can be divided into "biblio," which refers to books or bibliographies, and "metrics," which refers to measurement. This very simplified definition of a growing set of analytical tools is too often misunderstood by students and novices. Bibliometrics is not one analytical methodology; it is a diverse group of methodologies. Bibliometrics references the various methodologies of measurement and investigation applied to the artifacts of human communication forms, previously thought of primarily as books or other textual representatives. Using this very broad definition is intended to permit inclusion of new information and communications forms such as databases, webpages, and other technologies for recording information as well as not limiting the notion of bibliometrics to bibliographies or only physical print materials. Bibliometrics tools are applied across disciplines; they have been used to "measure" scientific communication and research productivity, to trace the movement of information, to track author productivity, to identify networks of communicants, and to suggest trends in publication, social emphasis, organizational pathways, and more (Borgman and Furner, 2002).

Human information is stored in a variety of media amenable to measurement including text, film, electronic, aural recording, art, and other recordable or translatable formats. Some researchers separate the study of information and communication forms into separate groups such as data, information, knowledge, and documents or text (Lewis and Jones, 1996). But the application of bibliometric techniques has implications for all of these states. Basic analytical methods may identify patterns of word use, vocabulary, or syntactic structures to reveal clues about authorship of material that are still questioned, such as Shakespeare's writings (Koppel, Schier, and Argamon, 2009). Locating high- or low-frequency occurrences of specific phrases, words, or structures may indicate an area worthy of further exploration. Recurring patterns in data, subject, queries, citations, authorship, publication data, themes, characters, and so on may suggest researchable issues or relationships.

Concepts and methodologies from bibliometrics are found in applications of data mining as a component of knowledge discovery in databases (KDD) and related knowledge management (KM). Retrospective examination of database collections to identify any potential patterns or statistically significant variations may yield new insight into the objects of the database or identify construction and relationships within the database and possibly the entities the database represents (Fayyad, Piatetsky-Shapiro, and Smyth, 1996). The practical uses of bibliometrics include contributing to information for decision making regarding collection development, weeding, cataloging and classification, circulation patterns, indexing, exploration of scholarly communication, and much more. Bibliometrics is both a research and a practical tool. This chapter provides an overview of a few key notions of bibliometrics and its applications in various roles.

Measurement, Description, and Information

Measurement provides a method for describing an entity. How tall a tree is, how many rings in the trunk, the depth of its bark, or the number of leaves on a stem—all of these contribute to describing the tree and may also allow for inferences about its age or its relationship to other plants. How many books in a library collection relate a description of size. A count of how many books in a specific subject area and those published in a given time period provides more descriptive information, which could permit inferences to be made about the library's use, patrons, or collection development policies. The basis of all science and research comes from observation; one intent of observation is description, which may include measurement as a method.

Sometimes it is difficult to ascertain the appropriate method of measurement. For example, there is much debate about a proper method to measure student achievement or teaching success. If grades measure student achievement, should grades given by teachers be considered the measure of the success of their teaching? The question becomes what do grades measure and what do those measurements mean? If all of a teacher's students are given A's, does that mean the teacher is successful? Since the teacher awards the grades, there may be a conflict in looking at success from this view (not to suggest teachers give grades for any reason other than correct completion of syllabus requirements). Just because there are measurements does not mean they are appropriate or informative; the context and criteria must be clear and fit what is being examined.

Observation and description are research processes, not just measurement activities, and measurement is not sufficient to assure comprehension of an occurrence. Amount does not correlate to quality, and it is not acceptable to make inferences about quality based entirely on quantity. How many articles an author has published yields no information about the quality of those articles. How frequently an author is cited does not necessarily translate into a statement of quality or even expertise. An author may be cited frequently for a number of reasons, including that many other authors disagree with his or her writings. How frequently an author publishes provides information about his or her productivity but not about the quality of the product. How frequently an author is cited suggests how widely read the author may be, regardless of the quality of the writing. A combination of factors must be considered when applying quantitative measures to make qualitative inferences; there are contextual characteristics to be considered. Publication in peer-reviewed scholarly vehicles lends a different meaning to authorship frequency, especially coupled with high-frequency citations of the author's work over time in other peer-reviewed scholarly works.

Measurement supplies descriptive information, such as how frequently a word is used or how frequently an author publishes. Measurement permits comparisons based on quantity, frequency, length, and even characteristics of quality. Bibliometrics provides measurements and descriptions from the study of our information, communication records, and literature. Pao suggests that bibliometrics studies deal with three components, "1) the physical object … 2) its creation and subject content; and 3) its use" (1989, p. 14). The physical object currently would include electronic communications and media, such as radio, television, film, email, ejournals, epublications, tape, CD, blogs, and the like, which are "captured" or recorded in some manner that permits retrospective examination and evaluation. Creation and content evaluations would examine the productivity of authors, currency of content, content coverage, and spread of content. Studying uses and users is possibly the most complex of bibliometric concerns, as there are compound factors involved that seem to defy quantification, such as human information seeking behavior. These three broad classifications of study for bibliometrics actually represent a multitude of smaller investigative areas and applications. These studies have the potential to reveal maps of literature or communication: who cites whom; who co-cites; who suggests discipline foci and interest groups, paths of information exchange, or scholarly communication networks (Borgman and Furner, 2002). Article titles in journals may indicate subfields or areas of interest for the journal or the journal sponsors. Bibliometric studies may also suggest trends in authorship, publication, subject coverage, growth in a discipline, or ideas. Using techniques such as Bradford's (1948) "core and scatter," bibliometrics may identify the journals that are key to providing the most quantitatively comprehensive coverage of a subject using the least number of journals. Computer algorithms can be applied to create indexes based on word frequency and scaled rankings. The application of bibliometric techniques can be used in document-retrieval systems, acquisition programs, circulation statistics, and even user preferences. Various database records reviewed retrospectively may reveal purchasing patterns among clients, banking practice habits in regions, health and disease patterns among the clientele of an insurance agent or large employee system, or no patterns at all. Bibliometrics encompasses a wide variety of methods of analysis based on the record of information and communication that may be applied across the spectrum of disciplines, as suggested by article titles such as "Intellectual Structure of Human Resources Management Research: A Bibliometric Analysis of the Journal Human Resource Management, 1985–2005" (Fernandez-Alles and Ramos-Rodriguez, 2009) and "How is Science Cited on the Web? A Classification of Google Unique Web Citations" (Kousha and Thelwall, 2007).

Measurement: Objects and Representatives of Information

One area of bibliometrics examines aspects of the objects or representatives of information exchange. One method evaluates the history of the objects, that is, how many of these objects are produced now versus previously? More precisely, how many of x objects in y context are produced now versus previously? For example, how many electronic articles were published in juried electronic journals in the field of library and information science in 2008, and how many were published in 2000? As in any attempt at description and measurement criteria, parameters need to be clearly indicated to ensure that only those items intended to be counted or measured are included, and everything else is excluded. Clearly there are requirements involved in the previous inquiry; electronic articles were a relatively new publication form in 2000. Juried electronic journals were not only a specific journal format, but they also had a very selective inclusion policy. Limiting the discipline to library and information science further restricts the items eligible for inclusion in the count and also creates the parameters to allow us to have meaningful discussions about the results, as does the inclusion of time periods. Only electronically published articles in juried electronic journals from the field of library and information science would be counted. They would be counted by year, from 2000 through 2008. If there was a statistically significant change in the number of electronic articles published in juried ejournals of library and information science, it might be useful to seek adjunct information to discover what might have influenced the change. Regardless of what numeric results were obtained by pursuing this query, it would be essential to note factors surrounding the time period involved, the prevalence in general of juried electronic journals in 2000 versus 2008, the tenure criteria acceptable in 2000 regarding electronic publication versus print publication compared to 2008, and so on. The quantitative results are not meaningful without the context, especially if the context might have a significant influence on the numeric outcomes.

The numeric results of the analysis form only a partial basis for exploration but also contribute to laying a foundation and may suggest other territories requiring exploration. A practical application of information such as this would be to review the journal collection policy for this field of study to determine whether the increase in juried ejournals has impacted the print journals. Further study would be necessary to determine whether topics covered in the ejournals are the same as those covered in print journals. Has there been any change in the number, quality, or coverage of the print journals; are the ejournals just another format, or are they replacing the print journals? These are critical questions from a collection development and budget point of view, which may make use of bibliometric study results.

Another example of measuring objects or representatives would be research-ing the number of journals published in medicine between 1899 and 1999: how many were published each year, were there changes in the number of journals published, were there changes in the number of journals in a specific language, were there any changes in the number or identity of publishers of these journals, and so on. This type of study provides information about the growth of records in a field and might suggest transformations in the field itself. Further, it pro-vides estimates of the continuing growth patterns and the implications of such upon the collecting libraries, including predicting future shelf space and storage problems. Changes in publication patterns can be indicative of larger economic changes, shifts in formats, interests, and business strength. If the primary lan-guage of publication changes, could it suggest a change in a discipline's domi-nant scholarly group? Sometimes measuring and observing create more questions to consider rather than resolving any of them.

A method thought to be practical for evaluating the usefulness of specific journals examines citation half-life and use half-life. Citations are references to another document (using the widest possible definition of document). These ref-erences to another document indicate a relationship and suggest the citing author has consulted the cited document, thereby being a possible measure of use. A suggestion that one author has consulted another's writings may be a means for mapping idea transmission, or interest groups, or nothing at all. (Linda Smith's 1981 *Library Trends* article discusses various considerations and assumptions about citations to consider in undertaking any citation-based research. The article is still a clear and useful resource that all potential citation researchers should review.) Half-life studies attempt to evaluate the length of time in which a journal is used, either as a resource as indicated by citation, or physical use as indicated by circulation (Pao, 1989). Tsay (1998) examines jour-nal "life" based on uses as demonstrated by circulation and citation. The premise of half-life in bibliometrics is to determine when half of all the active literature of a field has been published, or the time period that includes half or more of the references (citations) made. Short half-life, whether citation-based or use-based (which means more than 50 percent of the use or citations occurred in a short period of time), implies that "new volumes of a title are generally used more often than older volumes" (Tsay, 1998, p. 1285). Half-life studies may suggest which journals are most used, but they may also exaggerate use since there are more publications available today than previously. It has been suggested that half-life studies could identify which journals are least used, resulting in a list of items to consider for discontinuation. Caution should be taken in applying such a plan; the mission of the institution, the orientation and behavior of the users, and any possible other contributors to low use, such as inaccessibility, should be considered.

Citation analysis may be used to identify the "most" discussed issues in a field and topic area. It may also be a way to establish what the focus of interests, or new topics, in a discipline was at a given time or to determine the influences affecting the field. Dumas (1993) used a combination of citation analysis and subject classification to examine and characterize the British and American social work literature published between 1984 and 1991. He was seeking to identify the "core" themes of the literature and any changes or trends that might be evident though an evaluation of the citations. Such information may be valuable when attempting to ensure inclusiveness of a collection. The study was also significant for applying bibliometric techniques to social work literature.

Measurement: Creation and Content

Another measure using citations involves counting the number of times a specific article or author is cited, which may indicate some authority on a subject, whether the item is central to a discipline area, or even a topic of a significant debate. The number of times an author is cited may indicate that he or she is an authority in an area, is a prolific author, is controversial, or is a primary source for some topic. The number of times an author is cited has been viewed as an estimate of his or her stature or scholarly contribution to a field. Quantity of citation alone is not an appropriate measure of scholarly success. Years of discussion and research comparing "citedness" with academic productivity and scholarly stature suggest that quantification has some potential merit, but serious recurring questions plague the various methods (Borgman and Furner, 2002, p. 9; Smith, 1981).

Author productivity may be measured by how frequently the author publishes. A simple count of publications, as mentioned before, does not indicate quality, only quantity. However, it is possible to compare frequency of publications among authors within a field. This type of measurement evaluates the distribution of authorship in a field. Alfred Lotka in 1926 (in Meadows, 1987, p. 113–119) examined a sample of the author name index of *Chemical Abstracts* to determine the number of individual authors and their publication frequency during the period 1907 to 1916. The outcome of this study indicated approximately 60 percent of the authors in the sample produced only one publication, 15 percent had two publications, 7 percent had three publications, 4 percent had four publications, and 2 percent had five publications. Authors of six to 44 publications each represented the balance: 9 percent of the authors produced six to 44 publications each. Later studies of authorship performed on samples from a major university catalog and another using a sample of Library of Congress MARC records suggest that the number of authors producing one work was between 50 and 75 percent (Vickery and Vickery, 1987). Newer studies might show that this productivity relationship has changed. One could theorize a shift in author productivity in recent time with a new stress on publications as part of increased demands for university tenure and funding, but much more sophisticated measures would have to be undertaken to investigate whether a change in the production relationship has occurred. On the other hand, if in reality only a few authors are responsible for the majority of publications, there may be implications for collection development. Vickery suggests it would first mean having all the authors, including specifically all the single item authors, represented in a collection would be "very arduous" (p. 234). Alternatively, it might be interpreted to mean that collecting only the prolific authors would provide satisfactory coverage of a topic. Again, it is not necessarily a good assumption because it negates possibly critical contributions from the single item authors. Quantity is not an indication of quality, whether the amount is large or small.

Quantity can convey information about items to aid in identifying content. How many times would we have to see the word "cat" in a document to think the document might have something to do with cats? This does not necessarily mean that the document is about cats but just that there is some concept or relationship inherent in the document that requires the word "cat" or "cats" to occur more frequently than other words. If you remove all the noncontent bearing words (such as "a," "an," "the," "and," "which," "that," "what," and so on) and arrange all the content bearing words with similar meanings together and then by how frequently they occur, it may be possible to ascertain something about the document content. The following list represents such an extraction from a section of a previous chapter. The numeral preceding any word indicates how many times the word appeared in that specific form. The words with associated meaning are grouped together; the semicolons separate the associated groups:

> Two classification systems, 2 classification, 2 organization, descriptions, organizational scheme, collection structures, criteria, scheme; 2 relationships, 2 relevance, relevant, aboutness; user, 2 users, users' needs, users' abilities, information seekers; recall, 2 retrieval system, retrieval of information; subject area, subject domain; 2 representativeness; 2 systems; inquiries, inquiry; information; knowledge environments; parameters; technologically based.

Note that the most common words have to do with classification, organization, scheme, and structure; the next most common words have to do with relevance and aboutness; the third most common have to do with users; and the fourth most common have to do with retrieval. Based on this list of words, could we determine which chapter section the list comes from and what the section was about, or at least guess something about the content? It is not a completely reliable method because language is very complex with several patterns intrinsic to a specific language or even discipline. People use language very differently, but the method has many applications, with constraints.

What is the value of such an activity? Evaluating word and phrase frequencies may provide insight into the "aboutness" or the subject matter. Phrase frequencies may be specific to disciplines, or word choices may indicate a subdiscipline or sublanguage (Losee and Haas, 1995). Identifying content words can be important in the appropriate classification of an item and in the development of sufficient indexing or cross references, and it may also be critical in the retrieval of the item. One of the ways to determine whether a document has any value in resolving a question is by trying to place the content, the aboutness, of the item in relation to the question. If the interest is cats, the summary of phrases indicates that the item represented by the phrases above is not likely to be about cats but rather about classification and organization and possibly retrieval. As a result, that item would not be considered as likely to have information about or related to cats.

Citation analysis has also been used to evaluate documents for subject content. The assumption is that having a sufficient number of citations in common, or from a particular topical area, implies that the current document must have content relationships with the cited material. If the majority of the citations in a paper are to other documents concerned with bibliometrics, then perhaps the paper being evaluated is also concerned with bibliometrics. This is not an adequate determinate of subject content by itself as it does not provide any depth of content description. A paper with many citations related to bibliometrics has something to do with bibliometrics, but what specifically? Is it an overview, a critique, a bibliometric study, or what? Subject analysis is more than a surface estimation of content and requires significantly more investment than mere citation matching.

Tools to assist in locating information, without having to examine an entire document, include document surrogates such as catalog records, citations, abstracts, summaries, indexes, database search systems, web search engines, metatags, and more. The implementation of these surrogates in a retrieval attempt is complex and dependent upon both the ability to synthesize the actual document into a representative surrogate and to relate it to retrieval inquiries. For example, the creation of indexes for information retrieval is two-pronged: First, an item has to be analyzed for subject content, and second, indexing terms reflective of the content of the item have to be selected. Determining the subject content of an item may be theoretically accomplished by examining and distilling the content of a document into representative characteristics. However, when individuals have unique interpretations of the meaning of a document, of what is representative, or of the most critical importance in conveying the subject content, it is difficult to be assured that any two readers would select the same descriptive terms. Further, there is the issue of whether the terms selected correspond to an investigator's interpretation of a question. What happens when the potential user seeks documents with subject identifiers that are not used by the indexer or classifying agent?

The problems inherent in subject/content analysis have yielded an assortment of schemes to address them, including controlled vocabularies, thesauri, classification systems, bibliometric techniques, and machine indexing that use the actual document text (Taylor, 1999). Experiments have been performed using the overlap and transition range of high-frequency and low-frequency words as indexing terms, noting the most common content words in relation to the least frequent content words. A related approach counts word frequencies for each unique word and compares the normalized percentage values to a standard of relative frequency in the language. If the value is higher than the standard, the word may be used for indexing. Another method uses only the top 5 percent of content bearing words appearing in a ranked frequency list generated from a document to create index terms. It is possible to have computers count words and apply statistical and mathematical schemes to perform automatic indexing. In fact, document relatedness may be evaluated by comparing high-frequency words and matching documents with significant similarity in words and occurrence (Pao, 1989). Interest in automatic indexing is now linked to the World Wide Web, which is a virtually infinite information space. Methods to identify documents, sites, homepages, or links responsive to a search request are critical to continued development of the web's potential (Chen, Chung, Ramsey, and Yang, 1998).

A traditional approach to analyzing documents for content involves examining the components: title and subtitle, table of contents, introduction, any provided index terms, phrases, or figurative content. Characterizing the subject content of the item with terms or phrases from the document that will be representative of the content to a prospective user is critical to future retrieval. Whether placed into a card catalog system or an electronic database, content description of the document must reflect the document. A searcher relies on the analysis and representativeness of these aspects to locate a document that is useful to address an information need.

A correspondent system for the web involves examining the HTML header areas, sometimes searching the entire document by performing a keyword count based on the search keywords input by the user. The application of this type of search and match has encouraged the use of metadata fields (data about the data) that could be used to "organize" the web. Problems and concerns about maintaining free-flowing information and workable structures to aid retrieval keep the discussion of the use and implementation of metadata a research interest. In 1999, Chowdhury suggested that authoring software be employed to allow webpage creators to enter the keywords, descriptors, or whatever metadata they felt relevant at the top of the HTML page. In the early 2000s, the evolution of user tagging began as a result of tagging services such as Delicious (delicious.com), Flickr (flickr.com), and Technorati (technorati.com). User tagging became a new labeling and retrieval system of sorts, opening a whole new era for bibliometrics (or webmetrics), user behaviors, and information access. "Tagging is the process by which the resources in a collection are tagged—i.e., assigned tags in the form of words, phrases, codes, or other strings of characters—with the dual intention (i) that the tags individually or collectively represent features of the tagged resources (or of resource-tagger relations), and (ii) that such representations or descriptions may be exploited by search services that enable people to discover the particular resources that are of interest to them at particular times" (Furner, 2007, p. 1). Other approaches include intelligent agents that extend the basic counting concepts of bibliometrics by automatically indexing the content of a page and comparing it by using a number of statistical programs to determine the closeness or relatedness of one page to another. Some systems collect URLs (uniform resource locators or web addresses) of pages that have high keyword counts matching the search inquiry; they then solicit user evaluation of the retrieved pages to construct a tighter search plan by using the identified pages as models for further matching. The potential for exploring the web using bibliometric techniques and sophisticated new computing tools continues to be a challenging and fertile area for research.

The evolution of the web and all information/communication related tools creates multiple areas of potential analysis. For example, Luzon (2009) seeks to explore "academic weblogs and to determine how links are used for distribution of information, collaborative construction of knowledge, and construction of the blog's and the blogger's identity" (p. 75) to find new paths of scholarly communication created through access to the web. Investigation of how online survey results and participation may be impacted by "forced-response" surveys asks the question: What does it mean if you cannot refuse to respond and does it influence your responses (Stieger, Reips, and Voracek, 2007)? There are many new ways to approach the question of information retrieval, publication assessment, the meaning of peer-review, and what seems to be an ever-changing set of communication paths, standards, and interests—many of which will be susceptible to bibliometric analysis and will, in the future, be critical to the survival of information services.

Bradford's Law

An early bibliometric measure devised by Samuel Bradford (1948) has yielded interesting results when applied in different venues than he had originally intended. Bradford identified a pattern in some ways similar to Lokta's discovery about author concentration. A relatively small number of journals will contain the highest concentration of articles on a specific subject, while a larger number of journals will have a lower concentration. This "core and scatter" translates into a pattern wherein a small collection of journals could be identified that contains a larger number of articles on a specific subject than a larger number of other journals. According to Bradford, "it is possible to arrange periodicals in zones of decreasing productivity, in regard to papers on a given subject, and the numbers of periodicals in each zone will increase as their productivity decreases" (Bradford, 1948 in Meadows, 1987, p. 147). Bradford found in his study of applied geophysics that nine journals yielded 429 of the referenced articles, forming the first zone; 59 journals yielded 499 of the referenced articles, forming the second zone; and 258 journals yielded 404 (p. 150). Essentially, the number of journals needed to produce approximately the same number of articles increased, creating "zones" of a very rough approximation of the same number of articles. Bradford theorized that a nucleus of journals and zones of scatter for a subject could be determined. Bradford's work has been interpreted to mean that one can select the journals in the nucleus zone to provide the most coverage of a topic. With limited budgets, it might be economical to purchase the journals with the most concentrated coverage first; however, limiting the selection to only the journals with high concentrations of articles may cause other problems. The notion of core and scatter was a byproduct of Bradford's attempt to determine "the extent to which articles on a given subject actually occur in periodicals devoted to quite other subjects" (p. 146). Examining only the journals in which one might expect to find research on a specific subject means that other articles, which may be of importance, will be missed. Bradford indicated that the number of these articles would be large: "We can only draw the general conclusion that a large number of articles are produced by periodicals which, *a priori* are 'unlikely'" (p. 150). In fact, consider Bradford's results: Of 1,332 references identified, the nine-journal "nucleus" identified only 429, or just 32 percent, of the referenced articles. Two-thirds of the material was not in the "core zone," and therefore applying the concept of most coverage for the least number of journals actually means not providing more than 60 percent of the referenced articles. Core and scatter type behavior has been noted in journals, in author productivity, and in citation frequency as well as other areas. Bradford's law has been applied to a variety of subject areas with similar, though not identical, results. Research continues to investigate whether there is an underlying rationale for this pattern of dispersion (Brookes, 1969; Pao, 1989).

Core and scatter zones have been the basis for collection development tools used in small or special libraries. For example, using a core and scatter zone list of medical journals, it has been thought possible to identify which journals would be the minimum "core" of journals necessary to provide the most articles of a specific portion of the field. If the intention is to provide access to two-thirds of the resources of the field, then the journals should be selected from the core and scatter zones that will produce that proportion, or the first two zones, rather than just the first or nucleus zone. However, in Bradford's experiment, that would mean subscribing to 68 journals rather than nine to obtain two-thirds coverage of a topic. Adjunct to this was Bradford's interest in identifying the "unlikely" sources of information on a topic, hence the examination of more and more journals to locate information on the topic. Naturally, there are flaws in this approach to collection development; critical research will appear in journals in the outer scatter zones, which is a fundamental discovery of Bradford's experiment that is not always emphasized. Important ideas are not always readily accepted and may not surface in the "core" journals until the idea is accepted. Meanwhile, important time has been lost. Campanario (1996) found that some highly cited articles, considered of value to the field, originally had difficulty being published. The structures in place to maintain the quality of journals may contribute to delaying publication of new or controversial ideas as these may be difficult to verify, posing the potential of ridicule for the publishing body. A journal, having a large number of articles available about a topic by established researchers, may not be interested in publishing the works of lesser known authors or those with less established reputations, especially if the ideas are controversial. Relying entirely on the "core" portion of core and scatter may not be desirable, as there are many factors involved in journal publication other than what Bradford's law necessarily reflects. Core and scatter has important implications but should be tempered, as should most bibliometric methods, with additional information, more than one measurement system, and common sense based upon the underlying requirements of the collection, facility, or research.

More Citation Analysis

Citation analysis, mentioned earlier, may be used as a method to trace the flow or dissemination of information. Citations reflect connectedness of some form from document to document. When two items are cited together in another item, the first two are considered to be co-cited. Co-citation may represent a link from an earlier work to a later work, it may suggest common interests among the two cited authors, or it may be a map to joining journal content, depending on the frequency of the occurrence of co-citation. Even single citation can be traced from document to document and from journal to journal to create a topography of the movement of an article's concepts through a document system or a field (Smith, 1981). Following citations over time and across documents may provide information about information transfers from theoretical to applied work (van der Wurff, 1997). Tracing citations may indicate the growth of an idea as it matures by use; the more a particular article is cited may indicate some component of the article as being a central concept or foundational moment. Co-citations may indicate connections among ideas or interests that might provide different approaches to topics.

Using citation analysis can assist in establishing subject interest cohorts and research fronts as well as in identifying potential high-yield journals or authors. Citation analysis has been an issue in attempting to assess the scholarly productivity and "impact" of authors for some time. Frequent citation of specific works has come to be interpreted as being suggestive of an author's impact upon a discipline (Baird and Oppenheim, 1994; Garfield, 1983; Garfield and Welljams-Dorof, 1992; MacRoberts and MacRoberts, 1996; Reedijk, 1998). One measure of an individual's productivity or impact should never be sufficient to make career-impacting decisions. In 2005, Hirsch proposed a "new" citation index to provide a measure of author productivity and impact: "I propose the index h, defined as the number of papers with citation number $\geq h$ as a useful index to characterize the scientific output of a researcher" (p. 16569). According to Jasco, "This means that an author with $h=16$ has 16 publications each of which received 16 or more citations. The h-index varies widely from discipline to discipline and even within disciplines and research areas" (2008, p. 785). The h-index has evidenced significant interest and debate (Vinkler, 2007), as it is tested and applied across disciplines; ISI Web of Knowledge reports the article was cited in 462 articles (February 15, 2010).

Measurement: Users and Uses

Research about users and uses of information may be the most complex area of interest to the librarian and other information professionals. The level of complexity should be evident by the terminology and its lack of clarity. What is meant by "users" and "uses" of information? It could be demonstrated that everyone "uses" information, and therefore, everyone is a "user" of information. In attempting to study uses and users, it became apparent that definition would be difficult (Pao, 1989).

In the most general context, users are the people who attempt to find information or use a document, its surrogate, or representatives. This constitutes an enormous and broad class for which actual research would have to be very clearly defined in each study. Consider the following: Would one expect the people in an academic library to have the same needs and interests as people in a public library or in a museum setting? In a high school setting, would one expect the information needs of the freshmen class to be the same as that of the senior class? One of the issues becomes how to define the users and what about the users may be contributory to the study. Allen (1969) railed against using generic classifications such as "scientists" when the subjects being studied were not research scientists, but rather technologists, and the two groups do not exhibit the same communication behaviors. Information and communication behavior are areas of interest in user studies because a user's membership in a group may contribute to the manner in which he or she selects, investigates, or applies information resources. One area of bibliometric research involves tracing the behaviors of certain users to determine how best to address their information requirements and how best to enhance the information systems they may use. What comprises information behaviors is any activity involved in identifying and/or attempting to satisfy an information desire, interest, or need. It is thought that users might be classified by some characteristic, such as membership in an economic, age, educational discipline, or other type of group. If users could be grouped in this manner, it has been assumed that studying the information behavior of a sample of such a group could reveal how to better satisfy their needs. Studying how pediatric dentists interact with certain web-based databases could aid researchers in designing better interfaces, improving organizational design and so on to serve pediatric dentists. Researching information behavior based on group characteristics assumes the group will be homogenous enough to have shared behaviors, information interpretations, and responses. How realistic is this?

Information behavior is affected by many factors. A study to identify which information resources were most commonly consulted by science and engineering faculty might suggest other sources that would be fruitful to them. However, there is evidence that information seeking is limited to what is readily accessible or nearby (Lange, 1987/1988). What is determined to be readily accessible is related to how critical the information is viewed, as in high-steel construction workers or pilots seeking weather details from federal weather sources, presumably because their lives depend upon accurate weather information. When the individuals felt the information was critical, they would invest more time and energy in obtaining it (Schamber, 1991). Researchers have found that the selection of sources for information is related to proximity or perceived ease of access; the measure of "ease"of access may be impacted by the sense of criticality. Experience with a source increased the likelihood of it being considered accessible, as did academic discipline and perceived utility. Travel distance required to access a source was a factor, with items physically at a distance considered less accessible than items in close proximity. On the electronic front, availability, location, and competition for access to a workstation was a consideration, as were personal experiences with a resource, personal comfort, and a sense of expertise with a system (Abels, Liebscher, and Denman, 1996). An earlier investigation examined information behaviors of library and information professionals who used email-distributed conferences for information seeking purposes. Problems with access were blamed for a low response rate, less than 6 percent, which also suggests that it might have been premature to explore a change of resource use based on the internet. However, the respondents indicated that the use of the econference systems did enhance information resources (Kovacs, Robinson, and Dixon, 1995). New methods of communication will require intense investigation to determine the behavior basis and implications; consider YouTube, Twitter, Facebook, MySpace, blogs, wikis, and whatever tomorrow may bring. Each technological system with different limitations and requirements attracts a variety of audiences, which then turn the tool into something else.

When undertaking user studies, one is trying to identify information behaviors—such as individuals' methods of seeking information, determining resources used, and detecting what influences the behaviors and resources—as well as any constraints that might contribute to the behavior. The idea of information need has been a thorn in settling on a definition as well. User studies to explore behavior often have to confront the phrase "information need" as part of the user's makeup and part of the user's need to use information. Studies of users' behaviors and information needs are often performed as surveys, questionnaires, and interviews. There has been use of documentary sources such as circulation records, citations, and content analysis as well. Even simulation and role playing have been used (Gorman, 1995; Rohde, 1986).

As electronic resources have increased, more energy has been spent on evaluating how information seekers use electronic resources and what the impact is on professional or scholarly activity (Kaminer and Braunstein, 1998; Spink, Robins, and Schamber, 1998). Allied to this is a growth in recognition of the importance of easy-to-use interfaces to information systems, whether online public access catalogs, vendored databases including Dialog and LexisNexis, or the internet. So the tools and the requisite skills of the user have become part of the concerns of user studies. This also includes cognitive tools and analytical techniques employed in selecting or applying information (Wang and White, 1999).

Retrieval involves the selection of information from a variety of sources. It also depends on the characteristics of both the seeker and potential source as well as all the handlers in between. How can a document be used if a potential user has no way to retrieve it? The user may not be able to frame the information request sufficiently to match the classification, cataloging, indexing, or other retrieval mechanism. Equally, the retrieval mechanism, the search agent, the classification, or the subject identifier selection may not be appropriately reflective of the document. The user and the uses are special cases in each individual setting, with contributing complications from every turn, not to mention all the many instances of human interaction.

Finding fruitful and meaningful ways to examine "users" and "uses," objects of information, creation and content is still very much developmental and dramatically impacted by new electronic resources with all the attendant complications. How to determine how users interact with traditional print materials has been difficult and has never been satisfactorily resolved. Why is one document selected over another? Is it dictated by the user's sense of relevance to the information need, or is it ease of access? How can this be evaluated? Is a document used if it is moved from a shelf and left on a reshelving cart? What is the measure of use? How is circulation indicative of use? Add to this electronic systems, and one wonders how user selection can be determined, measured, and evaluated. Documents are no longer mere pieces of paper, or papyrus, or stone tablets, but more mediums than previously imagined. As many ways as there are to define a user, there are also as many to define a use. Whether measuring either will yield any useful information depends on the quality of the criteria invoked and the clarity of the definitions employed. These objects and representations of information and communication being the documentation and literature of our times, seeking to describe them by measurements and comparisons may yield new information, new theories, or the basis for prediction. Keep in mind, however, that describing things, even with quantitative measures, does not always lead to understanding or meaningful results.

Summary

Bibliometrics may be used to measure and describe documents, surrogates, and even user behaviors. The act of description and measurement may reveal aspects of information units, which could be explored for other applications or interpretations. By measuring and evaluating features of information units, it may be possible to infer patterns of intellectual activity or interest. Tracing citations or co-citations may reveal research fronts, even disciplinary transformations. Applying measurement techniques does not ensure that there will be meaningful results, only that there may emerge new indicators of activity or areas to be reviewed. Bibliometrics opens a door and offers a path by which to examine components of the information and communication enigma.

References

Abels, E. G., Liebscher, P., and Denman, D. W. 1996. Factors that Influence the Use of Electronic Networks by Science and Engineering Faculty at Small Institutions. Part I. Queries. *Journal of the American Society for Information Science* 47(2):146–158.

Allen, T. J. 1969. Information Needs and Users. *Annual Review of Information Science and Technology* 4 (pp. 3–29).

Baird, L. M., and Oppenheim, C. 1994. Do Citations Matter? *Journal of Information Science* 20(1):2–15.

Borgman, C. L., and Furner, J. 2002. Scholarly Communication and Bibliometrics. In B. Cronin (Ed.) *Annual Review of Information Science and Technology* 36 (pp. 3–72). Medford, NJ: Information Today.

Bradford, S. C. 1948. *Documentation*. London: Crosby Lockwood.

Bradford, S. C. 1948. The Documentary Chaos. *Documentation*. 106–121. London: Crosby Lockwood. Reprinted in A. J. Meadows (Ed.), *The Origins of Information Science* 142–157. London: Institute of Information Scientists and Taylor Graham, 1987. Foundations of Information Science, vol. 1. Series Editor B. Cronin.

Brookes, S. C. December 6, 1969. Bradford's Law and the Bibliography of Science. *Nature* 224 (5223):953–956.

Buckland, M. 1991. *Information and Information Systems*. New York: Praeger.

Calhoun, C. C. 1995. Serials Citations and Holdings Correlation. *Library Resources & Technical Services* 39(1):53–76.

Campanario, J. M. 1996. Have Referees Rejected Some of the Most-Cited Articles of All Times? *Journal of the American Society for Information Science* 47(4):302–310.

Chen, H., Chung, Y., Ramsey, M., and Yang, C. C. 1998. A Smart Itsy Bitsy Spider for the Web. *Journal of the American Society for Information Science* 49(7):604–618.

Chowdhury, G. G. Summer 1999. Template Mining for Information Extraction from Digital Documents. *Library Trends* 48(1):182–208.

Dumas, T. 1993. In Focus: Using Citation Analysis and Subject Classification to Identify and Monitor Trends Within a Discipline. In *Integrating Technologies: Converging Professions. Proceedings of the 56th Annual Meeting of the American Society for Information Science, October 24–28, Columbus, OH* 30:135–150.

Fayyad, U. 1996. Data Mining and Knowledge Discovery: Making Sense Out of Data. *IEEE Expert* 11(5):20–25.

Fayyad, U., Piatetsky-Shapiro, G., and Smyth, P. 1996. From Data Mining to Knowledge Discovery in Databases. *Ai Magazine* 17(3):37–54.

Fernandez-Alles, M., and Ramos-Rodriguez, A. 2009. Intellectual Structure of Human Resources Management Research: A Bibliometric Analysis of the Journal Human Resource Management, 1985–2005. *Journal of the American Society for Information Science and Technology* 60(1):161–175.

Furner, J. August 2007. User Tagging of Library Resources: Toward a Framework for System Evaluation. World Library and Information Congress: 73rd IFLA General Conference and Council "Libraries for the Future: Progress, Development and Partnerships." 19–23 August 2007, Durban, South Africa. Retrieved February 15, 2010, from archive.ifla.org/lV/ifla73/papers/157-Furner-en.pdf

Garfield, E. 1983. How to Use Citation Analysis for Faculty Evaluation, and When Is It Relevant? Part 1 and 2. *Essays of an Information Scientist* 6:354–362, 363–372.

Garfield, E., and Welljams-Dorof, A. 1992. Citation Data: Their Use as Quantitative Indicators for Science and Technology Evaluation and Policy-making. *Science & Public Policy* 19(5):321–327.

Gorman, P. N. 1995. Information Needs of Physicians. *Journal of the American Society for Information Science* 46(10):729–736.

Hirsch, J. E. 2005. An Index to Quantify an Individual's Scientific Research Output. *Proceedings of the National Academy of Science* 102(46):16569–16572. Retrieved February 15, 2010, from www.pnas.org/content/102/46/16569.full.pdf+html

Jasco, P. 2008. Testing the Calculation of a Realistic *h*-index in Google Scholar, Scopus, and Web of Science for F. W. Lancaster. In *The Evaluation and Transformation of Information Systems: Essays Honoring the Legacy of F. W. Lancaster*. Lorraine J. Haricombe and Keith Russell, eds. *Library Trends* 56(4):784–815.

Kaminer, N., and Braunstein, Y. M. 1998. Bibliometric Analysis of the Impact of Internet Use on Scholarly Productivity. *Journal of the American Society for Information Science* 49(8):720–730.

Koppel, M., Schier, J., and Argamon, S. 2009. Computational Methods in Authorship Attribution. *Journal of the American Society for Information Science and Technology* 60(1):9–26.

Kousha, K., and Thelwall, M. 2007. How Is Science Cited on the Web? A Classification of Google Unique Web Citations. *Journal of the American Society for Information Science and Technology* 58(11):1631–1644.

Kovacs, D. K., Robinson, K. L., and Dixon, J. 1995. Scholarly E-Conference on the Academic Networks: How Library and Information Science Professionals Use Them. *Journal of the American Society for Information Science* 46(4):244–253.

Lange, J. M. 1987/1988. Public Library Users, Nonusers, and Type of Library Use. *Public Library Quarterly* 8(1/2):49–67.

Lewis, D. D., and Jones, K. S. 1996. Natural Language Processing for Information Retrieval. *Communications of the ACM* 39(1):92–101.

Losee, R. M., and Haas, S. W. 1995. Sublanguage Terms: Dictionaries, Usage, and Automatic Classification. *Journal of the American Society for Information Science* 46(7):519–529.

Lotka, A. J. 1926. The Frequency Distribution of Scientific Productivity. *Journal of the Washington Academy of Science* 16(12):317–323. Reprinted in A. J. Meadows (Ed.), *The Origins of Information Science*. 113–119. London: Taylor Graham and Institute of Information Scientists. 1987. *Foundations of Information Science*, Vol. 1. Series Editor B. Cronin.

Luzon, M. J. 2009. Scholarly Hyperwriting: The Function of Links in Academic Weblogs. *Journal of the American Society for Information Science and Technology* 60(1):75–89.

MacRoberts, M. H., and MacRoberts, B. R. 1996. Problems of Citation Analysis. *Scientometrics*. 36(3):435–444.

Pao, M. L. 1989. *Concepts of Information Retrieval*. Englewood, CO: Libraries Unlimited.

Reedijk, J. 1998. Sense and Nonsense of Science Citation Analyses: Comments on the Monopoly Position of ISI and Citation Inaccuracies. Risk of Possible Misuse and Biased Citation and Impact Data. *New Journal of Chemistry* 767–770.

Rohde, N. F. 1986. Information Needs. *Advances in Librarianship* 14:49–73.

Schamber, L. 1991. User's Criteria for Evaluation in Multimedia Information Seeking and Use Situations. Unpublished Doctoral Dissertation. Syracuse University.

Smith, L. 1981. Citation Analysis. *Library Trends* 30(Summer):83–106.

Spink, A., Robins, D., and Schamber, L. 1998. Use of Scholarly Book Reviews: Implications for Electronic Publishing and Scholarly Communication. *Journal of the American Society for Information Science* 49(4):364–374.

Stieger, S., Reips, U., and Voracek, M. 2007. Forced-Response in Online Surveys: Bias from Reactance and an Increase in Sex-Specific Dropout. *Journal of the American Society for Information Science and Technology* 58(11):1652–1660.

Taylor, A. G. 1999. *The Organization of Information*. Englewood, CO: Libraries Unlimited.

Tsay, M-Y. 1998. Library Journal Use and Citation Half-Life in Medical Science. *Journal of the American Society for Information Science* 49(14):1283–1292.

van der Wurff, B. March 1997. Out of Particles. Centre for Science and Technology Studies (CWTS). [online, April 1999] Retrieved February 15, 2010, from sahara.fsw. leidenuniv.nl/cwts/noframes/cernintr.html

Vickery, B. C., and Vickery, A. 1987. *Information Science in Theory and Practice*. London: Butterworth.

Vinkler, P. 2007. Eminence of Scientists in Light of the *h*-index and Other Scientometric Indicators. *Journal of Science* 33:481–491.

Wang, P., and White, M. D. 1999. A Cognitive Model of Document Use during a Research Project. Study II. Decisions at the Reading and Citing Stage. *Journal of the American Society for Information Science* 46(4):244–253.

White, H. D., and McCain, K. W. 1989. Bibliometrics. In M. E. Williams (Ed.). *Annual Review of Information Science and Technology* 24:119–186.

Wiebe, J., Hirst, G., and Horton, D. 1996. Language Use in Context. *Communications of the ACM* 39(1):102–111.

Chapter 10

Information Economics

Melanie J. Norton

Traditionally, information economics has focused on information products and processes, evaluating the efficiency of information transfer systems as processes of input, output, and added value or scrutinizing an economic transaction to ascertain equity (King, Roderer, and Olsen, 1983). Another view of information economics depicts the impetus of information and its related technology as affecting economic, social, political, and cultural constructs the world over, not just within the framework of processes and products but as symptomatic of a cycle of information and knowledge growth (Castells, 1993; Tapscott, 1996). To discuss information economics, there are several concepts that require examination. First, information has dramatic economic implications. This is the information age, or information economy, with stakeholders, participants with something to risk, not entirely unlike other economic periods. Second, there are characteristics of economics that are important in the discussion of the information age, such as resources and uncertainty. Third, concerns about the assignment of value and assessment of cost are central to information economics. Fourth, and last here, though not last in the larger discipline, the combination of economics and information significantly impacts decision making in organizations and hence organizational information behaviors. This chapter will address each of the first two components at a rudimentary level, while the third and fourth areas will be covered in separate chapters. An explanation of the use of models as used in a variety of disciplines will supplement this chapter and provide a foundation for posing some information and economic models. The rationale for venturing into this arena in an introductory text is simply that the concepts of economics pertinent to information and the area of information economics will only continue to grow and acquire more importance to the information professions. Accepting this as the case is the first step in recognizing where the information professions may lead.

Economics

Economics in the broadest sense may be considered the activities undertaken to provide for the satisfaction of desires. As such, the study of economics has created theories and models to explain the activities, to examine the functions and interactions, and to delineate the character of economic systems. Economic systems are structures, or a series of structures, through which interactions occur that contribute to the satisfaction of desires (Redman and Redman, 1981). In general, economics is based on two related activities: production and consumption. Production is the creation of items to be consumed, and consumption is the obtaining, typically through purchase or barter, of the items produced. However, consumption may also refer to the use of resources. Resources are the materials—land, labor, and capital—that are used in production. There is a cycle implied in these activities that is rooted in the resources. Economics as a study is interested in "principles governing the allocation of scarce means among competing ends when the objectives of the allocation are to maximize the attainment of those ends" (p. 1). Scarce means are resources. In economics, resources are considered scarce "because they are limited, all uses cannot be satisfied at the same time" (p. 1). There are only so many dollars in a budget, only so much space in a building, only so much land available to grow certain crops. All of these could be considered scarce resources because they are limited in availability and can be used for only one action at a time. Certain resources, such as air, stand outside of this assertion since air is not considered scarce and is therefore considered to have a zero value in economics. However, other thoughts in the area of resources have turned up a new variant: information.

Information may be considered a resource, albeit an unusual one, because it is not scarce in the traditional sense. Information can be applied in more than one situation, is not readily containable, is easily transported, and exhibits characteristics that are not within the traditional model of resources. Information can be compressed and summarized. Information can be used in place of other types of resources; robots working on factory lines instead of people is one example of information replacing labor (Cleveland, 1982). Further, information in certain cases can be considered a commodity, an article of trade, an item for consumption (Cleveland, 1982; Schiller, 1988). Innovations in technology, specifically electronics, telecommunications, computer, and related information system components, have influenced the manner in which human beings undertake both economic and social activities. The resulting changes have modified the economic structures previously accepted and are indicative of significant and continued transformations on a global scale for some time to come. The traditional basis of economics, as previously defined, is rooted in production and consumption based on resource scarcity, demand, supply, and exchange; it has become more complex as the attributes of information and its technologies become more integrated into the economy (Castells, 1993; Cleveland, 1982).

The Information Economy

It has long been established that information and its related industries and activities are critical to expanding the economic components of the United States and the global economy (Black and Marchand, 1982; Carnoy, Castells, Cohen, and Cardoso, 1993; Cleveland, 1982; Cooper, 1983; Lamberton, 1984; Lanvin, 1995; Porter and Millar, 1985; Robinson, 1986; and Rubin and Sapp, 1981). Researchers around the world have concluded that information and its industries are economic entities with significant current and future prospective for economic growth and power (Goodman, 1987; Lanvin, 1995; Nora and Minc, 1980). Over the last three decades, it has become evident that economic growth in traditional sectors, such as agriculture, manufacturing, and trade, is dramatically and intrinsically bound to the capacity to use information and its technologies competitively. Improved information resources such as faster and more accurate weather forecasting, more detailed soil analysis, new insight into erosion control, stock feed formulation, and more efficient farm machinery contribute enormously to the agricultural productivity of the United States. The National Agricultural Statistics Services (NASS) Year 2000 Readiness report indicated 32 percent of farmers in the United States were using computerized systems. The automated farm systems in use included recordkeeping; irrigation; feeding systems; storage systems for grain, vegetables or produce; milking machines; milk storage; heating, cooling, and ventilation for livestock; and global positioning systems (National Agricultural Statistics Services, 1999). By 2009, 69 percent of farms earning $250,000 were using computers; farms earning less than $100,000 reported only 38 percent using computers (United States Department of Agriculture, 2009). Manufacturing and industry use information technology to improve timeline estimates on projects and to enhance competitiveness by saving money for customers by meeting or beating deadlines (Villano, 1999). Use of better gathering and implementation of information from point-of-sale by large retailers improves product purchasing, helps maintain balanced inventory, identifies regional product preferences and customer profiles, and produces real savings by having the appropriate products in the right places in the correct quantities. This information flow leads to greater customization of factory orders to serve particular retailers or wholesalers. In turn, this enables better factory floor project management and market sensitive production. All of these are improved supply chain practices that save time and money by having production activities in sync with demand, as well as putting materials in regions where they are known to be marketable (Caldwell and Violino, 1999; Engler, 1999; and Stein and Sweat, 1998). The actual enterprises involved in the creation, accumulation, application, and manipulation of information, as well as its related technologies and related offspring, are actually economically productive in ways not previously recognized (Castells, 1993).

Just as there was a significant number of laborers working in the agricultural sector who shifted to the industrial sector and its factories in the 19th and early 20th centuries, in the second half of the 20th century, labor has shifted from agriculture and factories into the service, knowledge, or information sectors. This movement into offices, sometimes into virtual ones, and a variety of service positions has been the result of changing technology, especially in the area of information exchange, telecommunications, and automation. The manner in which factories operate has been changed by automation, and the management of those facilities has been modified by information exchange and telecommunications. Decisions are based on information from agents in distant places and are no longer restricted by limited communication facilities (Castells, 1993). Information that provides insight into corporate conduct influences the value of stocks, managerial portfolios, and public image. The underlying infrastructures of governments and economies are being impacted as a result of increasing communications potential and larger and more diverse markets (Bar, 1995; Garcia, 1995; and Nicolaidis, 1995). Providing access to the new multiple layers of information has weighed upon the budgets of libraries and educational and research organizations (Henderson, 1999). New technology spawns new opportunities, new challenges, and more new technology.

The information economy has the potential and impetus to dramatically change the globe. This is not to suggest that it is an evenly distributed or balanced phenomena, because it is not. In the United States, there are distinct economic borders that separate people into technology haves and have-nots. In 1997, the distribution of U.S. households owning computers was only 35 percent. These statistics were skewed toward higher ownership based upon level of education: 65.6 percent of owners had attended graduate school, 56.2 percent were college graduates, and 22.5 percent were high school graduates. Ethnically, of the 35 percent owning computers, 48 percent were Asian, 35 percent were white, and 17 percent were black (Monthly Labor Review, 1999). In contrast, the Digital Futures Project Report 2009 revealed that only 15 percent of homes did not have computers (USC Annenberg School for Communication, 2009). U.S. Census data available on computer ownership stops at 2003; questions specifically asking about computer ownership were not asked in 2007 or later, but rather inquiries focused on internet access. The U.S. Census reported that, in 2003, 62 percent of homes had computers and 55 percent of homes had internet access (United States Census Bureau, 2009). By 2007, 62 percent of households had internet access, but distribution of access was still influenced by educational and ethnic background. Of those with bachelor's degrees, 88 percent had internet access while only 32 percent of those with less than a high school degree had access (United States Census Bureau, 2007). Ethnic distribution had a similar pattern as the 1997 numbers: 80 percent were Asian, 70 percent were white, 54 percent were black, and 53 percent were Hispanic

(United States Census Bureau, 2009). There are people and nations with limited access to the fiscal resources required to support a high-tech economy. Despite media hype, there are still large portions of the globe with serious infrastructure concerns that limit or impact technological access, such as poor transportation systems for materials or electronics; insufficient educational tools to promote technological development; and a dozen other more pressing human needs such as food, housing, and safety (Garson, 1995). There are also serious cultural implications as the information age and economy indiscriminately disseminate the advertising and cultural icons of the nations with sophisticated broadcast systems, radio, television, satellite, and internet (Haywood, 1995). This is not to diminish the importance of the information economy but to remind us that there are positive and negative aspects to this creature, and it will have far-reaching economic and social effects that should not be overlooked.

Stakeholders

Ultimately, the information age has the potential to affect everyone on the planet in some way and thereby in the broadest sense, it will make everyone a stakeholder. In a smaller sense, the technological information evolution is certainly impacting participants in both developed nations and emerging economies. Direct stakeholders include telecommunications industries, which may optionally hold the most sway over future development, along with the computer hardware and software manufacturers; the industrial sector, now dependent upon automation and information for efficiency and the appearance of cost savings; the research industry in any field, bound to the past and the future by the information technology and the impact of its economies; governments of all levels; and people who have access to information resources and the information economy and those who do not yet, and might not ever. The stakeholders all have something to gain or to lose related to their willingness and their current ability to risk. Their abilities are based on what their economic resources are, what fiscal or fiscally comparable things they have to invest, and how well they can move that investment into growth, or at least stability.

Corporations, small businesses, nonprofits, educational, and governmental bodies are all stakeholders. To fully explore the notion of stakeholders, consider a business that produces computer chips. If its research and development department fails to keep current with changing technology and changing design methods, or lacks creativity, the product will become obsolete within 18 months. If the product is considered obsolete, fewer products will be purchased; if this cycle goes too far, the business will fail. Everyone who worked for the business is out of work, and everyone who relied on those workers to buy goods from them (e.g., restaurants, car dealers, grocery stores) suffers a loss of income. If there is not a resolution, at least partial, a cycle of economic downturn occurs, and all the stakeholders become very apparent because everyone who is affected is a stakeholder. The level of stakeholders' involvement may vary. This is a large view of stakeholders; more often a smaller view is easier to comprehend. In the smaller view, the backers and workers of business and their direct contacts would be the stakeholders.

Resources

Traditional economic resources are "means of supplying what is needed" (Allen, 1984, p. 636), and these resources are considered limited, which contributes to a value system for exchange of resources. Silver, an ore, is a natural resource with limited availability in nature and enormous usefulness in society. It is a component of a variety of medical, photographic, and pharmaceutical materials, as well as being treasured as a precious metal. This resource has a physical, tangible character, which is also finite; it is possible to extract all of the usable silver ore from the Earth. When that happens, the value of the mined ore, as well as the value of the objects containing this ore, will increase as the silver becomes more scarce. Alternatively, finding resources to replace silver in critical products would decrease the demand and possibly prevent an ore crisis. One of the ways to determine whether there are alternatives for silver in various processes and products for which it is used requires research into the aspects of the ore and its handling that makes it useful. Such research involves significant investigation of the ore, its properties, its uses, and any related metals or materials that might be used as substitutes.

Modern information technologies, computer analysis systems, measurement devices, databases, chemical analysis methods, and information-based tools provide avenues for the exploration of alternatives to tangible scarce resources. Information is a resource in that it contributes to satisfying needs and desires, but it is very different in most other aspects. Tangible, physical resources, such as ore, lumber, machines, equipment, land, minerals, gems, are limited as in scarce; they can be depleted and diminished. A truck can be in only one place at a time and can be used for one activity at a time, and these tangible things cannot be held by more than one person at a time. These are not the characteristics of information. According to Cleveland (1982), information is expandable, that is, all the information is never fully acquired, information grows, it compounds upon itself, and it is added to over time; it is not scarce. (However, the volume of information available can actually make usable information nearly inaccessible, but this is not entirely the same as being totally depleted as an ore might become.) Just as information is expandable, it is also compressible; its formats can be modified, can be distilled, abstracted, and summarized, as into a formula. There will be some loss of information with such compression. It is not possible to compress a truck, or an ore, in the same manner.

The application of information can be used to substitute for resources, such as new information about silver alternatives or substituting automation for human labor. Information may be transported at the speed of light. Information is diffusive; it spreads, it changes, and it has been the greatest threat to oppressive governments. Information can be conveyed via a commercial, a photo, a body language expression, or hidden in the words of a novel or a newspaper. Information is shareable, unlike tangible goods. If someone is given a ring, the giver no longer has the ring, only the receiver; if someone is given an idea, both the giver and receiver have the idea. Additionally, the receiver may be able to improve upon the idea, expand it, and find a new application for it. These differences make information a unique resource, which can and does modify how we function with both tangible and intangible resources and virtually every aspect of our economic and cultural endeavors (Cleveland, 1982).

Uncertainty

The concept of uncertainty is integral across the spectrum of economic theories, especially in the areas of decision making, organizational theory, theory of finance, risk aversion (insurance theory), game theory, price theory, and even equilibrium theory (McCall, 1982). The works of Kenneth J. Arrow, J. Marschak, and R. Radner in the description and application of the notions of uncertainty have had profound effects on the field of economics. Indeed, the work of these individuals did much to bring the concept of uncertainty into virtually all areas of economic study (McCall, 1982; Heller, Starr, and Starrett, 1986).

What is uncertainty? What is its role in information economics? Arrow defined information as "the negative measure of uncertainty" (Arrow, 1984). Stated alternatively, lack of information is the measure of uncertainty. As Arrow points out, while there are theoretical quantifications for uncertainty (for use in mathematical modeling of economics activities primarily, such as decision making), there is no well-established quantitative measure for information. Arrow concedes, however, that while Shannon's measure of information does not provide a value for information, it may be applicable in determining the cost of acquisition of information. Despite the lack of measures applicable to information, the concept of uncertainty is simply the lack of information that might be pertinent to the economic activity at hand.

The concept of uncertainty is usually represented by applications of probabilities, that is, the likelihood of x condition, or outcome, occurring. We must consider this for the sake of analysis and discussion; economists have typically chosen to use models and methods that permit them to obtain a result, regardless of the actual parameters of the issue under study. Arrow emphasizes this in his discussion of Decision Theory. "There is no point in posing a problem for which we cannot find the solution, so we tend to modify our formulation of the problem in order to make it practical" (1984, p. 56). This usually means eliminating those aspects of a situation from a model that are difficult to measure or to evaluate. This view strengthens the application of uncertainty as a probability function as it permits economists, and those engaged in economic decision making, to establish artificial parameters to the probability. These parameters are easily viewed through Teams and Game Theory, that is, as rules to the game (Phlips, 1988).

In various situations, the information that might reduce uncertainty is also an issue of uncertainty and is as critical as the information itself (Arrow, 1984; Green and Laffont, 1986; Rothschild, 1986). Consider uncertainty about game rules or the lack of adequate definition of the parameters. If "rules include the set of payoffs, the set of strategies and the number of players," then an example is "An auction in which the bidders do not know what value the other bidders attach to the auctioned object ..."; this means that the "players do not know each others' payoffs" (Phlips, 1988, p. 9). This problem of uncertainty about parameters is handled by redefinition of the game so that each player knows the possibility of a result, in this case the payoff parameter "that is uncertain" (p. 9).

Two inferences can be drawn from the discussion so far. First, it is necessary for modeling and analytical reasons to establish artificial parameters to cope with uncertainty. Second, establishing such artificial parameters may contribute to uncertainty. By substituting additional probabilistic properties for information, the information available to reduce uncertainty may be diminished. The underlying assumption that permits multiple substitution of probabilities for information is that each of the players is now operating from the same substitutions, thereby replacing not only missing information (the quality of uncertainty) but also equalizing the playing field in submission to equilibrium theory (Newman, 1983).

Suppose there are four card players using a single 52-card deck, and the object of the game is to obtain groups of four matching cards, regardless of suit. Each player may first draw five cards, then after that, each player may draw one card and keep it or return it to the deck face down. First, all four players are aware that there are 20 cards in hand, which means there are only 32 cards in the deck. There are 13 possible sets of four cards. This information provides each player with the possibility of pulling the cards needed from the deck as they play. If cards are returned to the deck face down, then each player, as he or she takes a turn, learns a new card, gains information, while the other three players do not; however, the balance of uncertainty is maintained because each of the three players also gains card knowledge in the process of their turns. The balance is slightly changed if the returned card is returned face up because then all the players have the same information at the same time about the new card. However, some uncertainty remains because each player still holds his or her own unique cards, which the other players do not know about. Over the course of the game, as more cards are revealed, uncertainty will decrease. Depending on the rules of the game and the deck, the players can devise ways to estimate the tolerable level of risk taking to achieve a desired outcome. When rules are unclear, or circumstances can be modified without all the players being aware of the changes, then information inequity occurs and the playing field is not level.

Information economics is concerned with the effects that information (uncertainty reduction) or the lack of information (uncertainty) can generate (Arrow,

1984). Essentially, information economics attempts to take into account the variations created by the presence, absence, extent, and distribution of information in economic structures. Some of the characteristics of information (Cleveland, 1982), such as its expandability, work to undermine equilibrium or balance. For example, in the redefinition of the game, applying agreed-upon probabilities in substitution for areas of uncertainty could actually provide information for one of the players. When card players agree that one-eyed jacks will be wild cards, they are substituting probabilities that increase the likelihood of more wild cards, which increases uncertainty (Myerson, 1986). The game returns to a state of disequilibrium caused by an imbalance in uncertainty distribution, which is a violation of the validity of the probability substitutions for the uncertainty variant.

The tradition of research in uncertainty as a component of information economics continues to adhere to the use of the models where uncertainty is replaced by probabilistic structures. The research covers the areas of game theory, decision making, organizational theory, risk aversion (insurance theory), and finance theory, among many others. Newer works continue to apply the traditional models of uncertainty, as well as other traditional models of economics, to issues of cost consideration in information production, information evaluation, planning and information, and cost-benefit analysis of information, to name a few (King, Roderer, and Olsen, 1983; Kingma, 1996). Until new models or approaches are devised, the replacement of uncertainty variants with probabilistic structures will continue. This is not necessarily irrational, since even these models provide information about uncertainty aspects by virtue of their failings (Arrow, 1984).

Models

As we seek to better understand the world around us, we attempt to create imitations of our world, of circumstances, systems, organisms, ourselves, and our societies. From these imitations, which are usually more simplistic representations of our perceptions, we attempt to extrapolate further information about the world. This imitation is not limited to attempts to duplicate or even simulate an arena of study; rather, it includes attempts to apply forms and imagination to an arena that is not typically viewed in the light of the imitative form we may choose. The application of Shannon and Weaver's (1949) theory of information transfer, a statistically based examination of the flow of electronic signals and noise in a telecommunication structure, to the more general and nonelectronic transfer of information among individuals would be such a case (Wilkin, 1977). The initial intention of their work was to find ways to estimate the amount of signal necessary to overcome unintended signals in the conducting channels to ensure clarity of communication. This notion was seized upon in other fields as the basis for the sender-channel-receiver model considered essential to understanding human communication and information behavior.

The imitations are referred to as models. Models have been used by physical scientists for centuries as ways of representing the world, even the universe, while attempting to use the models as a means of explaining and understanding phenomena. Admittedly, many models were flawed, limited at their inception by the limitations of the era and the men who envisioned them. Aristotle's and Ptolemy's geocentric systems, which placed the Earth as the center of the universe, are classical flawed models yet were held as truth for centuries. Even when Copernicus set forth a new model with the Sun as the center of the universe, his model demanded planetary motion be perfectly circular. Kepler ultimately resolved some of the contradictions that circular planetary motion demonstrated, but longingly persisted in modeling the universe on a geometric model of nested polyhedrons. Many of the models that were proposed were heavily influenced by the political and religious climates of the time. Even Kepler was seeking some spiritual force in the motion of the planets, some higher order of mystical comprehension of the unknown (Boorstin, 1983). Those models, though far short of what is now understood, led ultimately to knowledge today.

Social sciences have lagged behind in modeling. Many of the models used in the physical sciences are mathematically based. It has taken considerable time and debate to bring mathematical structures into the social sciences. Moreover, it has taken time to recognize that modeling need not be entirely math-based; models may be exploratory structures that encourage inquiry and speculation. Models do not have to be static, nor are models the solution to issues but rather a method for examining issues.

The intent of this section is to look at models and the issues surrounding models relative to the social sciences. There will be a brief exploration of model history with some applications of models to issues in the library and information field. Models hold tremendous potential as diagnostic and test tools in the practical and theoretical work of library and information science.

Debating Models in Social Science

In 1967, a symposium on the Process of Model-Building in the Behavioral Sciences was conducted at Ohio State University. The symposium was to discuss the process of model building, and as such, it had to engage in a certain amount of definition. The underlying premise that undefined models are often accepted without explanation as accurate approaches to problems was a topic of serious concern. The participants attempted to discourse upon the activities and criteria that should be undertaken in model building. What ensued was an enlightening collection of diverse views that underlines the continuing conflict about the construction and role of models.

Stogdill (1970) considered models to be the same as theories but only shorter lived. Stogdill suggested that models should be based in scientific method with problems conceptualized logically and empirically. Moreover, he saw model building as a creative process that is not clearly understood. Luce (1970) described models as atheoretic, that is, methods for testing isolated properties of a theory, which may not be adequately representative of the theory. Atheoretic models are employed as a mechanism for exploring subsets of a theory; the results may or may not be expandable beyond the original subset. Ashby (1970) contended that models are constructs devised to approximate a portion of a real system for the purpose of convenience and the reduction of information that is inherent in the creation of the artifice. For the purposes of investigation, Ashby accepted models as useful and legitimate tools if scientific methods of analysis appropriate to the problem under study were applied. In the framework of appropriate scientific analysis, Ashby perceived the value of a model as directly related to its ability to reflect the real world. The strength of that reflection is being demonstrated via the model's ability to be tested and its trueness to the system being modeled. Morris (1970) submitted that models need not be part of reality but rather distinct from reality. The abstract model is developed into a state that reflects reality through a process of testing (whether the model is adequately descriptive of the problem) and through the ability to treat the model as a deductive tool. Morris' notion of models suggested the use of analogy drawn from established precepts. Morris further indicated that while fields such as engineering have many prior models to work from, the emerging sciences do not. C. West Churchman took exception to all the above characterizations of models. He questioned whether it was appropriate to model reality, since the model could only be a subset and could not take into account "the real world which is very complex and largely unknown" (1970, p. 135). Yet, as Churchman pointed out, people want to draw from this unknown to create an artifice by which to study the unknown. Churchman contended that reality should be "all the relevant challenges of the model" (p. 137), and he quotes E. A. Singer: "Reality is the repository of all unanswered questions." Churchman proposed that models are built in direct response to questions and are the result of an organized trial and error system attempting to respond to a question.

A synthesis of all of these opinions offers the best available description of models. Models are investigative tools. The reliability, acceptability, and validity of the results of the application of these tools should be suspect as we are investigating unknowns from various perspectives. At the same time, the usefulness and creative stimulation that models offer should not be underestimated. Models that adhere to scientific methodology based on accepted scientific theories and laws might, from a scientific point of view, be considered superior to models composed without proper foundation in the known. However, if models were limited to the known, there would be little point to using them at all (Churchman, 1970). It is in exploration that models are useful, but models are merely tools and do not prove nor disprove. It is essential to be aware of the shortcomings and appropriate application of these tools whether they are grounded in fact or fiction, or a mixture of both.

Applying Models

Models do not necessarily need to spring from the known, but they should be designed and applied with some rigor to secure their usefulness. This can be extremely difficult. The application of models can be divided between those that are testable, in the scientific sense, and those that are not. John Maynard Smith (1982) contrasted simple models used for creative impetus or investigation versus models dealing with critical areas that might directly affect lives. Modeling the breakdown of a nuclear reactor demands more attention to detail and reality than modeling a web engine information exchange. In applying various game theory models to evolutionary behaviors, Smith took great pains to detail the structure of the models: the assumptions, strategies, and limitations, which the design of the model and his applications of them imposed. The use of game theory models was an opportunity to explore a problem from a different viewpoint; basically, two models are better than one. But this conclusion can only be drawn because of prior analysis that was undertaken before bringing in the game theory model. Smith used the models as methods of testing and attempting to predict certain outcomes, but he did not use the models as the definitive result, rather as a path to inquiry. Specific shortcomings of a model should be clarified at the outset to ensure there is no confusion about the expectations and the potential extrapolations of the results. For example, applying game theory models to biological systems would entail specifying how the model cannot work and what assumptions or implied circumstances are involved. By stating the assumptions and design of the models that Smith proposed to employ in his inquiry, he gave those who would study his work a method for evaluating, criticizing, and replicating, or even modifying, his models with new information. The foundations of modern science rely upon such capacities. That Smith managed to arrange his models with such formality relies upon an aspect of models that Ashby (1970) pointed out: Models allow for the reduction of information. A model need not encompass all the complexities of the phenomenon it represents; rather, the model permits the extraction of parts for examination. As long as the fact that the model is not a total representation of the phenomenon is recognized, fruitful exploration may result. It is when the model is supposed or reported to be fully representative in every way of the phenomenon under consideration that grave pseudo-information is produced.

Models and Information

Models are employed in a variety of settings concerned with information. Information retrieval models based on computer-implemented retrieval tend to be categorized as traditional or interactive. The traditional model, the initial evolution of computer retrieval, resulted from the limitations of the machine. Retrieval activities were based on primitive matching algorithms that depended on the quality of the record surrogate and the capacity of the system to manipulate the records. This yielded results that were often completely disconnected from the actual search interest. Studying this retrieval scenario led to the recognition that relevance was an important but overlooked (or under-computed) aspect of successful retrieval (Spink, 1997). Users of systems such as Dialog developed techniques to improve the relevance of retrieval by progressively refining their searches. This weighing of results, seeking after more items that are similar to the ones selected for the second run, when put into a machine algorithm produced an automatic retrieval system. This is a relevance feedback method and was strongly based upon what the user deemed as relevant. Variations of this model continue to this day.

A newer model is developing that allows for interactive feedback on a variety of measures; preliminary research with this approach suggests important advantages. Multiple types of interactive feedback may significantly improve search results. It is evident that the cognitive involvement in the interactive model provides more feedback opportunities than a single automatic relevance conducted through direct programming (Spink, 1997). By creating a system upon which to test the retrieval process, a model produces results that can be explored using as many configurations as the researcher can imagine and justify.

Case study models are another tactic for examining issues. A common case study model usually involves reference desk questions or difficult patron queries. Aluri (1993) points out that the reference setting is actually a single element in a much larger system and may be impacted by a list of variables, ranging from physical environment to conflicting philosophies and practices. To model a reference interview or to construct a method for evaluating reference work would entail accounting for all the variables and how they interact with the ability of the reference personnel to perform. Setting a scene with various scripts to work out the best way to handle a situation could be a powerful model. It is also possible to extend these types of models by using actual documented occurrences and reenacting them to determine if an alternative solution could have changed the result. It is also a way to explore all the possible options for situations before they come to pass; this could provide important input to policy design. Recognizing the complexity of a situation may be the primary result of attempting to devise a testable model.

Models in an Economics Context

Modeling may be adventurous and creative, but these limitations imposed on the model must be clear or extrapolations that lead to confusion are created. One such case would be Harlan Cleveland's (1982) discussion of information as a resource in an economic sense. In economics, resources are considered scarce "because they are limited, all uses cannot be satisfied at the same time" (Redman and Redman, 1981, p. 1). Certain resources, such as air, stand outside of this assertion since air is not considered scarce and is therefore considered to have a zero value in economics. According to Cleveland, information may be considered a resource, albeit an unusual one, because it is not scarce in the traditional sense; it can be applied in more than one situation, is not readily containable, and exhibits characteristics that are not within the traditional model of resources. Further, information in certain cases can be considered a commodity, an article of trade, or an item for consumption (Cleveland, 1982; Schiller, 1988). How information is evaluated in economics may depend upon which economic approach is applied. Hence, a model must be clarified to be fully explored. But to clarify the model, a further venture into economics is required.

There are two primary approaches to economics. One of these is macroeconomics, which concerns itself with studying the components of a system as a whole, or an average, rather than the individual parts. Macroeconomics tries to examine and to investigate the relationships and interactions among these aggregate entities (Redman and Redman, 1981).

For example, government policies concerned with large groups, such as policies governing the telecommunications industry, would be a macroeconomic topic. Essentially, macroeconomics considers the larger economic system by focusing on national economics, or global economics, or on entire industries in collective. The interrelationships of the various components of the economy are critical to the macro view. Macroeconomic models are built to imitate the larger economy as well as the relationships among the components that construct the economy.

Another approach is microeconomic, or the study "of the individual firm and industry" (Redman and Redman, 1981, p. 7). It examines wages, prices, and income in a particular firm or unit setting. Microeconomics is concerned with the specifics of the individual units that comprise the economy. The study of microeconomics approaches economic analysis through the examination of the firm or the market, outside of the confines of the larger economy (Redman and Redman, 1981).

Whether from a macroeconomic or microeconomic view, working with models affects the perspective of analysis; the models are predominately the same, merely adjusted to reflect the larger or smaller extrapolation that will be generated. Both approaches use idealized, generalized, and abstracted perfect structure models that are supposed to be representative of the economic entity under study. Information from a general macroeconomic view would be a national policy issue, a resource, and potentially an interrelationship in the formulation of macro outcome. In a microeconomic view, information may be a resource or a commodity, and as the alternative to uncertainty, it might be a critical feature of a microanalysis. However, with few exceptions, information as a component of the models in macro- or microeconomics is typically treated as a noncontributor, and information's negative, which is uncertainty, is represented merely as an unknown value that is carried around in the equations (Bickner, 1983; Chick, 1983).

Many of the economic models that have been applied to information do not account for the dynamic nature of information as outlined by Cleveland (1982) and Arrow (1984). In particular, the microeconomic version of models is too limited in scope to account for the diverse and almost unpredictable qualities of information. Information does not act in a vacuum or even in a frozen time frame. Information is not necessarily limited to the firm or to the market, and, as such, it may have effects outside of the model; these may ultimately rebound upon the model. These assertions about economic models are not new and are typically overlooked in general, but with the emerging potential of information, it is no longer acceptable to apply models that ignore primary aspects of information, and they could therefore dramatically affect the outcome of a model application. Macroeconomic versions of models are often just as artificial as the micro-versions, but the nature of the approach involves taking more variables into consideration and therefore yields more dynamic results.

The limitations of the models from either micro- or macroeconomics are rarely (if ever) stated when applying them. This omission leads to misunderstandings when other fields, such as the information fields, attempt to employ the models from economics. In applying game theory models to biology, Smith (1982) was extremely cautious to outline the shortcomings of both game theory and the impact that it could have on examining a biological system from that model's viewpoint. No confusion was allowed to enter into the discourse via omission. As previously indicated here, much confusion has been allowed to enter into areas employing economics models. Indeed, as already stated, models are used to reduce the information that needs examination, or even act in a non-representative fashion, but the reduction of points, the variance from representation, the limitations, and resulting possible pitfalls must be identified. Further, certain characteristics essential to the problem being modeled should not be omitted. As Morris (1970) suggested, a model must be adequately descriptive of the problem it is applied to, or the resulting assumptions could be completely false. A determination of the descriptive qualities of the problem depends upon a careful analysis of the problem prior to any attempt to simulate it.

A case where the application of a model may suggest misleading conclusions would be the application of the Cobb-Douglas production model to public libraries (Hayes, 1979). The Cobb-Douglas model deals with production as a function of capital and labor. It operates on "production per employee" and "capital investment per employee"; both are generally considered in a strictly quantitatively measurable environment such as an automobile factory, where each part and each product can be assigned costs in both material and labor. The application of the model could be viewed as an adventurous investigation into its applicability to libraries. Depending on how it was applied, it might have some illustrative power, but equating a library system to a primary production system would require significant clarification of all the parameters and very careful evaluation.

The application of the Cobb-Douglas model might be creative and may in time, with extended foundation, be a useful model to modify for use in library management settings. The problem, however, requires further analysis and definition before we should go into such a model. Employing mathematical models requires clearly defining the sources of the numbers, as well as being certain of the appropriate interpretation of any resulting statistics.

Economic models can be applied with reasonable success to the information fields. Lancaster's (1971) work in cost-effectiveness explains how such an analysis can be undertaken. As with Smith's (1982) carefully documented work, Lancaster clearly establishes the path that must be traveled and the special circumstances that must be considered. He specifically identified what the sources of cost are and supports that identification with examples. Cost-effectiveness is defined with the variables identified and the role of a cost-benefit model identified. Additionally, the basic steps involved in the analysis are clearly stated and further explained. Lancaster actually creates a model that could be applied to information fields via his careful explanation of how to view the components of a cost-effectiveness model with information fields in mind.

Models Summary

Despite diversity of opinions about models, they have been used throughout human history as investigative tools. When models are constructed with attention to classical scientific method, as recommended by Ashby (1970) and Stogdill (1970), and demonstrated by Smith (1982) and Lancaster (1971), they can be employed in hypothesis testing and data gathering. Methodically constructed models could be utilized in all fields of inquiry as long as there is a method to the structure. The method should be the result of a comprehensive analysis within the limitations of that analysis. The model may lead the investigator into further analysis or down a garden path, but the foundation model must be clearly defined regardless of its source derivation. What is key to Lancaster's work, to Smith's work, and to the work of many other successful modelers is the comprehension that models are not the "solve-all." Models are investigative tools with limitations that must be identified and ultimately dealt with, within the framework of the problem being modeled.

Summary

Economics as a study is complex, made more so when considered with information as a component. Information economics will evolve as a different creature than previous economic forms because of the potential for cross-pollination on all fronts of activity. Aspects of information and its contrary uncertainty will have to be addressed in a more specific manner rather than having the possible outcomes ignored. The implications of information economics to all spheres, social, political, and financial, are tremendous and unpredictable because the transformation of information into an evolving resource, difficult to model or to control, suggests that we will not be able to rely on previous systems of integrating the notions of information into economic constructs.

References

Allen, R. E. (Ed.). 1984. *The Pocket Oxford Dictionary of Current English.* 7th Ed. New York: Oxford University Press.

Aluri, R. 1993. Improving Reference Service: The Case for Using Continuous Quality Improvement Method. *RQ* 33(2):220–236.

Arrow, K. J. 1984. *Collected Papers of Kenneth J. Arrow: The Economics of Information,* vol. 4. Cambridge, MA: Belknap Press of Harvard University Press.

Ashby, W. R. 1970. Analysis of the System to Be Modeled. In *The Process of Model Building in the Behavioral Sciences* pp. 94–114. Columbus, OH: Ohio State University Press.

Bar, F. 1995. Information Infrastructure and the Transformation of Manufacturing. In W. J. Drake (Ed.), *The New Information Infrastructure: Strategies for United States Policy* pp. 55–74. New York: The Twentieth Century Fund Press.

Bickner, R. E. 1983. Concepts of Economic Cost. In D. W. King, N. K. Roderer, and H. A. Olsen (Eds.), *Key Papers in the Economics of Information* pp. 10–49. White Plains, NY: Knowledge Industry Publications.

Black, S. H., and Marchand, D. A. 1982. Assessing the Value of Information in Organizations: A Challenge for the 1980's. *The Information Society* 1(3):191–225.

Boorstin, D. J. 1983. *The Discoverers.* New York: Random House.

Caldwell, B., and Violino, B. March 1, 1999. Hyper-Efficient Companies. *InformationWeek* 728:40–51.

Carnoy, M., Castells, M., Cohen, S. S., and Cardoso, F. H. 1993. *The New Global Economy in the Information Age: Reflections on Our Changing World.* University Park, PA: The Pennsylvania State University Press.

Castells, M. 1993. The Informational Economy and the New International Division of Labor. In *The New Global Economy in the Information Age: Reflections on Our Changing World* pp. 15–43. University Park, PA: The Pennsylvania State University Press.

Chick, V. 1983. *Macroeconomics After Keynes.* Cambridge, MA: MIT Press.

Churchman, C. W. 1970. When Does a Model Represent Reality? In *The Process of Model Building in the Behavioral Sciences* pp. 133–138. Columbus, OH: Ohio State University Press.

Cleveland, H. 1982. Information as a Resource. *The Futurist* 16(2):24–39.

Cooper, M. 1983. The Structure and Future of the Information Economy. *Information Processing and Management* 19(1):9–26.

Engler, N. January 25, 1999. Emerging Enterprise: Supply-Chain Help. *InformationWeek.* Retrieved February 15, 2010, from www.informationweek.com/718/18iusup.htm

Garcia, L. 1995. The Globalization of Telecommunications and Information. In W. J. Drake (Ed.), *The New Information Infrastructure: Strategies for United States Policy* pp. 75–92. New York: The Twentieth Century Fund Press.

Garson, G. D. 1995. *Computer Technology and Social Issues*. Harrisburg, PA: Idea Group Publishing.

Goodman, S. 1987. The Information Technologies and Soviet Society: Problems and Prospects. *IEEE Transactions on Systems, Man and Cybernetics* SMC-17(4), July–August:529–551.

Green, J. R., and Laffont, J. 1986. Incentive Theory with Data Compression. In W. Heller, R. M. Starr, and D. Starrett (Eds.), *Uncertainty, Information and Communication (Essays in Honor of Kenneth J. Arrow,* vol. 3) pp. 239–249. New York: Cambridge University Press.

Hayes, R. M. 1979. The Management of Library Resources: The Balance Between Capital and Staff in Providing Services. *Library Research* 1:119–142.

Haywood, T. 1995. *Info-Rich—Info-Poor. Access and Exchange in the Global Information Society*. London: Bowker Saur.

Heller, W., Starr, R. M., and Starrett, D. (Eds.). 1986. *Uncertainty, Information and Communication (Essays in Honor of Kenneth J. Arrow,* vol. 3)*. New York: Cambridge University Press.

Henderson, A. 1999. Information Science and Information Policy: The Use of Constant Dollars and Other Indicators to Manage Research Investments. *Journal of the American Society for Information Science* 50(4):366–379.

King, D. W., Roderer, N. K., and Olsen, H. A. (Eds.). 1983. *Key Papers in the Economics of Information*. White Plains, NY: American Society for Information Science, Knowledge Industry Publications, Inc.

Kingma, B. R. 1996. *The Economics of Information: A Guide to Cost-Benefit Analysis for Information Professionals*. Englewood, CO: Libraries Unlimited.

Lamberton, D. M. 1983. National Policy for Economic Information. In D. W. King, N. K. Roderer, and H. A. Olsen (Eds.), *Key Papers in the Economics of Information* pp. 302–318. White Plains, NY: American Society for Information Science, Knowledge Industry Publications, Inc.

Lamberton, D. 1984. Economics of Information and Organization. *Annual Review of Information Science and Technology* 19:5–29.

Lancaster, F. W. 1971. The Cost-Effectiveness Analysis of Information Retrieval and Dissemination Systems. *Journal of the American Society for Information Science* pp. 12–27.

Lanvin, B. 1995. Why the Global Village Cannot Afford Information Slums. In W. J. Drake (Ed.), *The New Information Infrastructure: Strategies for U. S. Policy* pp. 205–222. New York: A Twentieth Century Fund Book.

Luce, R. D. 1970. What Are Mathematical Models of Behavior Models of? In R. M. Stogdill (Ed.), *The Process of Model-building in the Behavioral Sciences* pp. 115–132. Columbus, OH: Ohio State University Press.

McCall, John J. (Ed.). 1982. *The Economics of Information and Uncertainty (A Conference Repo*rt). Chicago: University of Chicago Press.

Monthly Labor Review. April 1999. Computer Ownership up Sharply in the 1990s. Bureau of Labor Statistics. United States Department of Labor [online] stats.bls. Retrieved February 15, 2010, from www.bls/opub/ted/1999/Apr/wk1/art01.htm

Morris, W. T. 1970. On the Art of Modeling. In *The Process of Model Building in the Behavioral Sciences* pp. 76–93. Columbus, OH: Ohio State University Press.

Myerson, R. B. 1986. Negotiations in Games: A Theoretical Overview. In W. Heller, R. M. Starr, and D. Starrett (Eds.), *Uncertainty, Information and Communication (Essays in Honor of Kenneth J. Arrow,* vol. 3*)* pp. 3–24. New York: Cambridge University Press.

National Agricultural Statistics Services. USDA. 1999. Year 2000 Computerized Systems Readiness Report. [online] Retrieved February 15, 2010, from usda.mannlib. cornell.edu/usda/reports/nassr/other/computer/y2k0299.txt

Newman, G. 1983. An Institutional Perspective on Information. In D. W. King, N. K. Roderer, and H. A. Olsen (Eds.), *Key Papers in the Economics of Information* pp. 275–301. White Plains, NY: American Society for Information Science, Knowledge Industry Publications, Inc.

Nicolaidis, K. 1995. International Trade in Information-Based Services: The Uruguay Round and Beyond. In W. J. Drake (Ed.), *The New Information Infrastructure: Strategies for United States Policy* pp. 269–303. New York: The Twentieth Century Fund Press.

Nora, S. and Minc, A. 1980. *The Computerization of Society* pp. vi–12. Cambridge, MA: MIT Press.

Phlips, L. 1988. *The Economics of Imperfect Information.* New York: Cambridge University Press.

Porter, M. E., and Millar, V. E. 1985. How Information Gives You Competitive Advantage. *Harvard Business Review* July–August:149–160.

Redman, B. J., and Redman, J. C. 1981. *Microeconomics: Resource Allocation and Price Theory.* Westport, CT: AVI Publishing.

Robinson, S. 1986. Analyzing the Information Economy: Tools and Techniques. *Information Processing and Management* 22(3):183–202.

Rothschild, M. 1986. Asset Pricing Theories. In W. Heller, R. M. Starr, and D. Starrett (Eds.), *Uncertainty, Information and Communication (Essays in Honor of Kenneth J. Arrow,* vol. 3*)* pp. 97–128. New York: Cambridge University Press.

Rubin, M. R., and Sapp, M. E. 1981. Selected Roles of Information Goods and Services in the United States National Economy. *Information Processing and Management* 17, 1981: 195–213.

Schiller, D. 1988. How to Think about Information. In V. Mosco and J. Wasko (Eds.), *The Political Economy of Information* pp. 27–42. Madison, WI: University of Wisconsin Press.

Shannon, C. E., and Weaver, W. 1949. *The Mathematical Theory of Communication.* Urbana, IL: University of Illinois Press.

Smith, J. M. 1982. *Evolution and the Theory of Games.* New York: Cambridge University Press.

Spink, A. 1997. Study of Interactive Feedback during Mediated Information Retrieval. *Journal of the American Society for Information Science* 48(5):382–394.

Stein, T., and Sweat, J. November 9, 1998. Killer Supply Chains. [online] Retrieved February 15, 2010, from www.informationweek.com/708/08iukil.htm

Stogdill, R. M. 1970. Introduction: The Student and Model Building. In *The Process of Model Building in the Behavioral Sciences*. Columbus, OH: Ohio State University Press.

Tapscott, D. 1996. *The Digital Economy: Promise and Peril in the Age of Networked Intelligence*. New York: McGraw-Hill.

United States Census Bureau. 2007. Computer Use and Ownership: Current Population Survey (CPS) Reports. October 2007: Detailed Tables, Appendix Table A. Retrieved February 15, 2010, from www.census.gov/population/www/socdemo/computer.html

United States Census Bureau. 2009. Computer Use and Ownership: Current Population Survey (CPS) Reports. October 2009: Detailed Tables, Appendix Table A. Retrieved February 15, 2010, from www.census.gov/population/www/socdemo/computer.html

United States Department of Agriculture. 2009. Farm Computer Usage and Ownership. Retrieved February 15, 2010, from usda.mannlib.cornell.edu/usda/current/Farm Comp/FarmComp-08-14-2009.pdf

USC Annenberg School for Communication. 2009. Annual Internet Survey by the Center for the Digital Future Finds Large Increases in Use of Online Newspapers. Retrieved February 15, 2010, from www.digitalcenter.org/pdf/2009_Digital_Future_ Project_Release_Highlights.pdf

Villano, M. March 15, 1999. A Lead-Pipe Cinch. *CIO* 12(11):51–60.

Wilkin, A. 1977. Personal Roles and Barriers in Information Transfer. *Advances in Librarianship* 7:257–297.

Chapter 11

Interpretations of Value

Melanie J. Norton

Establishing the value of information has presented complex and unique problems for economists and information scientists for most of this century (King, Roderer, and Olsen, 1983). Defining information and relating it to a value, benefit, or cost structure have so far presented significant theoretical problems. Information value, if characterized as being measured as the usefulness or utility of information, cannot usually be ascribed until after the information has been obtained and applied. This presents a paradox: how to place a value on information and how to measure that value cannot necessarily be accomplished at the same stage of economic interplay. In fact, when information is valued in this fashion, dependent upon the usefulness of information, the value can be as dependent on the recipient of the information as the information itself (King, Roderer, and Olsen, 1983; Repo, 1986).

Various attempts have been made over the years to confront these fundamental issues. In 1945, Hayek discussed the market mechanism as a way in which information is valued. Boulding (1956/1973) presented ideas of how information is individually valued. Marschak (1968) attempted to use a Shannon-like model to define information in economic terms. Kenneth Arrow (1984) recognized information as an entity, integrally linked to uncertainty and economics, in need of clearer definition and valuation. Fritz Machlup (1979) examined the issues involved in measuring the value of information and offered several cost-benefit analysis considerations for use in this effort. Historically, these authors have created the paths used to review information value and attempted to cope with the complexities of the value of information.

Attempts to clarify the definition of information to attend to the issue of valuing it have engaged economists and information scientists in cost-benefit analysis discussions, commodity versus resource debates, probability theory, game theory, and multitudes of various other controversies (Arrow, 1984; Bates, 1988; Cleveland, 1982; King, Roderer, and Olsen, 1983; Repo, 1986; Spence, 1974). Debates over the appropriateness of neoclassical economic considerations in describing the value of information and adventures into Keynesian and Baysian models have only served to further complicate the discussion (Lamberton, 1983; Newman, 1983). Essentially, all of these inquiries have contributed to describing information and information value, which might eventually yield a working, though probably not a definitive, approach to the issues involved. Re-examining some aspects and suggesting some alternative interpretations may provide a path to additional insight into the issues of information value. Key to any discussion of information value has to be the context of the consideration, which is one of the areas that economic modeling tends to simplify beyond recognition. Actual information value is steeped in enormous context, built by the actors, the environment, and the anticipated, or hoped for, outcomes. Without an understanding of these aspects, it is too easy to inappropriately interpret an economic exchange.

Value in Context

Value refers to the worth, utility, or desirability, which is assumed, demonstrated, or bestowed upon an entity, activity, or product (utility equals use or usefulness). Whether the thing being valued is a commodity or a resource has no specific tangible effect on the value. The overall status as a scarce resource, or an essential commodity, or a socially prized item may affect the trading price or exchange value, but the conditions of quantity and social opinion are the precipitous factors, not whether it is a thing of nature or a product of man (Bickner, 1983; Repo, 1986). *The value of information, regardless of whether it is considered a commodity or a resource, is the worth, utility, or desirability that is assumed about it, demonstrated by it, or bestowed upon it.* How is the value ascertained and how is it measured? How is the worth of information determined in selling, purchasing, or otherwise obtaining that information? How is that worth, that value, measured and acted upon? Information value is relative. It is dependent upon the *identity, role, or orientation* of the potential users and the information relationship to, or within, a specific identity at a specific time. Identity characteristics may include cultural, personal, and organizational components. The term "cultural" is used to refer to ethnic background and involvement. "Personal" refers to individual, in that though influenced by cultural considerations, it is not being wholly based upon the group, though personal and cultural components may be inextricably connected. "Organizational" means whatever structured environment the individual or culture may function within. Fundamental to a discussion of value of information in this context is the assertion that the value of information is tied to the individuals, cultures, or organizations, and thereby, tied to an identity, role, or orientation related to those aspects.

Traditions, information about the conduct of a particular group, pass from one generation to another as the continuance of a body of information that separates one culture from another. This conveyance may involve an individual as the medium, as in the carrying of oral histories over the generations. The value of information, in this case being culturally based, is prized as central to the congruity of the group's past, present, and future; the information is essentially priceless to the cultural entity and to the individuals that comprise that body. As such, the information is reproduced from generation to generation; as children reproduce the genetic traits of parents, reproduced information carries the traditions and histories of cultures. And just like the occasional aberration of an inherited trait, information can be affected by the reproduction. Information might have *no* value outside the cultural boundaries. Cultures may prize information that has no utility outside that culture, or has no correspondent outside the culture, or simply has no meaning taken out of the context of the specific culture. In this case, the information value *appears* sterile; it has no external value, and no external reproduction is likely.

The error in this is that even information that is not valued across cultures may be personally valued. A visitor to a culture hears a traditional story and carries it to other situations, to other cultures. Personal valuation of information will be based on personal interests, characteristics, education, history, etc. Personal views affect the value placed on information in a personal role and influence areas of agreement with the information. Concepts of self-image and group association will play a significant part in how the information is personally valued (Boulding, 1956/1973) and reproduced.

Renovation and Mutation of Information

Information transmitted out of its original corpus may be modified by the new carrier, either by intention (*renovation of information*) or by accident (*mutation of information*). In renovation of information, intentional modification is undertaken, such as adjusting all books to use politically correct gender descriptors; this changes the information conveyed and, depending on which side of the issue one stands, changes the value placed upon that information. Individuals may inject personal value into information value. Value can be changed when information is added, subtracted, or interpreted. When information is interpreted or applied interpretatively, it is modified and may increase or decrease in value. Attempting to change culturally valued information will be met with resistance, and such modified information will be devalued. External to the cultural base, interpretation may provide value, real or imagined, to information that is otherwise sterile outside of the cultural frame. One culture's interpretation of another culture's traditions may add value to the information about another culture, regardless of the correctness of the interpretation. Interest in the artifacts of another culture denotes information value associated with what can be determined about that other culture, but modern interpretations, no matter how well grounded in sustained research, may still be incorrect. However, until the information is disputed, the information value, assigned in this instance by an external culture, will be based upon criteria of the external culture. The external culture's interpretation may be considered sterile, relative to information value by the original culture.

Mutation of information occurs when information received is unintentionally modified through carrier failure, such as a bad phone connection. Mutation may be the result of misinterpretation of information as well. Renovation and mutation of information produce changes that may influence the value of information. Either occurrence could yield new information with new value. An error in a chemical formula could yield a new compound with higher information value than the original formula. An error in interpretation might lead to a different set of ideas and discoveries and have a different resulting information value, which could be positive or negative.

Organization and Value

Organizational components to be considered in valuing information are related to the structures that may affect the movement of information and the interpretations that the organizational body may attempt to force on information. Information value in the organization is determined by specific characteristics of the organization. Team organization versus top-down organization will influence how information is valued and how it is transmitted or not transmitted. Management formations, or cultural hierarchies, contribute to information value. Top-down styles keep the lower echelons less informed; there is less information available. If neoclassical supply-and-demand models are applied to information, this would increase information value in general, but information is not well suited to those models and frequently the information drifting down in top-down management systems is considered less valuable than other sources. Team management or cooperative management systems may have varying information value ranges based on the actual degree of trust among the cooperative units and the ability to transmit information intact, as these systems have more channels for transmission and verification than top-down. The sources of information that an organization finds acceptable will influence information value. If the information sources are all external or all internal, or any extremely imbalanced configuration thereof, the information may be drastically skewed, and the value of the information should then be appraised with extreme caution. However, if organizational information gathering techniques are skewed, it may not be possible for that organization to recognize that information value will be skewed as well.

The organizational component of identity is not limited to businesses or single cultures. The organization of a multicultural society, such as our own, influences how information is valued, in that information movement is affected by the structures of our society, and interpretations are imposed upon information by our information media. In certain groups, the information value of the front page of the *New York Times* is considered significantly greater than the information value of *USA Today*; in other groups, the opposite valuation is made. In parts of the academic world, the organizational structure rewards seekers of new information with little regard to the value of that information. In fact, in the research realm, the organization creates a special information value problem. Researchers may seek to maintain exclusive knowledge of information, prizing the information based on possible future value that is accrued by having exclusive credit for the discovery of the information. The information has value as a credential for the researcher, possibly even significant financial benefit. However, the information value may be even higher in the general knowledgebase, as was the case for a number of discoveries regarding acquired immune deficiency syndrome (AIDS) and how it is transmitted. There are risks involved with information value, both in the application and in the attempt. Such risks include placing value on what is valuable only to a closed culture or undervaluing information because it is misunderstood but is later clarified and found to be of extreme value. What must be recognized is that any information valuation system is composed of more than just information issues. There is a significant amount of scenario relativity; that is, who, what, where, and why should influence how any measures for information value are applied.

Measurability

Some aspects of information are measurable (i.e., values can be derived from the construction of a database based on cost-benefit analysis). How many person-hours, how much computer equipment, how much electricity, how much paper, and essentially, how much production and labor capital was put into the construction of the database can be determined. But what is the value of the information in the database, not the database as an entity, but the information it contains? Repo contends that "criteria for the determination of the value of information arise out of the process of use and seeking of it" (1986, p. 376). He further proposes that there are criteria for utilization: validity, quality, ease of use, and the degree of fit between the information provided and the environment in which it is being sought. This utility value is certainly valid after the database has been purchased, but how does the purchaser determine the value of information before it is purchased? The value of the information in the purchaser's eyes is important prior to purchase because it is contributory to the decision to purchase, as well as contributing to factors that will influence price acceptance. Basically, the purchaser needs information about the information in the database to make the decision to purchase. (This aspect of information is reduction of uncertainty at purchase. The database, it is assumed, is desired to assist in reduction of other uncertainty.) This need for information about the information is where the problem of the value of information is most complex, though it may appear simple. In the case of databases, it is possible to use pre-established criteria in evaluating the potential usefulness of a database. But the criteria must be based upon a level playing field; that is, that the representative database samples reflect the actual database content. If a database is actually electronic yellow pages, is that the database content anticipated when purchasing a targeted mailing list?

When purchasing a house, the buyer has made certain assumptions about the quality of the materials used in the structure, the quality of the workmanship, the longevity of the electrical systems, the furnace, and so on. Those assumptions are made, however, under certain contractual agreements that guarantee performance for a specified period of time. The buyer is accepting the risk that the builder can be held to the terms of the contract if something goes wrong with the house or with the finances of the contractor. Through legal agreement and the acceptance of some risk, the buyer is relying on the contractor and the courts to protect his or her investment in the house. The buyer purchases the house after inspection of it, but unless he or she monitored every step of the construction process, inspected the products used, and knew enough about the whole method of construction, it is still a risk; the purchase is made based on uncertainty—to an extent, the buyer is accepting a lack of information. Is this different from the purchase of the database, or of information in general? The buyer does not really know the performance level of the house until it is used. The purchaser does not really know the performance level of the information until it is used.

Further, if the purchaser fails to use the information or fails to apply the information most profitably, is it the vendor's fault? What if the purchaser uses the information to create yet another product that yields significant financial benefit to the original purchaser but no benefit to the original seller? These are issues of copyright and intellectual property. However, consider the house again: The contractor built and sold it. Now the buyer owns it. What if he or she adds a room, a pool, or redecorates? Can the builder claim a right to the increased value made of the house? No, the builder cannot.

Averaging Anticipated Value

Purchasers of information must make more complex decisions about information than about physical materials. Anticipated value or anticipated benefit of information must be considered. Determining an appropriate value may be attempted by calculating "… an average of all the possible values of some good or outcome weighted by their respective likelihood" (Bates, 1988, p. 78). Estimating all the possible values from the use of information and adjusting for the likelihood that such use will occur allows for consideration for variations in value based upon context of use and the possibility of other uses of the information. In theory, this method would provide a way to allow "the analyst to treat the value of information goods as fixed in subsequent analyses" (p. 78). Having the advantage of such a value based upon the probability of applications permits a balance of exchange values to be considered. These types of considerations are taken into account when purchasing a house or a computer or any other marketable entity. To some extent, using this type of valuation technique with information requires more comprehensive understanding of what the information has to accomplish and what possible outcomes may be obtained.

Lack of Prior Knowledge

What if the information that the purchaser needs is something that he does not have any prior experience with, or any prior data or estimations about? The "black box" of high school science class comes to mind: How does the purchaser know how to value what is in the black box without knowing anything about the contents? This is the recurring question: How does a purchaser, or vendor, determine the value of a black box, an unknown? This is the issue that has not yet been adequately answered. Despite the similarities between purchasing a house and purchasing information, there is the overriding, recurring issue of the depth of unknown referent to information. Information can be as simple as a house or a database from a reputable vendor who has identified precisely the depth of the data in the database, or information can be a black box. A black box is the unknown that is exposed when experimenting in science laboratories. How does one place value on the information created, acquired, or stumbled across in a laboratory experiment?

Many new products and much new information emerged from the NASA programs to reach the moon. Many of the products were the result of attempts to solve specific problems identified in the preparation for the flights. Commodities and information were created to address specific problems. Some of the solutions discovered addressed tangential issues or had larger economic advantages, such as Velcro. The many computer applications of hardware and software and medical data also yielded side benefits that we reap to this day. The value of the information to be gained in the effort was not known. There was an assumption of risk, an acceptance of uncertainty in venturing into the experiment. The people involved in the experiment, the agencies providing funding, and to some extent the general populace of the United States assumed that the information would be valuable—that is, it would be useful. It is often with this perception, or prediction of value, that value is implied. Value so derived may be overestimated or underestimated. In an economic view, determining the value of information remains a high-risk proposition that requires more information to reduce uncertainty.

Cost-Benefit Analysis

The interrelatedness of information value within a potential context or application suggests that the appropriate approach to valuing information should be constructed around cost-benefit analysis. A working analysis of this type would involve the creation of a scenario documenting the environment of the information application, including all the potential contributing costs coupled with estimations of potential benefit. The difficulty originates from identifying cost accurately and estimating benefits reasonably. To fully determine a value in this variety of systems, it is necessary to include the elusive "public good" notions typically associated with the communications arena.

Let us examine one example. The cost of placing computers into grade schools should include the cost of the machines, the modification to the electrical systems, long-term change in the cost of building utilities, costs for paper, wiring, and maintenance, plus the cost of training teachers to be able to use the systems and to teach the students. The cost of training seems to be always overlooked, but more than that is the cost involved in bringing computers into the curriculum in a meaningful way with tangible results for the students and the teachers. There is no question that there is value involved in the provision of the machines and the related information, but the value cannot be calculated without taking into account all the actual costs, even the ones economists like to overlook because they make the equations ungainly. The issue of benefit or measurable value can only be accurately determined if all the potential results are estimated. If the teachers are trained to use the equipment to teach the students, the investment in the teachers is recovered in one teaching cycle and will not need repeating if successfully accomplished the first time. With the teachers trained, it can be assumed that they will continue to grow as they teach, so the value of the initial training will in the long run at least be worth twice the initial investment. The equipment will degrade over time, but if it is used to its fullest, integrated into the curriculum so that students and teachers are maximizing results, the depreciation would be appropriate over time and still be a benefit as even an old system is useful when properly integrated and managed. The alternatives—that is, not having put the equipment into the classroom or not having trained the teachers adequately—would mean no benefit. Simply, training 20 teachers, who train 20 more students each for five years, means 2,000 students trained with the technology who would have more opportunity than 2,000 students without such experience. In a cost-benefit analysis, this can be distilled to numbers, but the environment and larger outcome must be considered to fully anticipate a value. Estimating values in this fashion is cumbersome, but it may be useful in reducing uncertainty or at least anticipating potential utility. This framework permits the insertion of the cultural or organizational elements, which may so dramatically influence a value situation.

Summary

Information value is intrinsically bound to the transmitter, the receiver, and the channel in specific relation to their identity models and their situations. The utility of any information, and therefore the value of information, is situationally bound. Understanding the possible components involved and preparing scenario analyses may enable the establishment of valuation parameters relative to specific characteristic components. Without comprehending the relativity of information value, we will not satisfactorily address the issue.

References

Arrow, K. J. 1984. *Collected Papers of Kenneth J. Arrow: The Economics of Information,* vol. 4. Cambridge, MA: Belknap Press of Harvard University Press.

Bates, B. 1988. Information as an Economic Good: Sources of Individual and Social Value. In V. Mosco and J. Wasko (Eds.), *The Political Economy of Information* pp. 76–94. Madison, WI: University of Wisconsin Press

Bickner, R. E. 1983. Concepts of Economics. In D. W. King, N. K. Roderer, and H. A. Olsen (Eds.), *Key Papers in the Economics of Information* pp. 10–49. White Plains, NY: Knowledge Industry Publications.

Boulding, K. 1956/1973. *The Image.* Ann Arbor, MI: The University of Michigan Press.

Cleveland, H. 1982. Information as a Resource. *The Futurist* 16(2): 24–39.

Hayek, F. A. September 1945. The Use of Knowledge in Society. *The American Economic Review* 35(4):519–530. Retrieved February 15, 2010, www.jstor.org/stable/1809376

King, D. W., Roderer, N. K., and Olsen, H. A. (Eds.). 1983. *Key Papers in the Economics of Information.* White Plains, NY: Knowledge Industry Publications.

Lamberton, D. M. 1983. National Policy for Economic Information. In D. W. King, N. K. Roderer, and H. A. Olsen (Eds.), *Key Papers in the Economics of Information* pp. 302–318. White Plains, NY: Knowledge Industry Publications.

Machlup, F. September 1979. Uses, Value, and Benefits of Knowledge. *Knowledge* (1):62–81.

Marschak, J. May 1968. Economics of Inquiring, Communication, Deciding. *American Economic Review* 58. In T. Saracevic (Ed.), 1970. *Introduction to Information Science* pp. 697–706. New York: R. R. Bowker.

Newman, G. 1983. Institutional Perspective on Information. In D. W. King, N. K. Roderer, and H. A. Olsen (Eds.), *Key Papers in the Economics of Information* pp. 275–301. White Plains, NY: Knowledge Industry Publications.

Repo, A. 1986. The Dual Approach to the Value of Information: An Appraisal of Use and Exchange Values. *Information Processing and Management* 22(5):373–383.

Spence, A. M. 1974. An Economist's View of Information. *Annual Review of Information Science and Technology* 9:57–78.

Chapter 12

Digital Accessibility: Information Value in Changing Hierarchies

Melanie J. Norton and June Lester
(Revised 2010 by Melanie J. Norton)

With access to authority levels merely keystrokes away, the rigid managerial hierarchy has experienced contractions of layers. Increased and nearly instant access, as well as heightened expectations for response, create demands for attention, which may impact management itself. Planning to provide more resources in the digital age requires new forms of resource control techniques, including better time management and evaluation of information value. So many voices can now be heard that new structures and economies must be considered. Addressing all the needs of all the players on the digital information field will require creativity. Will the modified management structures be able to address the digital revolution?

This chapter addresses the concept of information value in organizations and how that value is impacted by accessibility. The discussion will consider how changes in access, occurring because of information communication technology developments, may contribute to changes in the organizational structure for information gathering and how change in access leads to differing valuations of information. The purpose here is to raise issues for consideration, not to provide answers.

Impact of Digital Accessibility on the Organizational Hierarchy

Organizational structure is an information transfer system designed to service groups or individuals to permit the completion of the tasks and missions of the organization (Nadler, 1992). As Kaltnekar states, "organizational relations are defined by information and vice versa. In fact, organization processes mainly represent various activities relative to information: input, processing, transmission and above all numerous information flows connected with it" (1991, p. 516). Typically, until the advent of modern information technology, this was a relatively inflexible hierarchical channel through which information flowed, or sometimes trickled, depending on one's position in the channel. The role of the group or individual within the organization fairly well dictated the level, quality, and character of the information access available. The front line salesperson probably had little or no contact with the president of the company. What information reached the sales force was interpreted by the various layers of management. Lines of authority, whether business or military, were also paths for the movement of information. The position of an individual in a specific location in the channel also tended to form the image, or self-perception, that the individual held of his or her role in the organization and even lent to the creation of an image of the organization itself (Gardner and Peluchette, 1991). The combined images of self and organizational structures worked together to form the basis for the interactions of the individual with the organization. The individual needed to know whom to directly approach for information and who should be approached via a series of other individuals; that is, what channels of authority needed to be followed in obtaining or distributing information. Further, these combined images influenced the methods used in hierarchical communications. Speaking with one's immediate supervisor might be acceptable for addressing some issues; other issues required written communications. In either case, the individual's style of presentation and interaction was affected by the perceptions of both self-role and the organizational structure (Gardner and Peluchette, 1991).

Concomitant to these perceptions of role and structure is the notion of organizational culture, which includes the history and environment that formed the existing communications pathways (Nadler and Tushman, 1992). The value ascribed to any information traveling up or down the channel can be impacted by any or all of these components. For example, an individual's position in the hierarchy attaches certain value to information, regardless of the actual value. When someone in authority (or perceived authority) utters statements, these may be taken as fact with no further investigation. Though our society seems to be more cynical and less trusting of others, there is the odd tendency to accept as experts anyone with a large enough media outlet. Celebrity and visibility have become a path to being treated as an expert. The structure, the layers of authority, the hierarchy of communication, the style and method of presentation, the players and their roles—all these contribute to the movement of information in an organization, and each component influences the valuing of the information communicated through that system. Perceived authority lends more value to information, sometimes inappropriately.

The method of information movement or the communications system is the infrastructure base of the organization and is a major reason for having a formal structure (Gerstein, 1992); it is key to the decision-making functions of the organization (Kaltnekar, 1991). This system has been profoundly affected by the advent of information technology. According to Nadler, "information technology has begun to revolutionize organizational design by providing alternatives to hierarchy as the primary means of coordination" (1992, p. 5) and information transfer. Nadler also talks about several variations in the traditional organization that have emerged:

1. Self-managed teams

2. High-performance work systems that emphasize the integration of advanced tools such as expert systems with modified worker organizations

3. Increased joint ventures between companies

4. Greater collaboration inside and outside organizations

5. Outsourcing

Digital accessibility enables the movement of information and contributes to the value of self-managed teams. Making information available to a group of individuals, without the hierarchical chain of intervening interpreters, allows the group to use information, assumed to be less filtered, to engage in better problem exploration and problem solving. Self-managed teams tend to focus on specific aspects of business problems and involve partnerships rather than supervisor and subordinates. Making information available through less rigid channels enhances the implementation of self-managed teams, regardless of technology.

Essentially, the evolution of computer technology, and especially networking systems, has impacted every aspect of the traditional organization by influencing the communication pathways and therefore the availability of information. Electronic mail, electronic bulletin boards, shared files, and other similar systems allow information transfer without the typical channels of hierarchy, breaking down rigid organizational structures by circumventing that hierarchy and allowing information to flow through the electronic structure rather than through the traditional channels of authority. Openness with information allows organizations to expand the personnel involved in projects and to network outside of themselves. However, the availability of digital access, while presenting an opportunity to engage more members of an organization, does not always result in that engagement. Boundaries become blurred, both within the work groups and within the organization. Decision-making becomes less centralized, more dispersed, and certainly at some levels, less institutional in nature (Kaltnekar, 1991). The composition of the organization changes over time, even the "walls" of the organization may change to encompass the customers within the evolving communication net. As some organizations have experienced, the voice, email, or blog of the customers can indeed appear to be interior to the organization.

The potential for such close contact, whether among customers and organizations or workers within organizations, can have both positive and negative consequences. It might be assumed that despite the ability to do so, individuals will not rashly travel outside the bounds of the traditional communication structures and will not skip all the levels of the hierarchy to satisfy a desire to communicate directly with the ultimate boss, but there is actually little beyond common sense and organizational culture to prevent this. Though face-to-face encounters between the extremes of the hierarchy would be unlikely or confined to very specific situational circumstances, electronic encounters are not so constrained. Workers with information communication technology have the ability to interact with the various levels of the managerial hierarchy without restraint and in some cases nearly anonymously. Further, employees with externally faced network access could distribute information outside the organization, depending on configurations and data policies, as if they were representatives of the organization, whether it was part of their responsibilities or not. Coping with the issues that contributed to justifying information control by management, security concerns, privacy conflicts, and corporate citizenship become more complex because of digital accessibility's impact.

Customer contact into organizations was expanded substantially just by the general introduction of the telephone; add blogs, tweets, instant messaging, or any of the arrays of social networking tools designated as Web 2.0 and the consumer voice has life in every corporate boardroom and government office. Responsiveness to public commentary becomes a measure of survival potential. There is general agreement that customer input should be embraced and exploited to improve services and therefore the economic base. According to Brandt (2008), while "improving the customer experience is a top priority in a majority of companies. … A March 2005 Forrester Research survey found that "a majority of firms confessed to delivering 'sub-par experiences to customers'" (Temkin in Brandt, 2008). Essentially, while significant amounts of information are obtained from customers via complaint collection systems, surveys, and so on, many organizations have been less than successful in integrating the information gathered into meaningful response systems and have not improved customer satisfaction. The mechanisms to appropriately distribute the information and create successful responses to improve customer relations are still not working (Brandt, 2008). The same shortcoming can be noted for employees; although they may have the ability to submit information to the organization, it is not necessarily resulting in organizational improvement. Digital accessibility provides the potential for hierarchical information channels to change, but it does not guarantee the outcome. Through the power of Web 2.0, the "social network" that gives a voice to all, it is possible for employees or consumers to cause significant damage to corporate images or even political campaigns.

The newest technology, along with changing views of the criticality of the customer, seems to be opening more communication avenues to all levels of the organization. Customers can have near instant access to an organization via the web, email, or blog, and what they cannot access, they certainly can and do discuss. Failure to respond can be devastating. For example, one computer producer able to handle only 4,000 of the 10,000 calls a day being received was attacked on the internet with messages of complaint and displeasure that cost the company "more than half of the company's sales-related input and ... lost business" (DeYoung, 1995, p. 42). More recently, user displeasure could result in behaviors that are akin to denial of service attacks, situations where a network site has so much traffic pushed at it that the system cannot respond, preventing anyone from using the site productively (United States Computer Emergency Readiness Team, 2004).

There has been significant growth in the use of the web to share and gather information with potential customers. The advent of improved browsers and relatively easy HTML authoring tools has enhanced the ability of organizations to create sites and has increased the pressure to have a presence on the web. Organizations use the web as a distribution site for their products, information, or surveying activities. Estimating that more than 250 million consumers in the United States alone access the web for information about emerging products, potential purchases, reviews, and service reports means opportunities for closer contact between the customers and the manufacturers. Monitoring the activities of the customer on websites can provide early signs of purchasing habits or changes in customer attitudes. Growth in online access, applications, and use has generated an industry focused on gathering and investigating data about the activities of all users at all levels. "In May of 2009, Google commissioned Forrester Consulting to evaluate the use of Web analytics technologies within U.S.-based enterprise organizations" (Forrester Consulting, 2009, p. 3). One of the observations of the study was that "the practice of measuring visitor activity within online properties has become commonplace—so much so that nearly three-quarters of large enterprises consider the Web analytics technologies that enable their organizations to quantify visitor traffic across their sites to be indispensable" (p. 4). Web analytics are used to plan and assess products, determine consumer interests, and study internet traffic for marketing; they have implications for a variety of data mining purposes (Forrester Consulting, 2009).

Universities and educational institutions of all varieties use websites to recruit prospective students; to provide online admission applications, information about courses, schedules, degree programs, and conference meetings; and to offer online courses. Nonprofit organizations use websites to provide online contact points for volunteers, solicit donations, describe their operations, and invite general participation. Individuals advertise their services and products.

Federal and state government agencies, as well as cities, have an enormous electronic presence, providing access for their constituents to the documents and research products of government (though not always for free and not always easily searchable). Incorporation of this communication technology into the information transfer system has rapidly become ubiquitous as part of the organizational structure across all sectors, with significant impact on information flow and information value. The challenge of locating information may impact how deeply the searcher reaches and that too will impact the actual value of the information. If the user selects the first three items returned in response to a query, how likely is it that this information is the best response? Depending on the design of the search engine, the search request, and the database source, the material returned may have no relevance to the information request but will be accepted out of convenience and lack of information about the information system's construction. These considerations influence how organizations design and present websites; it is not sufficient to post information without a structure and a plan to attract the desired audience.

Today we are in an environment in which consumers are responsive and insistent and expect feedback as quickly as they can type in requests. Repeat email messages come less than ten minutes apart, as senders expect a resolution of their issues immediately. Messages or postings appear that seem to assume everyone else in the world is attending to email or bulletin boards at the same time. With the explosion of cell phones, increased access to the internet, and the use of blogs, tweets, and social networking tools such as Facebook, MySpace, and more, responding to customers or critics is an ongoing task that demands enormous effort. Organizations and individual employees devise schemes to provide timely responses to even the most trivial electronic inquiry because any message can be the predictor of a public display of anger, a public haranguing that can cost consumer confidence, or a frenzy of complaints from others who have felt slighted but who were not previously motivated to report. Electronic accessibility is inserting the consumer, the customer, or even the casual, unrelated computer user into the structure of any organization that has assumed an electronic presence. The impact of this electronic information stream varies. Out of self-defense, some administrators, high profile scientists, CEOs, and the like make public announcements that they do not respond directly to email, which does not particularly discourage all petitioners. A relatively new trend is for people to document their every moment via YouTube, Twitter, Facebook, texting, and so on. Famous people and plain folk provide opportunity for others to follow them, reading or watching the daily drama of their lives whether monumentally boring or insanely exciting.

On the other hand, the depth of customer investment into organizational online presence could be a powerful tool for the organization. Kent (2008), discussing blogs in particular, points out that these information technologies can be public relations tools: "Allowing or encouraging visitors to an organization's Web site to participate in how online news and information is framed is possibly the greatest strength of blogs and the feature of the most importance to public relations practitioners. Research on framing and agenda setting has shown that the ability to control what individuals *see*, is the first step to controlling what people *think*" (p. 35). However, Kent also points out that the usefulness of blogs has yet to be established and deserves significantly more research before assuming they are a powerful persuasive tool.

Several questions arise in reference to the changing communications scene in which there is increased accessibility both from within the organization and from the outside to the decision-making levels of the organization:

1. How does one manage the impact of this changed information system on the organization?

2. What channels of communication need to be kept in place, and which are obsolete, if indeed any are?

3. What information value system will be in place, and how will it differ from the information value system of the hierarchical organization?

4. If customers are to be internally involved in the organization, what are the boundaries?

Despite nearly two decades of online activity, these questions have not been well addressed. Evolving technology, expanded social networking tools, and enormous growth in the adoption of multiple information/communication resources make it unlikely the answers will be readily obtained or stable. If people have access to the technology, they can have access to the opinions of the world and have an audience at large. How is this impacting behavior in the formal and informal spaces of human interaction?

Most organizations have changed because of information communication technologies, but despite the predictions since the 1960s that information technology would decrease the levels of hierarchy and flatten the structure significantly, flattened is probably not the appropriate interpretation of what has occurred. Though some organizations have decreased the layers of hierarchy by one or two levels (Shimada, 1991), this has not positioned everyone on the same level of information access or organizational power. The information structure of the hierarchy, while in some cases changed, is not eliminated; there are still those more "in-the-know" and those who never will have all the information needed. Decision-making may appear to be more distributed due to improved technology, but it is not horizontal; it may at this point be more of a matrix or network arrangement. But even network matrices have levels and restrictions for exchange. Perhaps the most profound and unanticipated outcome of information communication technologies has been the insertion of the consumer further into the decision processes of organizations. Being forced to monitor and respond to public voices influences the exchange of information within and outside of the organization, as well as impacting the decisions of the organization.

Methods of communication and channels for control of information have changed not only in relation to the increased technology but also in relation to changes in the larger social environment. Information technology allows anyone with access to communicate with anyone else in the network. However, the organizational culture and common sense can serve to control these communications, at least within the limitations of individual respect for the customs. Agreed-upon standards and procedures for the use of electronic mail as well as other communication systems channels can limit inappropriate use. Just as there are rules to govern the use of phones in the workplace, or appropriate procedures for filing a complaint, similar rules and procedures can be delineated related to the use of information technology. However, emerging trends such as the ubiquitous cell phone, Wi-Fi connections that allow for free ranging television or broadcast reception, and texting through every event suggests that traditional codes of civility and conduct based on common sense are slipping away. In their Pew Internet & American Life Project *Networked Workers*, Madden and Jones (2008) report the majority of respondents to their research indicated checking personal email during work hours as common, with just less than half reporting "most or all of the messages they send and receive are personal" (Madden and Jones, 2008, p. iv). Corporate America responds with increased monitoring of employee communication tools, increased restriction on site access, as well as more restrictive policies. Discussion of the rights of employees to use the technology available at work for personal reasons has been an issue since the first computer. The ability to monitor the information networks that employees use is an element of digital accessibility that impacts the organization's hierarchy but tends to create restrictions rather than expanded access. In an effort to control employees' inappropriate use of the technology, the organization could inadvertently restrict access to information that may be pertinent.

Although enhanced digital accessibility has the potential of providing total elimination of hierarchical information flow, removal of all channels for control of communication could cause chaos. Whatever minimal control channels are necessary to provide organizational structure need to be maintained but with enough flexibility to allow communications advantageous to the organization. The issue of valuing the information that is to be communicated through the electronic systems has to be confronted at various levels. Customer input can help identify new markets or point out repairable shortcomings; members of the organization may see things that others miss, which could lead to new opportunities. As always, determining what information is valuable is dependent upon factors far beyond the control of the sender and often not fully understood by the recipient. Unless no information is discarded without examination, there is at least some chance that items of value will be lost. The task of examining all incoming information can overwhelm, undermining the ability to recognize valuable information. Individuals and organizations should have more training focused on best practices for accessing the growing information resources as well as direction on how to maximize efficiency in searching. Ongoing education and refresher courses covering technology, as well as information organizational schemes, would be a useful investment.

The increase in customer information that results from the juncture of digital accessibility, increased responsiveness to customer needs, and enhanced customer orientation as the focus of the organization poses significant challenges in managing information flow and in assessing information value. Streamlining information is more easily achieved in managing employee input, limiting communication and reports to what is determined to be critical, but it is not possible to completely streamline customer input. Further, this compression of information ensures that valuable information will be lost. The use of online surveys helps to delineate some of the customer input, but none of it can be overlooked. As mentioned before, ignoring customer input can be a costly error. Social networking tools such as blogs, wikis, forums, Facebook, MySpace, and so on all provide vehicles for unfettered expression of opinions, by consumers as well as employees. Failing to examine these could result in significant information loss, as well as invite broad dissemination of incorrect or misleading information.

The issue of boundaries for customers involved internally in the organization is in some ways a very difficult problem. Whether it is a for-profit or nonprofit organization, the consumer public can sow havoc when dissatisfied. There are few limits to the contacts the public can make, and using a global medium like the internet can lend volume to one's words. Being able to email or text the CEO or the president grants a sense of democratic power, but such power is not always responsibly exercised. How to cope with what might be serious charges or just angry misinterpretations is a challenge. As reports of interpersonal violence and even terrorist activities within the country increase, a heightened sense of danger means less leeway and shortened decision time in determining the proper action when possible threats are received. An angry email, a sarcastic posting, or any set of words that might be interpreted as threatening violence can result in loss of positions and freedom. The value attributed to disgruntled conversation and heated complaints has been increased by the larger social fears. Previously ignored tirades venting frustration are monitored for suggestions of threats of violence. Campus shootings such as at Virginia Tech and increased terrorism concerns make any threatening comment more potent.

Each organization will make decisions about all of these challenges predicated on the customer base, the receptivity to customer input, and the ability to divine the real from the unreal. The bottom line is that the customer cannot be ignored, should always be listened to, and must never be insulted. What happens after that is completely situationally dependent. The wise organization will have some means to analyze and evaluate the various situations arising from customer intervention in information flow. The boundaries will have to be set by the organization, but without a doubt those boundaries will be challenged.

Variations in the Pace of Infusion of Information Technology into the Organization

In addition to the increased accessibility provided by electronic systems and the resulting change in information flow and information value within an organization, another significant factor influencing changes in information flow has been the practice of not providing every member of the organization with adequate access or training necessary to participate in the new communication systems. Often cost becomes the justification for this selective dissemination approach. Despite the tremendous growth in availability of information technology, there is still a discrepancy between the media hype and the actual installation of information technology and literacy in organizations.

These transitional organizational states, where information technology is not fully installed or implemented, can have negative effects on the organization at both macro and micro levels. At the macro level, because there has been global growth in the implementation of information technology as a resource expanding tool, organizations ignoring information technology or not fully utilizing it risk losing markets, limiting growth potential, and failing to recognize and exploit opportunities. On the micro level, individuals without adequate information technology access are limited in job growth, job security, future employment potential, and basic critical information. When such workers are displaced, the lack of sufficient technology skills limits job openings and pushes the worker lower in the hiring pool. It is unclear how serious the lack of technology skills is in the workforce. It has been noted that when people are referred to online applications for jobs or to online registration for unemployment or other aid, they cannot maneuver the systems or interfaces without assistance, indicating that the workforce is not as technologically advanced as those agencies imagined (Johnson, 2009). Diminished workers who are not keeping current ultimately cost organizations in a variety of arenas. Individuals without information resources cannot contribute to the organization at the same level as other workers. Workers without the technology are relegated to the traditional information hierarchy, whereas those with technology may have access to the changing style of decision-making. In the marketplace, consumers with technology access impact organizations. The actual demographics of the computer-owning public are not known; the impact is difficult to control or predict. The entire arena is still evolving and is still new enough that it is not reasonable to characterize the computer-user population, especially as online services make access easier for less technologically oriented people.

Within the organization, information technology access is not just the possession of the machines; it also involves having or acquiring appropriate technical skills. As technology has evolved, the value of employees can be impacted by their success or failure to maintain and upgrade skills in keeping with the changing systems. Training and currency with information technology is considered critical by workers for job satisfaction and likewise critical by employers seeking to maintain a stable, functional information systems workforce (Earls, 1995). Within organizations, an artificial hierarchy based on possession of and skill with technology is created, and such an artificial structure impedes an organization's (or a society's) growth through negative impacts related to the differential valuing of information and information technology in comparison with other factors. Undeserved stature may be accorded to information that is transferred using the new technology, while information transmitted by traditional means or through the traditional hierarchy may be falsely devalued. The possession of technical skills may give individuals additional rank and authority, while diminishing the rank and authority of less technically skilled workers, regardless of other career-related criteria. Sometimes the trade-off is the loss of years of organizational knowledge and culture as a result of early retirement of key workers who for a variety of reasons are not given access to the technology or are not provided with adequate training. While such retirements might be viewed positively, the changing organization structure may not be as well positioned as some may think. The information lost with those types of retirements cannot be replaced or recouped by technology. The insight that a longtime employee might have into the current and future activities of an organization based on time in place and experiential knowledge is lost, and the value of this lost information may be unrecognized potential diversification or missed market opportunities.

Information technology staff are not necessarily in possession of enough information to appropriately outfit the entire organization, and the devaluing of non-technologically generated information may have longterm consequences. The unreasonable expectation that the information technology staff should be able to understand every individual task of the organization may have led to the unmet expectations of the early information technology years. More realistically, successful organizations are encouraging the involvement of non-information technology staff in information technology acquisitions, design, and implementation. This two-fold strategy empowers the employee, while investing him or her in the job, and recognizes a diversity of information values. Determining, with help from the information technology staff, what hardware and software will best help perform the job, causes the employee to take responsibility and also commits him or her to the organization (Kaltnekar, 1991).

It seems reasonable to assume that information technology should be integrated throughout the organization, regardless of any centralized information technology group, since the role and advantage of information technology itself is having it permeate the organization to maximize the flow of information and the exchange of ideas (Woodsworth, 1991). Though the supposition that information technology would flatten the hierarchy has been shown to be questionable, it is certain that information technology affects the structure, via the technology, via the skilled personnel it demands, and via the skills that the typical worker can now acquire to implement information technology (because the technology has improved even if the quality of the employee has not). Small organizations wishing to survive must keep as current as possible without negatively impacting their economic positions. This can best be achieved by flexibility and resolute attention to the mission of the organization, currency of the employees' training, and sensitivity to the customer base. Not to be overlooked is attention to the information itself, not just the technology. What the organization needs to know, what creative activities are ongoing, what each sector contributes, and how economically viable each contribution is mean as much to the survival of the organization as does investment in the technology.

Summary

Sometimes too much information or too much technology can decrease efficiency (McWilliams, 1995). Understanding the value to the organization of the information that flows through the channels that are enabled by technology is critical to managing technology to the advantage of the organization. The value of information is linked to its usefulness to the organization, and the user primarily determines information value. If information is inaccessible simply because there is too much of it, it has no value and may actually be a wasted cost due to the cost of collection, which suggests that organizations of all sizes need to evaluate the cost and benefit of information gathering. Just because it is possible to collect enormous bodies of information does not mean that it is profitable. While the web makes an infinite amount of information available, it is still not clear that organizations or citizens are fully benefiting from it. While access to more information should make each employee more valued, that is not necessarily the result and can actually contribute to inappropriate distribution. Digital accessibility is impacting organizations and societies, but the resulting changes in information hierarchies are unclear. Involving more participants in decision-making, or appearing to, suggests the hierarchy is being transformed from a linear to a relational matrix.

There are no quick and easy answers to any of the issues discussed here. Digital accessibility impacts organizational structure and the ways in which organizations gather, use, and value information in ways that we do not yet fully understand. In the present climate of rapid change in the extent and means of accessibility, determining both the nature of the changes and their impact is a challenge. The differing approaches to infusion of information technology provide a fertile field for examination of how information value changes in relation to differing structures and the extent to which those structures are a result of changes in digital accessibility. Research needs to be undertaken to determine how much flattening of the organizational hierarchy has occurred and how much of it has to do with information technology versus other changes in the social structure. Continuous review and evaluation of the impact of information technology in organizations and in all aspects of society needs to be conducted. We know that management structures are changing in response to the digital revolution, but so is society. The challenge is to cope with the changes in ways that will optimize the value of information to the organization, to society as a whole, and to the individuals who comprise both.

References

Brandt, D. November/December 2008. Getting More From the Voice of the Customer. *Marketing Management* 17(6):36–42.

DeYoung, H. G. October 9, 1995. The Trouble with Technology. *Computerworld* 29(41): 42–43.

Earls, A. J. June 1995. An Ounce of Training … Is Worth at Least a Pound of Success. *Computerworld* 29(22):51–55.

Forrester Consulting. September 2009. Appraising Your Investment in Enterprise Web Analytics. Forrester Research, Inc. Retrieved February 15, 2010, from www.google. com/analytics/case_studies/Appraising-Investments-In-Enterprise-Analytics.pdf

Gardner, W. L., and Peluchette, J. V. E. 1991. Computer-Mediated Communication Settings: A Self-Presentational Perspective. In E. Szewczak, C. Snodgrass, and M. Khosrowpour (Eds.), *Management Impacts of Information Technology: Perspectives on Organizational Change and Growth* pp. 168–205. Harrisburg, PA: Idea Group.

Gerstein, M. S. 1992. From Machine Bureaucracies to Networked Organizations: An Architectural Journey. In D. A. Nadler, M. S. Gerstein, and R. B. Shaw (Eds.), *Organizational Architecture: Designs for Changing Organizations* pp. 10–38. San Francisco, CA: Jossey-Bass, Inc.

Google Analytics. 2010. Retrieved February 15, 2010, www.google.com/analytics/index. html

Johnson, A. October 2, 2009. Lack of Computer Skills Foils Many Job Seekers. MSNBC.com. Retrieved February 15, 2010, from www.msnbc.msn.com/id/ 33106445

Kaltnekar, Z. 1991. Information Technology and the Humanization of Work. In E. Szewczak, C. Snodgrass, and M. Khosrowpour (Eds.), *Management Impacts of Information Technology: Perspectives on Organizational Change and Growth* pp. 493–533. Harrisburg, PA: Idea Group.

Kent, M. 2008. Critical Analysis of Blogging in Public Relations. *Public Relations Review* 34(1): 32–40.

Madden, M., and Jones, S. 2008. Networked Workers. Pew Internet and American Life Project. Retrieved February 15, 2010, from www.pewinternet.org/Reports/2008/ Networked-Workers.pdf

McWilliams, B. October 9, 1995. Information Entrepreneurs. *Computerworld* 29(41):20–25.

Nadler, D. A. 1992. Introduction: Organization Architecture: A Metaphor for Change. In D. A. Nadler, M. S. Gerstein, and R. B. Shaw (Eds.), *Organizational Architecture: Designs for Changing Organizations* pp. 1–9. San Francisco, CA: Jossey-Bass, Inc.

Nadler, D. A., and Tushman, M. L. 1992. Designing Organizations That Have Good Fit: A Framework for Understanding New Architectures. In D. A. Nadler, M. S. Gerstein, and R. B. Shaw (Eds.), *Organizational Architecture: Designs for Changing Organizations* pp. 39–57. San Francisco, CA: Jossey-Bass, Inc.

Shimada, T. 1991. The Impact of Information Technology on Organizations in Japanese Companies. In E. Szewczak, C. Snodgrass, and M. Khosrowpour (Eds.), *Management Impacts of Information Technology: Perspectives on Organizational Change and Growth* pp. 298–329. Harrisburg, PA: Idea Group.

United States Computer Emergency Readiness Team. 2004. Understanding Denial-of-Service Attacks. National Cyber Alert System, Cyber Security Tip ST04-015. Retrieved February 15, 2010 from www.us-cert.gov/cas/tips/ST04-015.html

Woodsworth, A. 1991. *Patterns and Options for Managing Information Technology on Campus*. Chicago: ALA.

About the Contributors

Dr. EunKyung Chung is an assistant professor of library and information science at Ewha Womans University, Seoul, Korea. She has presented or published research on semantic interoperability in digital libraries, text classification for digital libraries, and digital libraries education. She teaches courses in digital libraries, information retrieval and web searching, and database systems. With a background in both library and information science and computer science, her broad research interests are in integrating the technological aspects into traditional issues in the library and information science fields.

Dr. June Lester is a professor in the University of Oklahoma School of Library and Information Studies, where she has been on faculty since 1993, serving from 1993 to 2000 as director of the school. She teaches graduate courses in the foundations of information studies, information behavior, information policy, and academic libraries. She has extensive professional experience in management and information policy.

Dr. Teresa S. Welsh is an associate professor of library and information science at The University of Southern Mississippi, where she teaches courses in archival management, history of libraries, research methods, and information science. She earned her PhD from the University of Tennessee and has extensive experience with web repositories, telemedicine research, and information literacy. She has been an assistant director of the Katrina Research Center since its foundation in 2006.

Dr. JungWon Yoon is an assistant professor at the School of Library and Information Science, University of South Florida, and holds a PhD in information science from the University of North Texas. She is currently teaching courses on organization of knowledge, indexing and abstracting, and visualization of knowledge. Her research focuses on image representation and retrieval, and user behavior with image documents. She has been particularly interested in representation of connotative messages of an image, user-oriented representation of an image, and cross-cultural image retrieval.

Peter Zuber is the engineering librarian at the Harold B. Lee Library at Brigham Young University. He is the chair of the Users Studies and Assessment Team and holds multiple U.S. patents in engineering and science (Electrophotography and Color Theory). He earned his MLIS at The University of Southern Mississippi in 2007.

About the Author

Melanie J. Norton is an associate professor and the director of the School of Library and Information Science at The University of Southern Mississippi in Hattiesburg. She has served on various information technology initiatives and has previously chaired the committee examining appropriate implementation and strategic planning for university-wide technology. She advocates for campus-wide engagement in all technology initiatives and a commitment to sustained training of faculty and staff. Her interests in technology implementation have led to her placement on several focus and study groups for the university. Her experience includes initiating and leading the first fully online graduate program at Southern Miss. She managed a multimedia library and laboratory system for nearly a decade, as well as the development and management of the local area network. She has worked in a medical records library and a range of government, manufacturing, and retail settings.

Norton's teaching resume includes graduate and undergraduate courses dealing with collection development, computers in libraries, multimedia tools, internet resources, information ethics, and library automation. Additionally, she has taught graduate courses in systems analysis, information science, information and society, database search tools for public and special collections, and research methods. Her research interests include information economics, management of information, personnel management, and issues in the technology and human contexts of communication.

Index

Figures are indicated with italicized page references followed by *f.*

More Titles of Interest from Information Today, Inc.

Information Representation and Retrieval in the Digital Age, Second Edition

By Heting Chu

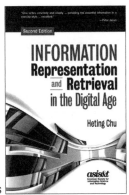

This second edition of Heting Chu's popular work on information representation and retrieval (IRR) features numerous updates and revisions, including coverage of taxonomies, folksonomies, ontologies, social tagging, Search/Retrieve Web Service, and next generation OPACs. She reviews key concepts and major developmental stages of the field, and then systematically examines information representation methods, IRR languages, retrieval techniques and models, and internet retrieval systems. In addition, she explains the retrieval of multilingual, multimedia, and hyper-structured information and explores the user dimension and evaluation issues.

320 pp/hardbound/ISBN 978-1-57387-393-2
ASIST Members $39.60 • Nonmembers $49.50

Digital Inclusion

Measuring the Impact of Information and Community Technology

Edited by Michael Crandall and Karen E. Fisher

Through an examination of efforts by community technology organizations in Washington State, *Digital Inclusion* offers a model for educating policy makers about the actual impacts of such efforts, along with suggestions for practical implementation. The case studies and analyses presented here will be of critical interest to community technology centers, libraries, government service agencies, and any other organization (or funder) that uses technology to deliver services to the information poor.

200 pp/hardbound/ISBN 978-1-57387-373-4
ASIST Members $47.60 • Nonmembers $59.50

Computerization Movements and Technology Diffusion

From Mainframes to Ubiquitous Computing

Edited by Margaret S. Elliott and Kenneth L. Kraemer

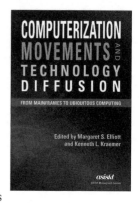

"Computerization movement" (CM) refers to a kind of social and technological movement that promotes the adoption of computing within organizations and society. Here, the editors and more than two dozen scholars trace the successes and failures of CMs from the maiframe and PC eras to the emerging era of ubiquitous computing. The studies presented here show the need for designers, users, and the media to be aware that CM rhetoric can propose grand visions that never become part of a reality and reinforce the need for critical and scholarly review of new technologies.

608 pp/hardbound/ISBN 978-1-57387-311-6
ASIST Members $47.60 • Nonmembers $59.50

Information and Emotion

The Emergent Affective Paradigm in Information Behavior Research and Theory

Edited by Diane Nahl and Dania Bilal

Information and Emotion introduces the new research areas of affective issues in information seeking and use and the affective paradigm applied to information behavior in a variety of populations, cultures, and contexts. Colletively, their contributions make *Information and Emotion* a unique source of research findings on the user perspective; the user experience; and how emotional aspects can be interpreted, mitigated, or enhanced through design that is informed by use, and by users who directly participate in information design.

392 pp/hardbound/ISBN 978-1-57387-310-9
ASIST Members $47.60 • Nonmembers $59.50
